BLACK AMERICA SERIES

LEXINGTON
KENTUCKY

(front cover) This picture was taken at King Alumni House on the campus of the University of Kentucky in the late 1940s. (Courtesy of Lilla Bentley.)

(back cover) This photograph of a civil rights demonstration was taken on Main Street. (Courtesy of Calvert McCann.)

BLACK AMERICA SERIES

LEXINGTON
KENTUCKY

Gerald L. Smith Ph.D.

ARCADIA PUBLISHING

ISBN 978-0-7385-1437-6

Published by Arcadia Publishing
Charleston, South Carolina

Printed in the United States of America

Library of Congress Catalog Card Number: 2002103389

For all general information contact Arcadia Publishing at:
Telephone 843-853-2070
Fax 843-853-0044
E-mail sales@arcadiapublishing.com
For customer service and orders:
Toll-Free 1-888-313-2665

Visit us on the Internet at www.arcadiapublishing.com

For my daughters, Elizabeth and Sarah

Contents

ACKNOWLEDGMENTS

Many people contributed in significant ways to this book. I begin by conveying my appreciation to the Lexington History Museum (LHM) Board of Trustees. Ed Houlihan, the executive director of the board, supported my suggestion to collect photos of African Americans. He wrote a grant funded by the Kentucky Humanities Council (KHC) titled, "In Black & White: A Photographic Collection of African Americans in the Bluegrass." This KHC grant enabled the LHM and the African American Studies and Research Program at the University of Kentucky to engage in the collection of photographs. Several people deserve recognition for their contribution to that worthy project. They include the following: Ellen Claire Allen, Keisha Carter, Yolanda Douglass, Amanda Elliott, Joan Grever, Shannon Guerrant, Allan Hetzel, Lisa Higgins-Hord, Evangeline Johnson, Betsy Houlihan, Mary Beth Marshall, Betty Lee Mastin, Calvert McCann, Dr. L.H. McIntyre, P.G. Peeples, Mr. and Mrs. Arthur Rouse, Sarah Newby, Margaret Kannensohn, Betty Smithers, Thomas Tolliver, and Eric Weig. The photos collected in that project will be listed on the Kentuckiana Digital Library web-page.

Preparing and writing this book entailed far more time than I imagined. Yet, the following people graciously welcomed me into their home as I sought information, answered my questions by telephone or e-mail, or trusted me to keep their personal photos for several weeks as I prepared the book. I am profoundly grateful for the contributions of the following people: Ellen C. Allen, Alice Wallace Bailey, Ronald Berry, Lilla Bentley, Annetta Bibbs, Ella S. Bosely, Gerri Botts, John Will "Scoop" Brown, Mary Brown, Russell Clark, Doris Coffey, Lutisha Coleman, Saunda Coleman, Yolanda Douglass, Sharon Engles, Amanda Elliott, Henrietta Fender, Dwight Hughes, Cleo Ingram, Julian Jackson, Reverends Henry and Lamont Jones, Kay Jones, Catherine Lewis, Lawrence Lewis, Catherine Livingston, Calvert McCaan, Jamaan McCann, Ruth Million, Sarah Newby, Barbara Olsen, Laura Tompkins Owens, Phaon Patton, Winston Powell, Charles and Marie Quillings, Rev. Horace R. Smith, Betty Smithers, Thomas Tolliver, Miley Travis, and Doris Wilkinson.

I am especially thankful for the professional assistance I received from Harold Barker, Lexington Fayette Urban County Government Archives; Jim Birchfield, Lisa Carter, and Jason Flahardy, Special Collections, University of Kentucky; Merelene Davis, Ron Garrison, and Norma White, *Lexington Herald Leader*; Jan Marshall and Robin Rader, Lexington Public Library; Charlene Smith and Mary Winters, Kentucky Historical Society; Betsy Morelock, Kentucky State University; and B.J. Gooch, Transylvania University. Sally Powell and Josh Phillips in the UK Photography Lab did a superb job printing negatives and scanning photographs for this book. The staff in African American Studies was also helpful. Tarica Dow, Joy Myree, Antiwan Walker, and especially my assistant, Evangeline Johnson, contributed to this work in important ways.

Lastly, I express thanks to my family. My wife, Teresa, has been the strongest advocate for this book. Thank you, sweetheart, for your love and encouragement. Our daughters, Elizabeth and Sarah, allow me to keep life in perspective. My parents, R.W. and Mary Crawford; grandmother, Mamie Mayfield; and mother-in-law, Octavene Turner have always been a constant source of love and support and I am grateful for the opportunity to share this book with them.

INTRODUCTION

In the spring of 1897, Mary E. Britton, a Lexington African-American schoolteacher, shared her thoughts about a book entitled *Biographical Sketches of Prominent Negro Men and Women of Kentucky* written by W.D. Johnson. Britton wrote, "Races, as well as individuals, are estimated according to their achievements in religion, literature, and the arts. Without a record of their progress along these lines, the world would be ignorant of those characters, both male and female, who have made history."

On November 11, 1902, Britton made history in Lexington when she was granted a license to practice medicine in the city. However, Britton was more than a physician and schoolteacher. On April 15, 1892, she penned a strong argument on behalf of African-American women against the passage of Kentucky's Separate Coach bill. Although the bill passed, Britton and her contemporaries worked assiduously to improve the plight of African Americans in Lexington despite their treatment as second-class citizens.

Because so little information is known about black life in Lexington, this book seeks to document through photographs the struggles and progress African Americans experienced from slavery to the passage of the state civil rights bill in 1966. In doing so, this work seeks to reach deep into the heart and soul of the black community to capture its fortitude, pride, dignity, and interracial diversity. Besides highlighting institutions, as well as professional and skilled African-American workers, this book presents the domestic and agricultural workers whose ordinary lives contributed to the establishment of businesses, churches, schools, and clubs.

These photographs are proof that African Americans in Lexington were persistent in their will to create a lifestyle they could enjoy and take pride in. Though they were forced to attend segregated schools, live in segregated neighborhoods, and occupy poorly paid jobs, African Americans stressed religious and educational values to their children, organized events and programs that boasted dignity and class, and demonstrated against racial inequality in difficult times. The spirit in which they lived their lives is a story worth seeing in pictures.

African Americans came to the Bluegrass of Kentucky as the servants of whites in the late 18th century. They cleared land, built cabins, erected fences, raised gardens, washed clothes, cooked meals, and fought Native Americans. In 1800, the slave population of Lexington numbered less than 450 blacks. By 1860, the city numbered 600 free blacks and 2,480 slaves out of a total population 9, 521 residents. A large number of African Americans lived in rural areas and worked in the hemp and tobacco fields of Fayette County.

Lexington served as a profitable slave market for people selling slaves further south. The auction block on Cheapside in downtown Lexington was the site of heartless sales of black slaves that involved the separation of families. In 1822, Rev. James H. Dickey witnessed a coffle of chained slaves, which included men and women, headed from Paris to Lexington. "A solemn sadness sat upon every countenance," recalled Dickey. At least two dozen slave traders were advertising in local papers and were making deals in the city by the end of 1858.

After the Civil War, Lexington's black population more than doubled. Some African Americans chose to live in black hamlets on the outskirts of the city, where they built their own churches and schools. Those who came to Lexington migrated to the city for different reasons. Some African Americans, no doubt, wanted to escape white retaliation; others sought relief assistance, educational and employment opportunities, or the possibility of reuniting with loved ones. Their arrival led to the development of several black neighborhoods in Lexington since whites wanted to distance their contact with newly freed blacks. Adamstown, Brucetown, Davistown, Goodloetown, Kinkeadtown, and Smithtown were among the African-American neighborhoods developed by white landowners in what was considered then as less attractive areas of the city.

Throughout the late 19th and much of the 20th centuries, employment opportunities for blacks were limited. Most worked as domestic servants, waiters, farmhands, cooks, common laborers, and factory workers. Those African Americans without a job risked being sold back into slavery. The June 12, 1881 Sunday morning edition of the *Lexington Press* carried an article entitled "On the Block, An Old Time Sight—Two Negroes Sold into Slavery." Henry Dudley and Henry Tucker had been "sentenced to twelve months slavery at public auction" the day before. Tucker was described as "a fine specimen of the mere animal man, bullet headed, bull-necked, strong limbed, and deep-chested, six feet three inches tall, and about 35 years old. Supposedly, "he could break 300 pounds of hemp a day." Tucker was purchased by the highest bidder for $112.50. Dudley sold for $112. The columnist wrote: "It is necessary to the well-being, health and comfort of the city that more of the loafers that blockade our streets be put on the block."

Despite this charge, African Americans were not "loafers." A professional class of African-American doctors, lawyers, teachers, politicians, and businessmen and women were an integral part of the community by the late 19th century. Black schools did a remarkable job educating children despite the meager resources they received. African-American social and charitable organizations permeated the city offering planned cultural programs, dinners, dances and friendly gatherings. The African-American church served as the most significant institution in the community. It represented spiritual leadership and economic independence. The church also served as a resourceful refuge for African Americans worn by the daily ritual of racial oppression.

But African Americans did not easily accept racial inequality in Lexington. On July 30, 1911, J. Alexander Chiles, an African-American lawyer, penned a letter to the editor of the *Lexington Leader* expressing his disappointment that the "colored truant officer was 'dropped'" and a white officer hired at a higher salary to monitor the black children. Chiles argued for retaining the black truant officer. He also wrote "Colored citizens have to pay the same prices for dry gods, food fuels, clothing, the same fares on city interurban and railroad cars [as] the white citizens, it is but fair, just, and equitable that they should be given some work on public works, and be paid the same price for their labor as other workers are paid; the colored teachers employed to teach colored children should be paid the same salaries for teaching the like grades as the white teachers receive for the same teaching . . .This is right, this is just; this is a 'square deal.'"

A couple of week later, Dr. John E. Hunter, a local black physician, echoed support for Chiles's comments in a letter to the *Lexington Leader*. Hunter was concerned that black doctors in Lexington were not being hired as health inspectors in African-American schools. "The Negro physicians of this city have not been a class of whiners for office by any means," wrote Hunter, "but have been busy and hard workers for the health of their people. From now on the negro physicians will at least expect the opportunity to look after the health of the colored school children, just as the colored men and women are employed to teach them."

As the 20th century progressed, Lexington's African-American population continued to face discrimination in employment, housing, education, and usage of public accommodations. Between 1920 and 1960, the city's black population declined as northern cities offered better opportunities. However, those African Americans who chose to remain in Lexington continued to build a vibrant and insulated community and fight for racial justice. The African-American church, school, family, and neighborhood were all part of a life that white Lexingtonians rarely saw, understood, or fully appreciated. It is my hope that this book will give present and future generations a greater knowledge of African-American life in the Bluegrass of Kentucky.

One

Images of Slavery

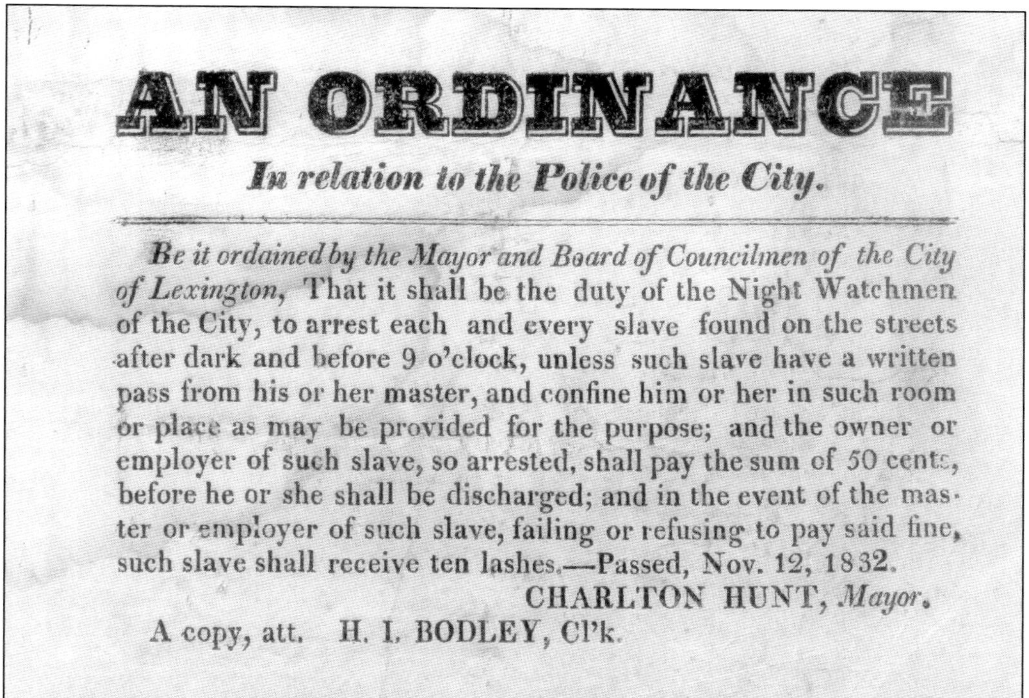

AN ORDINANCE

In relation to the Police of the City.

Be it ordained by the Mayor and Board of Councilmen of the City of Lexington, That it shall be the duty of the Night Watchmen of the City, to arrest each and every slave found on the streets after dark and before 9 o'clock, unless such slave have a written pass from his or her master, and confine him or her in such room or place as may be provided for the purpose; and the owner or employer of such slave, so arrested, shall pay the sum of 50 cents, before he or she shall be discharged; and in the event of the master or employer of such slave, failing or refusing to pay said fine, such slave shall receive ten lashes.—Passed, Nov. 12, 1832.

CHARLTON HUNT, *Mayor.*

A copy, att. H. I. BODLEY, Cl'k.

A Broadside for Slave Owners. Slave insurrections were a concern for city leaders. On July 8, 1800, they passed a resolution to establish a committee to "engage some proper person as a watch to patrol the street." Ten years later, a group of slaves in Lexington was arrested for their connection to a "dangerous conspiracy." In 1831, Nat Turner's insurrection in Virginia led to further alarm among southern whites. The broadside pictured here reflects the efforts of local whites to alleviate this concern. (Courtesy of Special Collections University of Kentucky.)

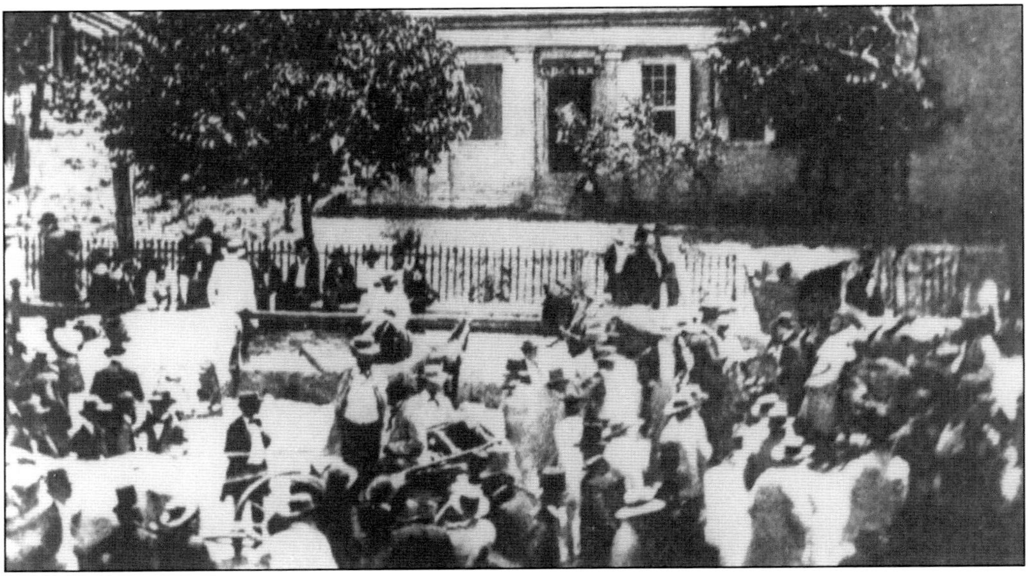

SLAVE SALES ON CHEAPSIDE. During the antebellum period, Cheapside, in downtown Lexington, was the site of court days, horse shows, and slave sales. On the northeast side of the street stood a whipping post. Jeremiah (Jerry) Delph and A.S Thompson were among the auctioneers who worked the auction block. On February 14, 1859, Thompson sold five slaves. One was a 13-year-old girl who sold for $1,160. This photograph is believed to depict the scene of a slave auction on Cheapside. (Courtesy of Coleman Collection, Transylvania University.)

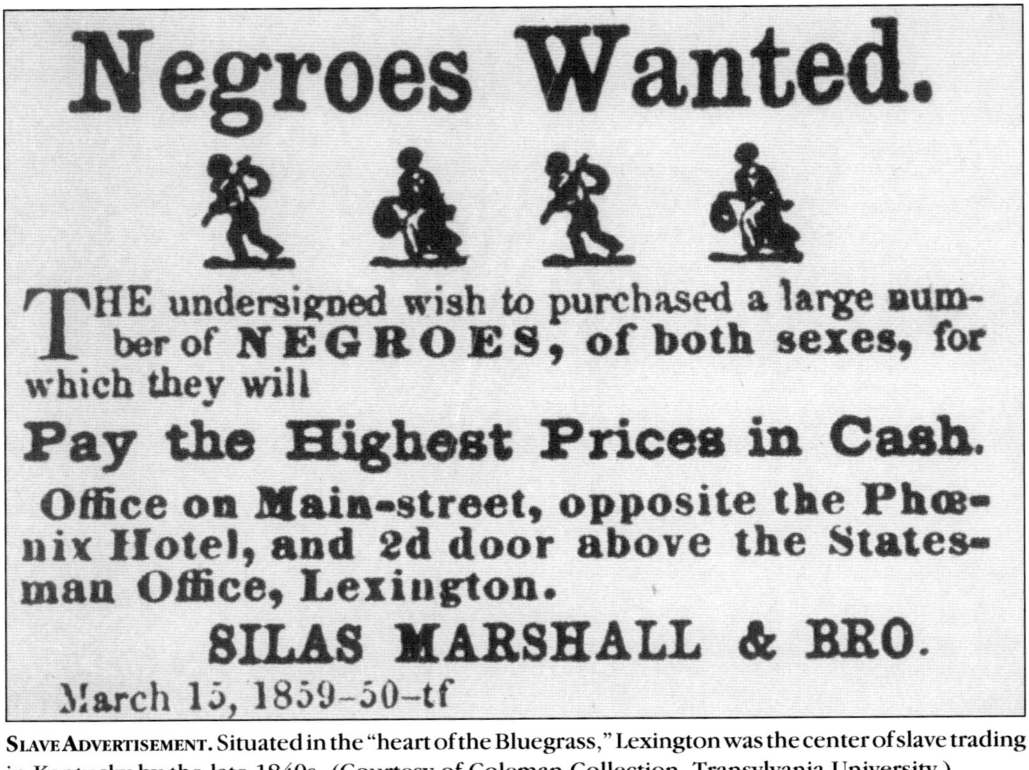

Negroes Wanted.

THE undersigned wish to purchased a large number of NEGROES, of both sexes, for which they will

Pay the Highest Prices in Cash.

Office on Main-street, opposite the Phœnix Hotel, and 2d door above the Statesman Office, Lexington.

SILAS MARSHALL & BRO.

March 15, 1859–50–tf

SLAVE ADVERTISEMENT. Situated in the "heart of the Bluegrass," Lexington was the center of slave trading in Kentucky by the late 1840s. (Courtesy of Coleman Collection, Transylvania University.)

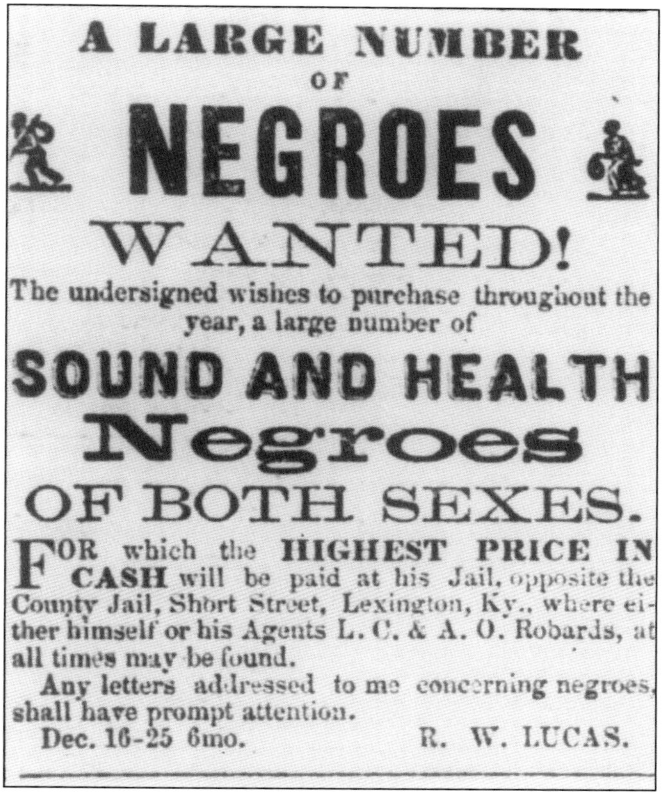

A LARGE NUMBER
OF
NEGROES
WANTED!
The undersigned wishes to purchase throughout the year, a large number of
SOUND AND HEALTH
Negroes
OF BOTH SEXES.

FOR which the HIGHEST PRICE IN CASH will be paid at his Jail, opposite the County Jail, Short Street, Lexington, Ky., where either himself or his Agents L. C. & A. O. Robards, at all times may be found.

Any letters addressed to me concerning negroes, shall have prompt attention.

Dec. 16-25 6mo. R. W. LUCAS.

Slave Advertisement. Lewis C. Robards was considered the leading "Negro buyer" in the city by the late 1840s and early 1850s. He purchased unhealthy slaves and sold them to buyers without disclosing their condition. Several purchasers of slaves took Robards to court because of his dishonest practices. (Courtesy of Coleman Collection, Transylvania University.)

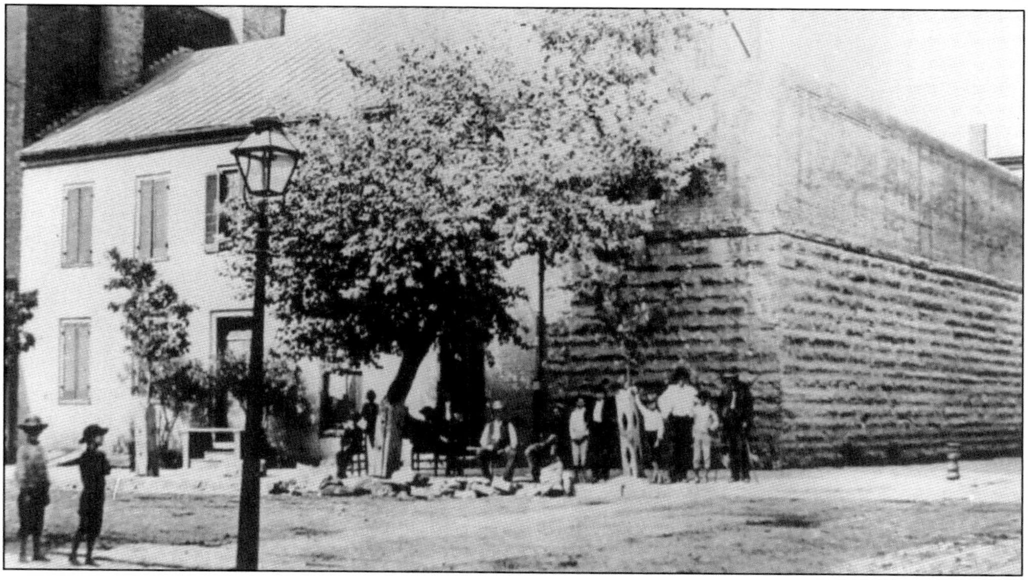

Megowan's Jail. This county jail was erected on the northeast corner of Short and Limestone Streets in 1819. A two-story building constructed of brick and stone, the jail was also used to hold runaway slaves and surplus bondsmen who were to be sold further south during the 1830s. Thomas B. Megowan was the jailer for 20 years. On February 1, 1877, the *Lexington Daily Press* reported that Megowan died at the age of 81, "broken down and impoverished." This photo was taken *c.* 1880. (Courtesy of Coleman Collection, Transylvania University.)

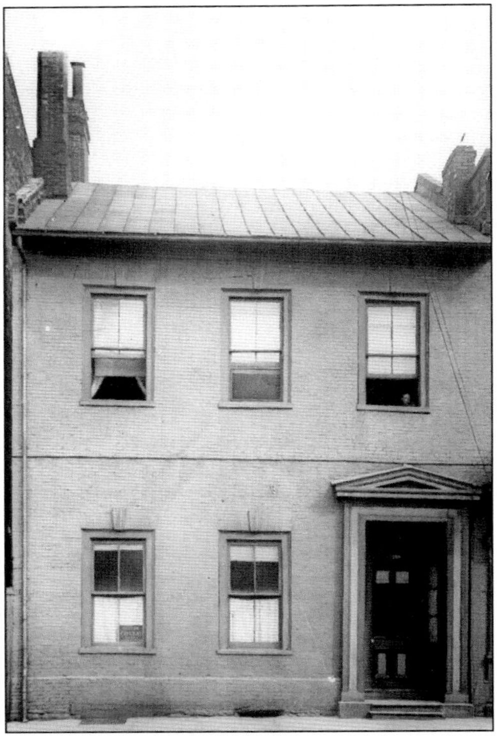

Pullman's Slave Jail. In 1849, Lexington slave trader William Pullman leased this jail to Lewis C. Robards. Slave pens eight-feet-square and seven-feet-high with barred windows and damp brick floors stood in the rear of the jail. Pullman was too ill to continue operations but claimed Robards was prepared to "keep Negroes by the day or week for anyone wishing to confine them in jail for sale or other purposes." In 1858 slave traders Blackwell, Murphy, and Ferguson occupied "Pullman's old stand." Pictured is Pullman's slave jail at 149 North Broadway Street, which ironically, served as the headquarters for the local chapter of the Freedman's Bureau. The building was razed in 1902. (Courtesy of Barton Battaile Collection, Lexington Public Library, Kentucky Room.)

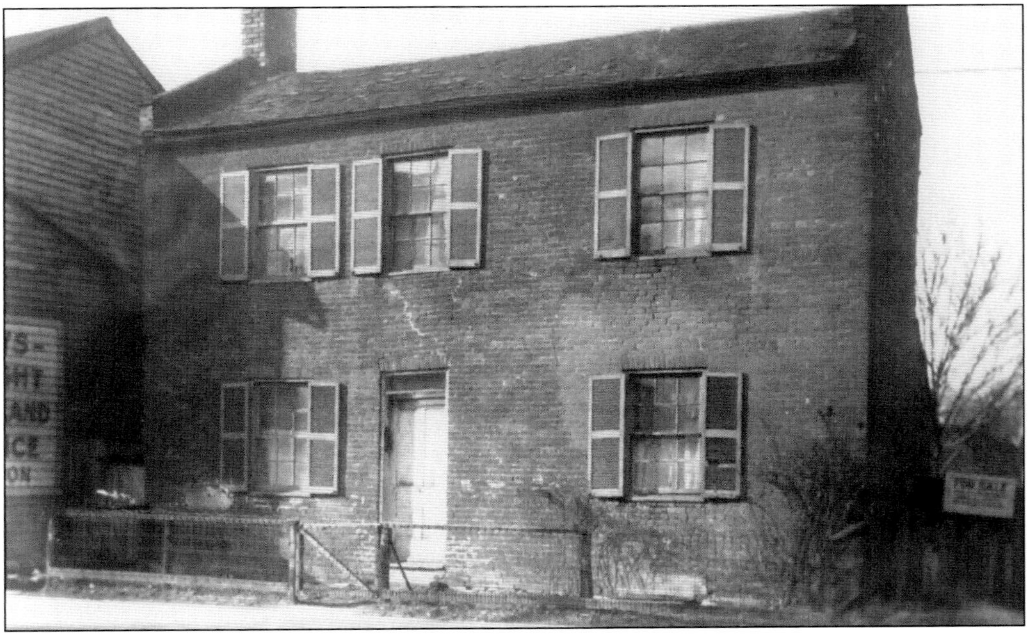

Robards' Slave Jail. Robards' jail expanded rapidly in Lexington. He purchased this building on West Short Street and the property next door. In one building, he kept what he called his "choice stock" of female slaves. He advertised his jail as "the largest and best constructed building for a jail in the West . . . . The rooms are large and airy, are neatly furnished and a fine yard is attached to the building." Faced with financial difficulties in 1855, Robards sold his jail and several slaves to the Bolton, Dickens & Co. (Courtesy of Coleman Collection, Transylvania University.)

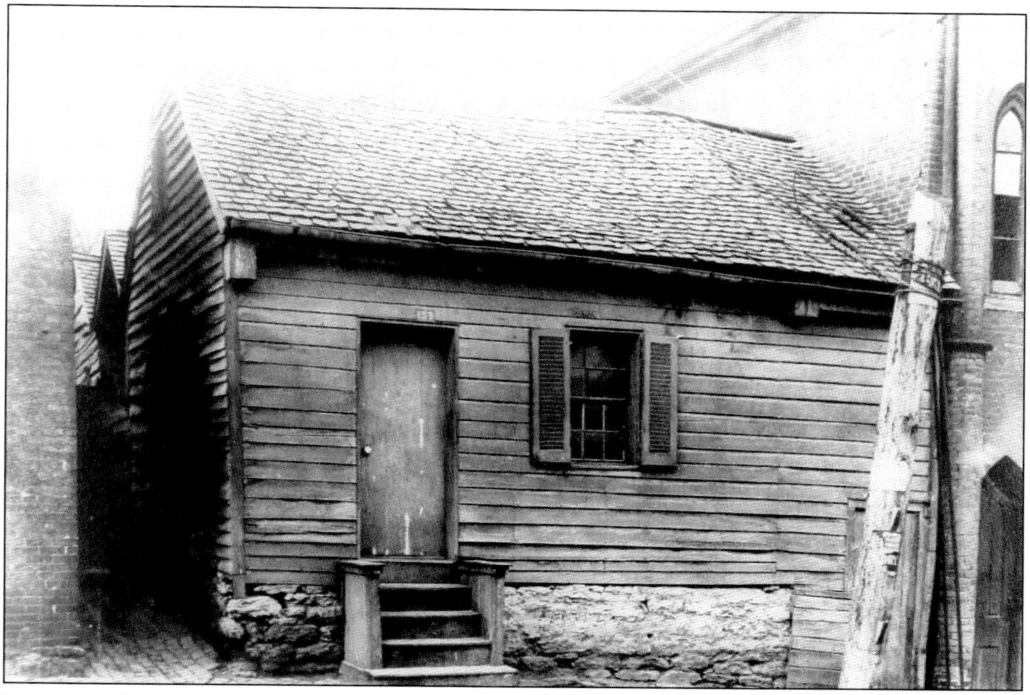

Slave Jail. The demand for slaves in the Deep South, the capture of runaway slaves, and the arrest of those who violated curfews created a need for places to hold slaves on a temporary basis. This house on the west side of Limestone Street was used to keep slaves for overnight purposes. (Courtesy of Barton Battaile Collection, Lexington Public Library, Kentucky Room.)

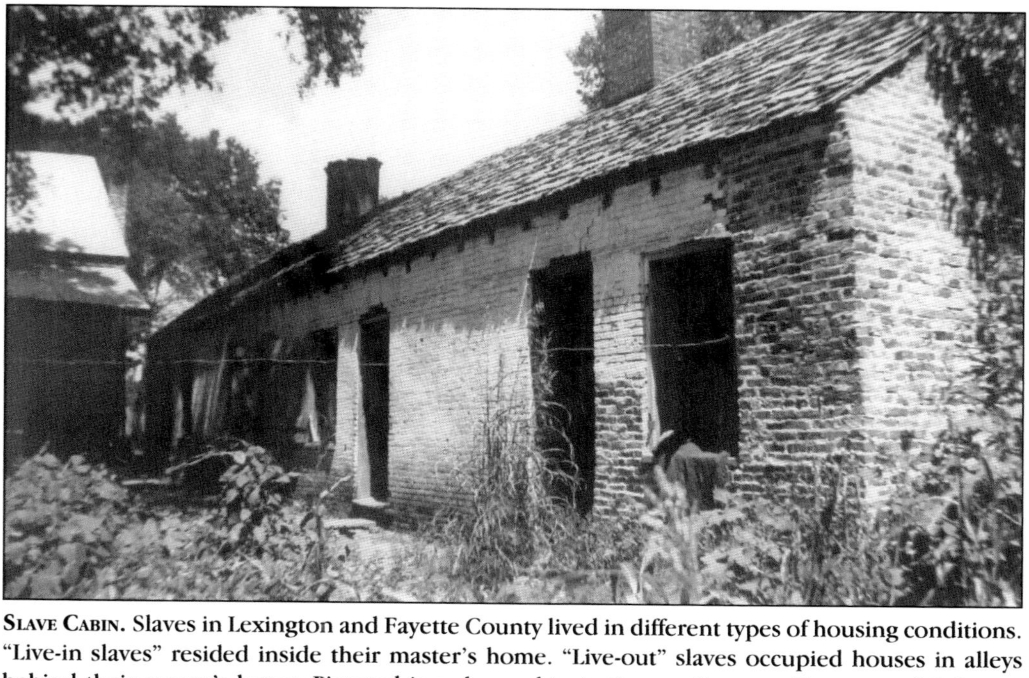

Slave Cabin. Slaves in Lexington and Fayette County lived in different types of housing conditions. "Live-in slaves" resided inside their master's home. "Live-out" slaves occupied houses in alleys behind their owner's home. Pictured is a slave cabin in Fayette County. (Courtesy of Coleman Collection, Transylvania University.)

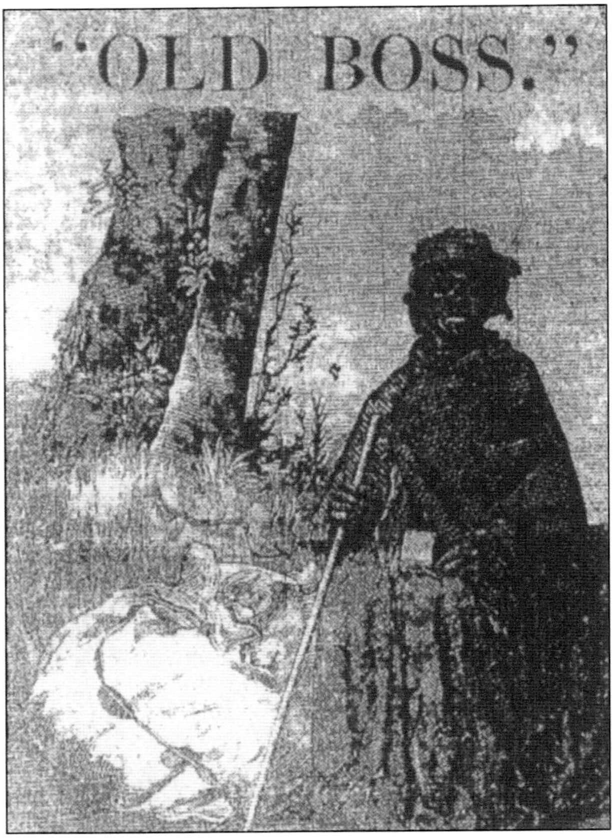

Nancy Anderson. Described in the June 30, 1938 edition of the *Lexington Leader* as an "eccentric Negro rag and paper picker," Nancy Anderson was known as "Old Boss." She was born in Jessamine County and came to Lexington in 1835. Relishing the behavior of this poor and illiterate woman, whites thought that her public commentaries on the streets of Lexington delivered in broken English were entertaining. A local drugstore even named a 5¢ cigar "Old Boss." Anderson's photograph was included among those of other distinguished white Lexingtonians sealed in the cornerstone of the Fayette County Courthouse on July 4, 1883. She died in 1888 following a tragic accident in which her legs were run over by a train. Despite the alleged affection people had for her, she was buried in a pauper's grave. Pictured is a box cover of Old Boss cigars with Nancy Anderson's image printed on the top. (Courtesy of *Lexington Herald Leader*.)

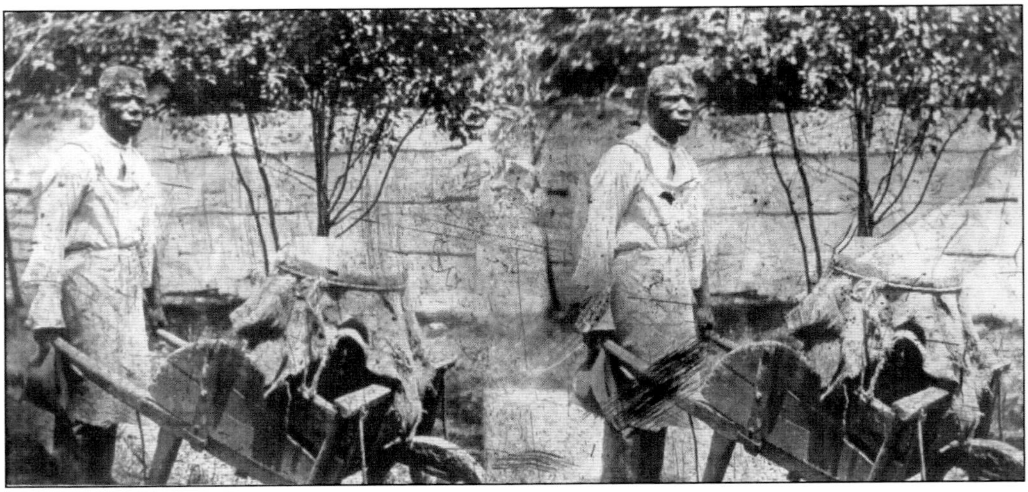

An African-American Man Working in Lexington, *c.* 1864. Stereographs were taken of battlefields during the Civil War. A twin-lens stereoscopic camera took pictures like this one, which captures an African-American man pushing what appears to be a wheel barrel. (Courtesy Bullock Collection, Transylvania University.)

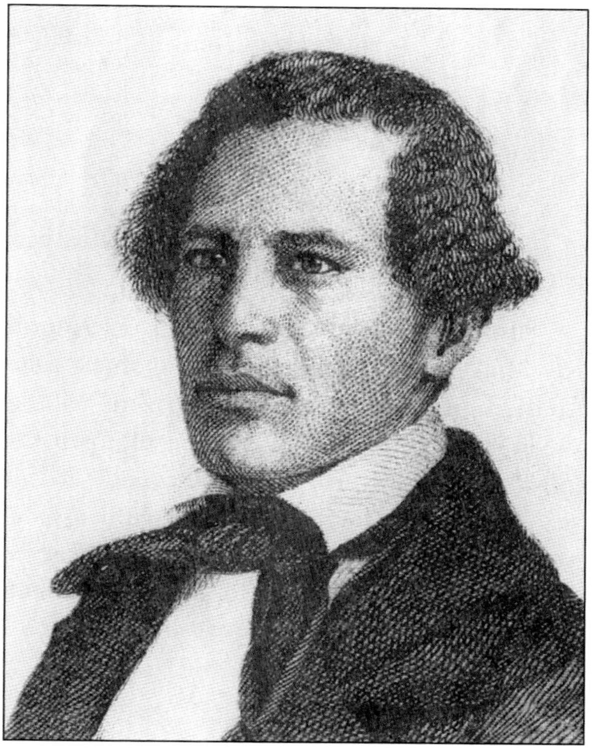

William Wells Brown. Brown was born a slave in 1814 on the farm of Dr. John Young, which was located on the outskirts of Lexington. Brown left the Bluegrass and became an abolitionist and an accomplished novelist and historian. In 1847, he wrote *Narrative of William Wells Brown, a Fugitive Slave, Written by Himself*. After publishing numerous works, Brown died in 1884.

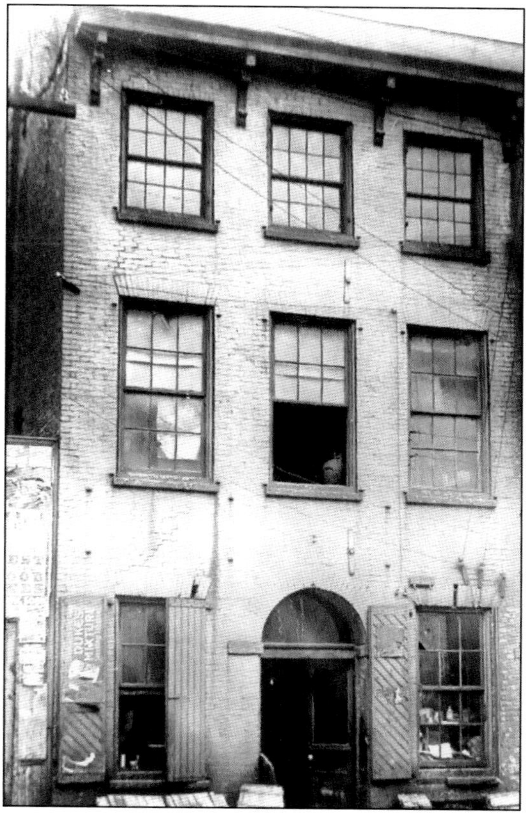

Office of *True American*, Newspaper. On June 3, 1845, Cassius M. Clay, a white man, began publishing an abolitionist newspaper from his office at No. 6 North Mill Street. Clay was a proponent of gradual emancipation but received strong criticism from other whites. While he was sick, a group of whites seized his printing press and shipped it to Cincinnati. Clay filed suit and was awarded damages of $2,500. Clay published the paper from Cincinnati between October 1845 and May 1846. (Courtesy of Coleman Collection, Transylvania University.)

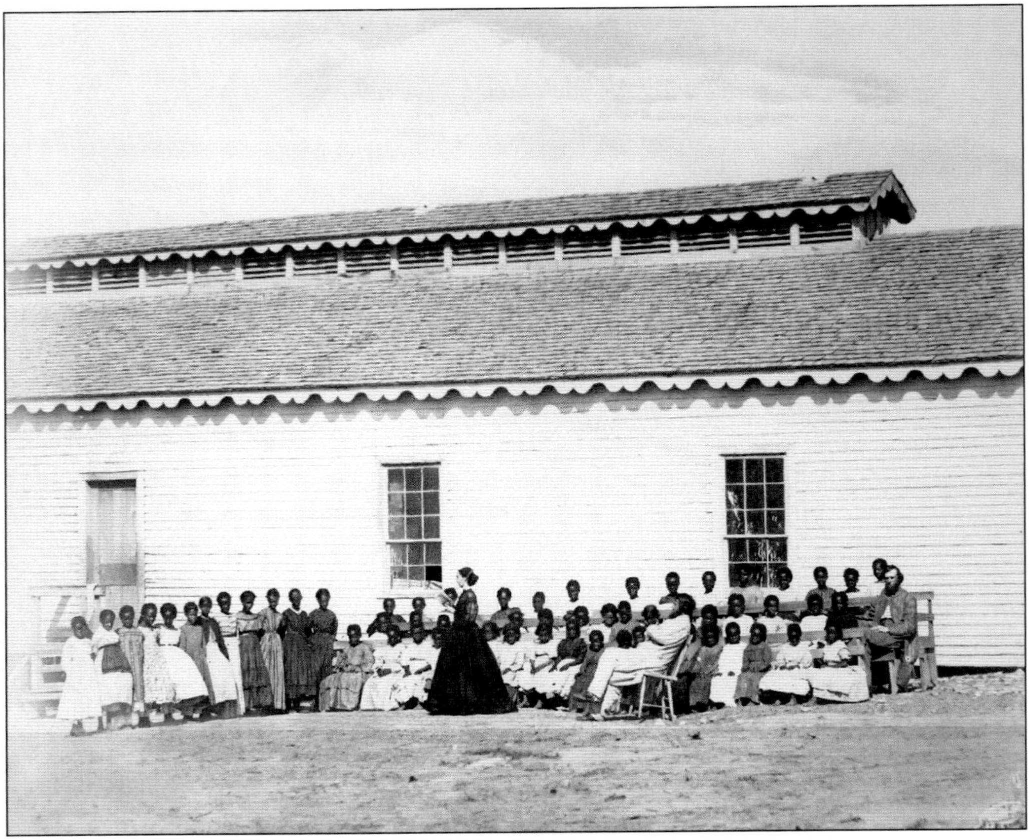

Camp Nelson. Located south of Lexington in Jessamine County, Camp Nelson was established by the Union Army in 1864. Initially, slaves from the Bluegrass were brought to the camp to build railroads. It became a recruiting station and a training camp for African-American soldiers on March 10, 1864. John G. Fee, an abolitionist and white missionary, recruited other missionaries to come to the camp to teach African Americans. Camp Nelson was designated a United States cemetery in 1867. A white missionary stands before African Americans in the *c.* 1864 depiction above. (Courtesy of Special Collections, University of Kentucky.)

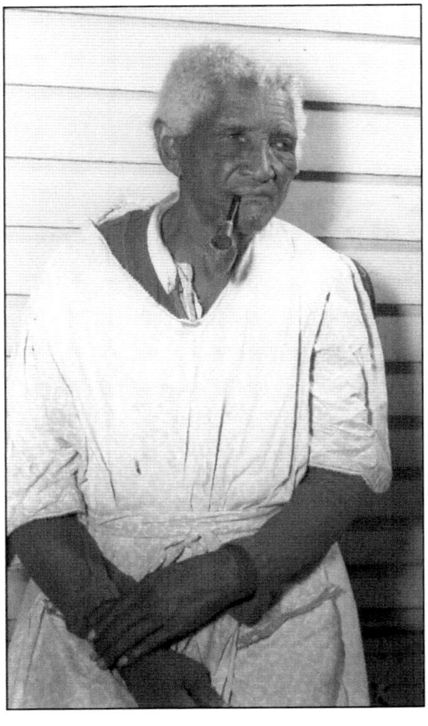

A Long Life. Leah Taylor, a former slave, was thought to be 105 years old when this 1949 photograph was taken. She was living on North Broadway with her son and his wife and was described as "spry and clear minded." Reflecting upon slavery, Taylor recalled long days "workin' in the fields like a horse." (Courtesy of *Lexington Herald Leader*.)

Two

Hands at Work

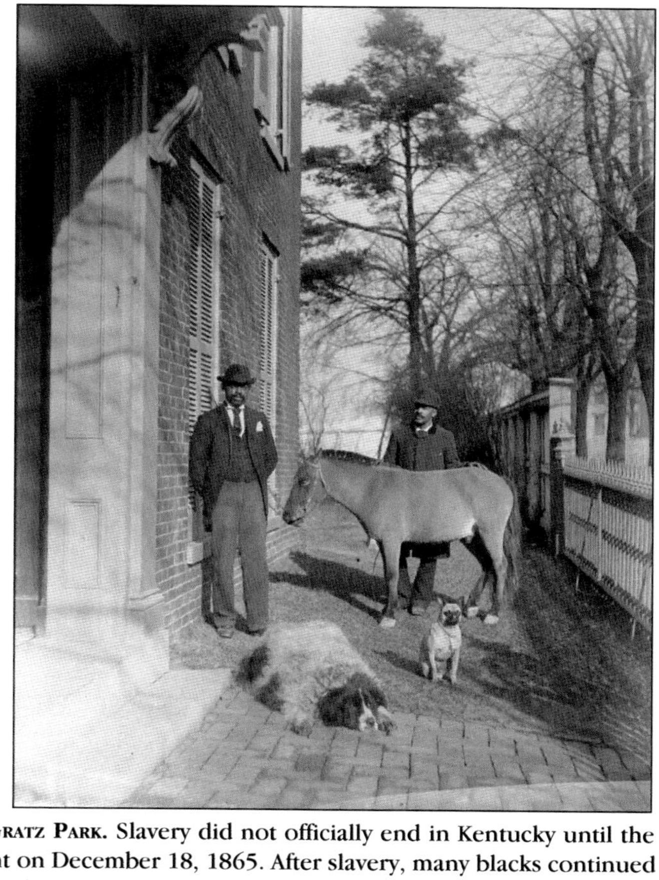

Standing Near Gratz Park. Slavery did not officially end in Kentucky until the ratification of the 13th Amendment on December 18, 1865. After slavery, many blacks continued to work for white families and live along alleys that lined white neighborhoods. This picture was taken *c.* 1888. (Courtesy of Barton Battaile Collection, Lexington Public Library.)

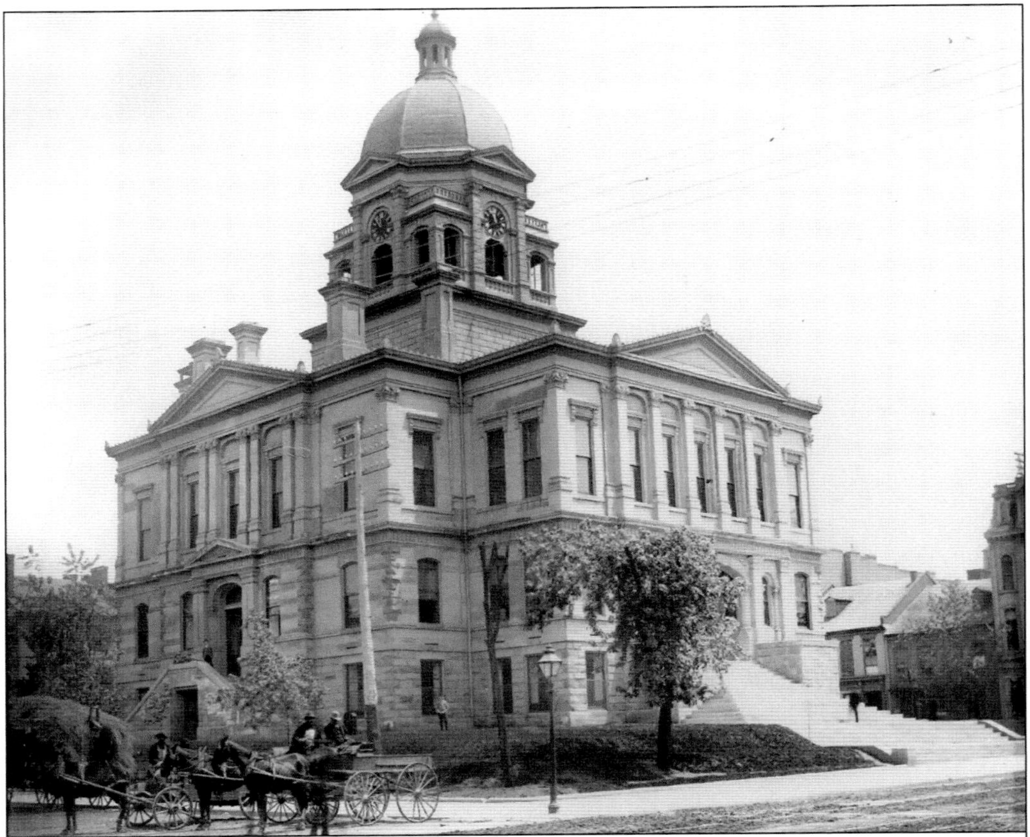

African-American Wagon Drivers. In the late 19th century, African-American men were hired to transport agricultural products, goods, and other materials, as well as passengers. Pictured is a small group of dray drivers parked in front of the court house on Main Street.

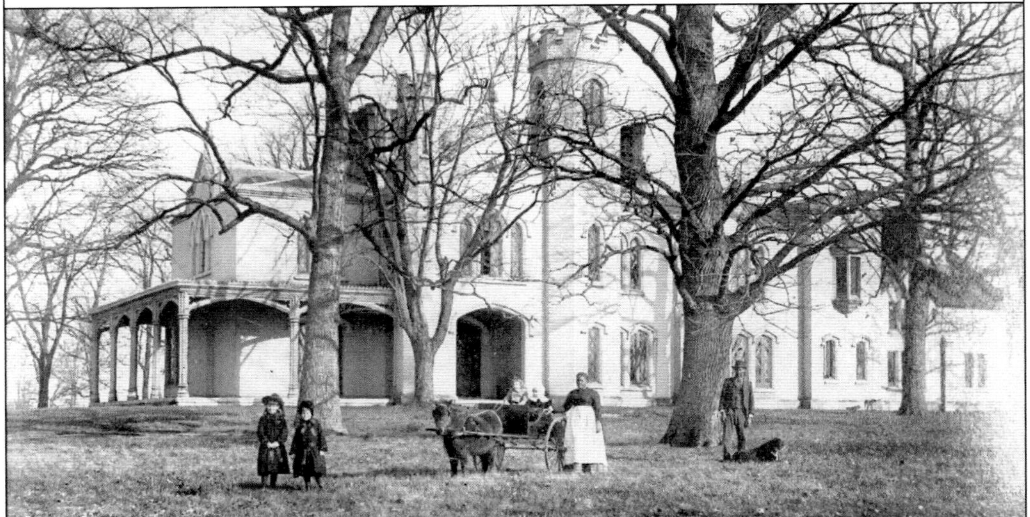

African-American Caretakers. Pictured is an African-American man and woman watching children play on Loudon Avenue and Bryan Station Road in what is known today as Castlewood Park.

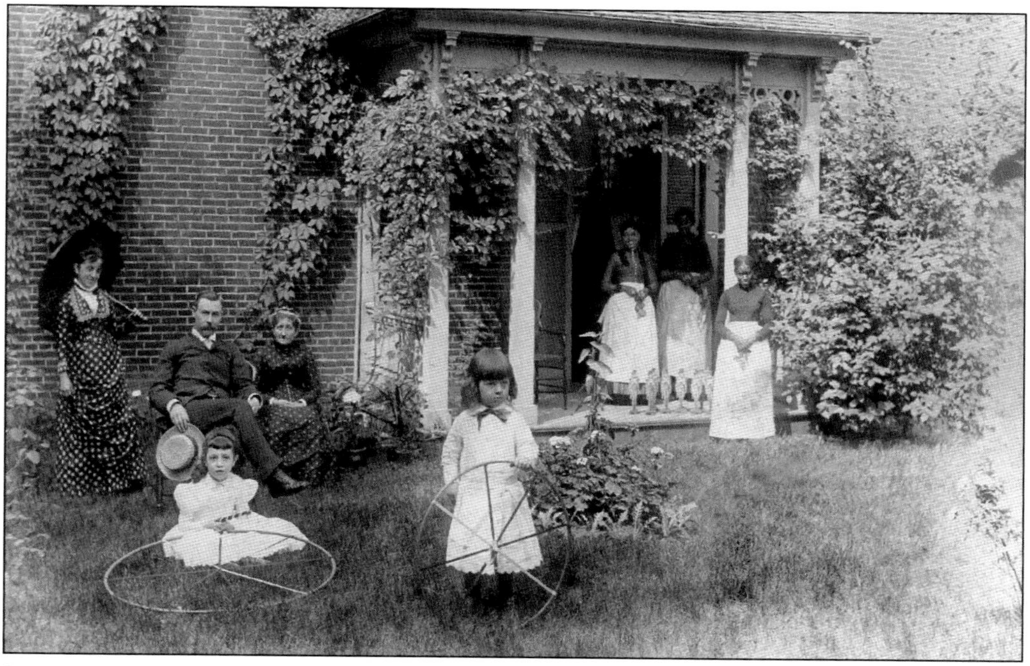

Domestic Servants. The primary occupation reserved for African-American women was domestic service. The hours were long, the pay was poor, and the work was demanding. Pictured in the background are three servant women in the doorway of the home of J. Hull Davidson, *c.* 1888. Davidson was the manager of the Phoenix Hotel and later served as mayor of Lexington in 1892 and 1893. (Courtesy of Barton Battaile Collection, Lexington Public Library.)

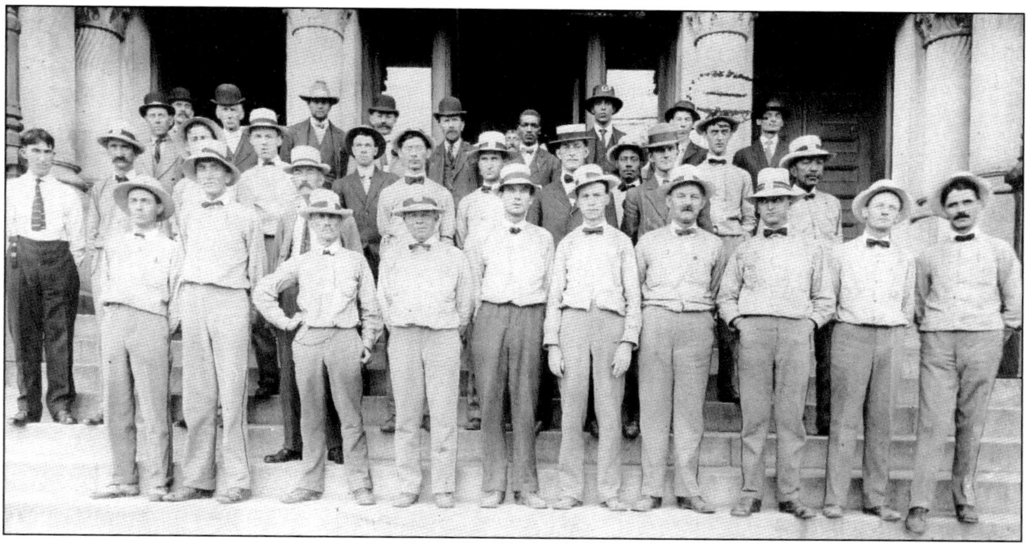

Letter Carriers. African Americans worked in post offices in Lexington, Frankfort, and Louisville in the early 20th century. According to the Lexington City Directory, Andrew Scott was a letter carrier in 1893. John B. Snowden worked with Scott as a letter carrier in 1902. Snowden was still delivering mail in 1919. This picture of Lexington postal workers was taken in 1910 and shows Scott on the second row, far right. (Courtesy of Barton Battaile Collection, Lexington Public Library.)

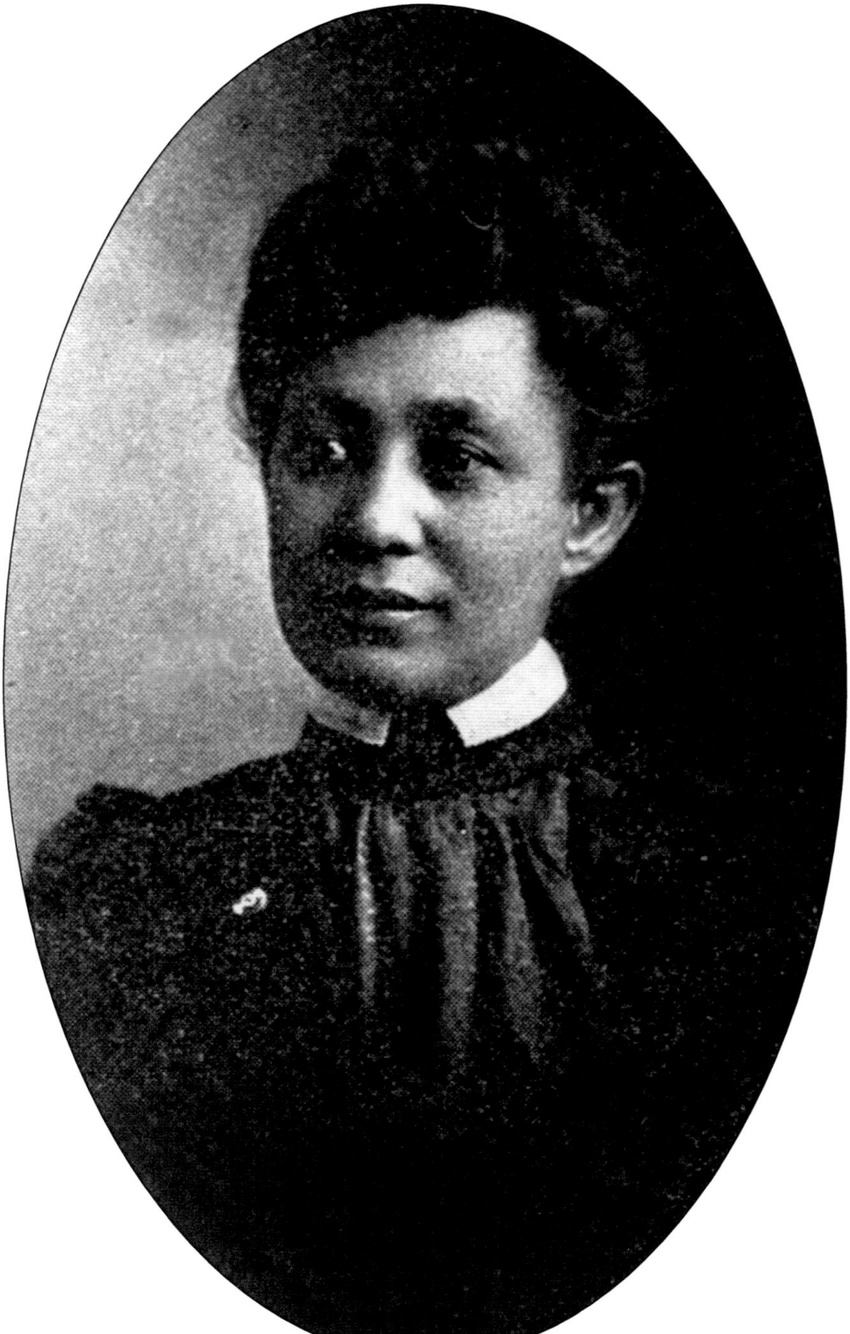

Dr. Mary E. Britton. Described as "industrious, frugal, honest, faithful, and charitable," Britton was a highly respected teacher, writer, activist, and doctor. On April 19, 1892, the *Kentucky Leader* printed her two-column letter to the Railroad Committee of the House of Representatives in opposition to the Separate Coach Bill. Britton later practiced medicine at 545 North Limestone. A devoted Seventh Day Adventist, she died August 27, 1925 at St. Joseph Hospital. (Courtesy The Negro Population of Lexington.)

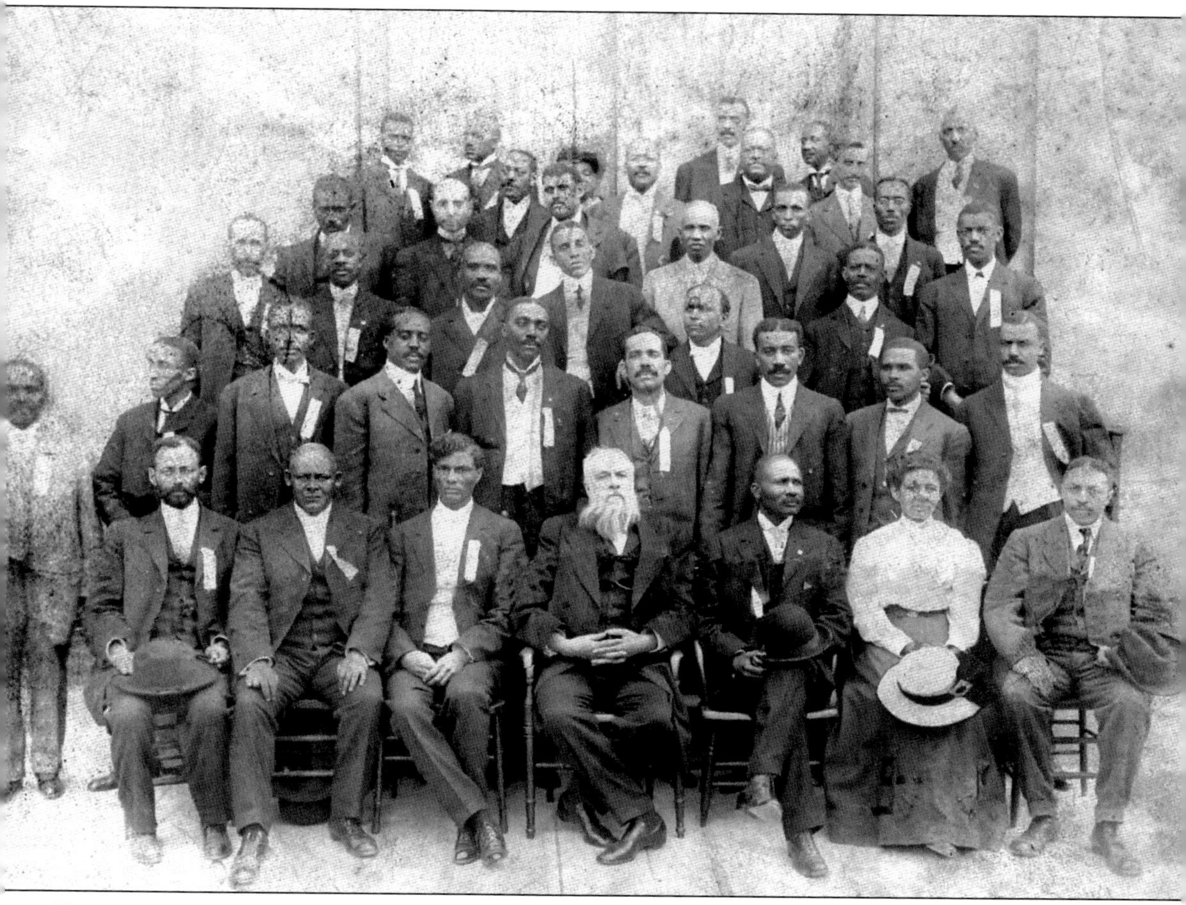

Meeting of the Medical Society of Negro Physicians. On May 12, 1910, African-American physicians, dentists, and pharmacists from several Kentucky cities that included Lexington, Louisville, and Covington met at the First African Baptist Church on East Short Street. Dr. G.W. Hubbard, dean of Meharry Medical College was one of the speakers. Pictured in this group photo on the third row, fourth person standing from the left, is Lexington physician, Dr. T.T. Wendell. (Courtesy of Thomas Tolliver.)

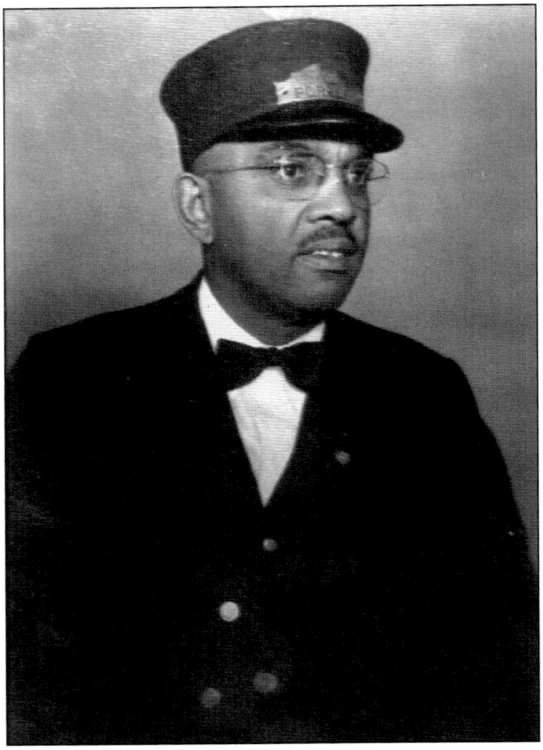

Tom Jackson, Pullman Porter. Throughout the early 20th century, a large number of black men worked on railroads as Pullman porters. Their job entailed serving the needs of passengers with a smile. Tom Jackson worked as a porter on trains for several years. He was also a treasurer at Shiloh Baptist Church. (Courtesy of Ella S. Bosley.)

African-American Waiters at the Lexington Club. Waiting tables was an occupation that was typically reserved for African Americans. The men in this photo were employed at one of Lexington's more exclusive dinning facilities. (Courtesy of Dr. T.T. Wendell Collection, Kentucky Historical Society, Special Collections and Archives.)

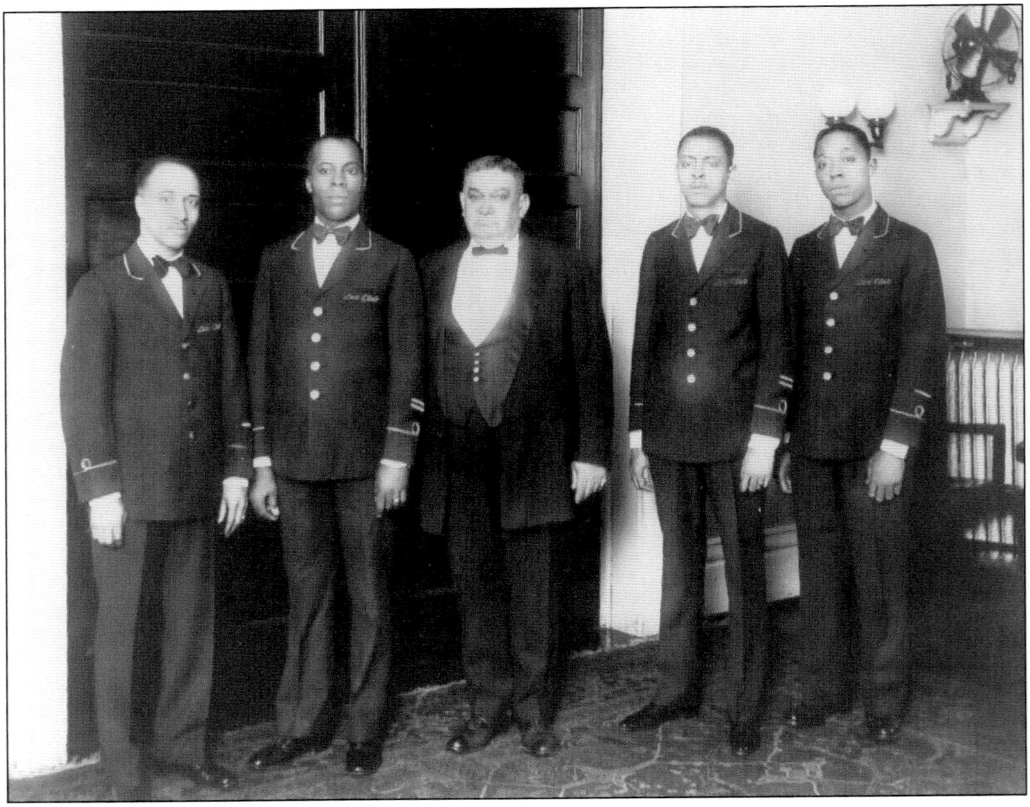

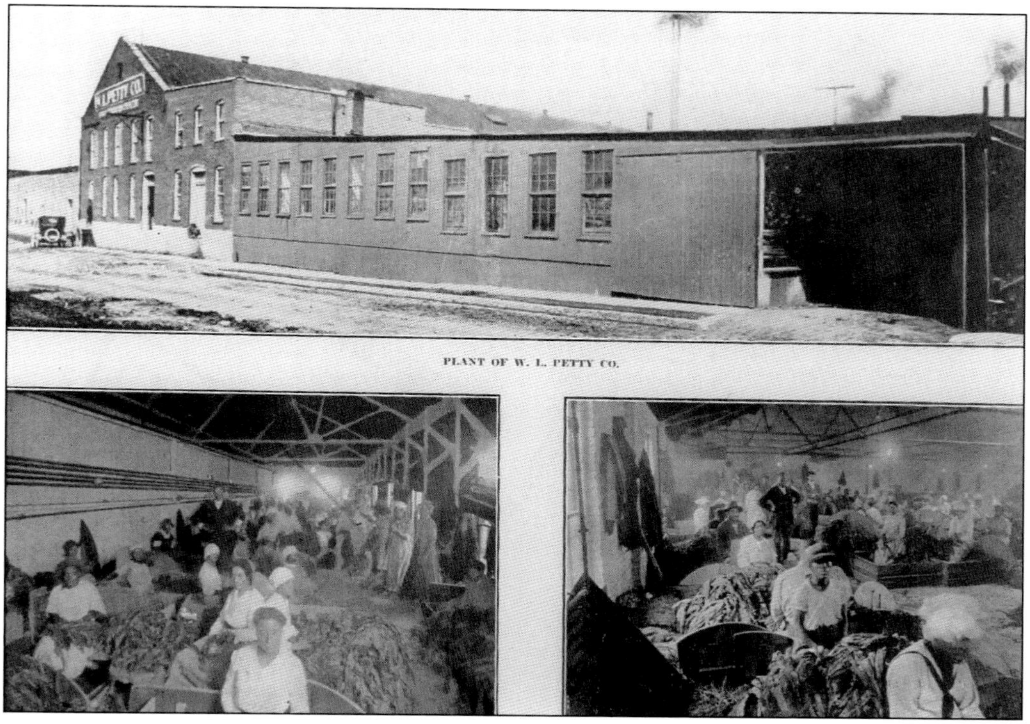

W.L. Petty Tobacco Steaming Room. Tobacco warehouses employed large numbers of African Americans, especially women. Many of these warehouses were poorly ventilated and did not include restroom facilities. Often workers earned less than $6.50 a week. Pictured are women working in W.L. Petty's Warehouse at 451 Chair Avenue near South Broadway. (Photo Courtesy of Barton Battaile Collection, Lexington Public Library, Kentucky Room.)

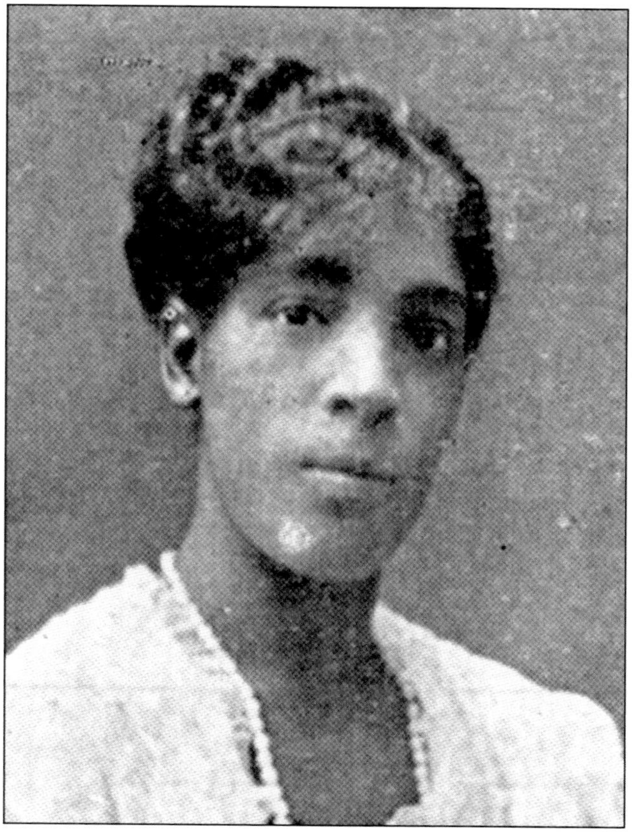

Madame Roberta Dallis. A successful African-American businesswoman, Roberta Dallis was listed in the *Dunbar Echo* as Lexington's "Oldest and Most Experienced Beautician" in the late 1920s. Her beauty parlor was located at 315 Wilson Street. (Courtesy of *Dunbar Echo*, Winston Powell.)

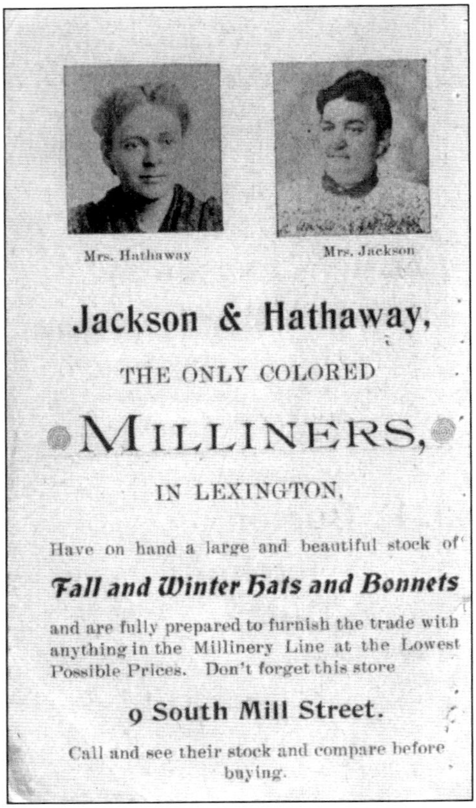

BUSINESSWOMEN. The Negro Business and Fair Directory for Lexington included this ad for "The Only Colored Milliners of Lexington" in its 1899 edition.

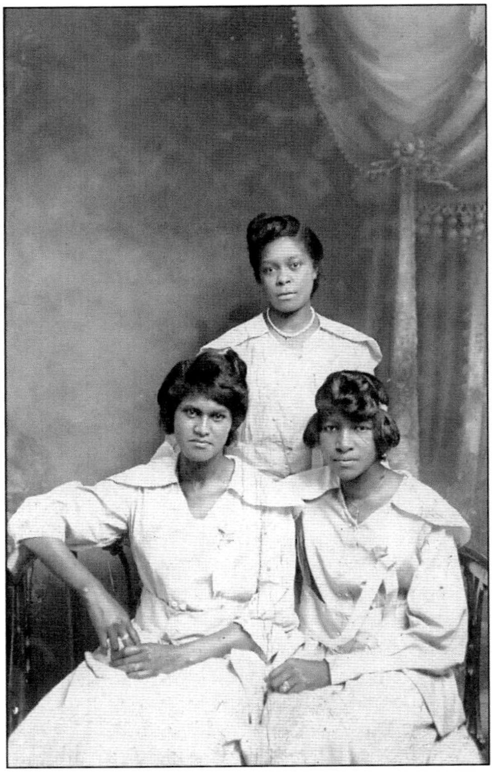

SCHOOLTEACHER. Alice Arnold, left, taught at Russell Elementary and Dunbar High School. She is pictured with two friends, Sarah Simpson and Ada Beasely, *c.* 1924. (Courtesy of Lilla Bentley.)

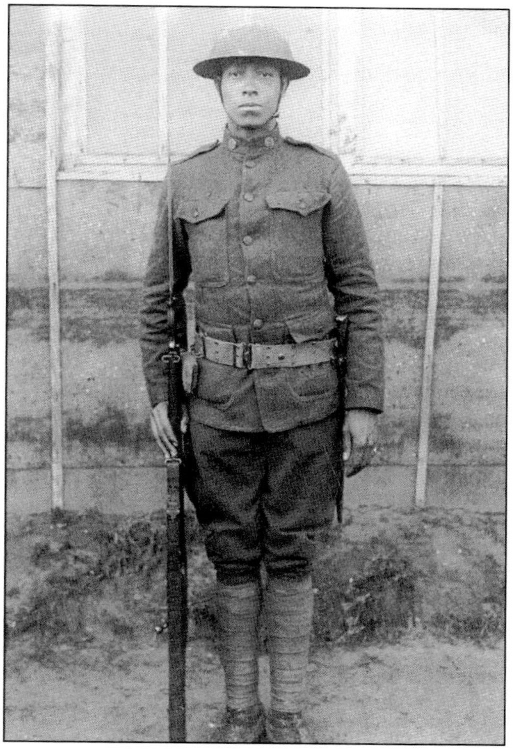

Corp. Enoch Cooper. On July 2, 1918, the *Lexington Leader* published the names of 250 "colored selectives and 46 alternates" scheduled to report to Camp Zachary Taylor in Louisville, Kentucky by July 19. Among the names released by the city draft board was that of Enoch Cooper. He is pictured here in his World War I uniform. Cooper was ordained a deacon at Shiloh Baptist Church in 1919. (Courtesy of Amanda Elliott.)

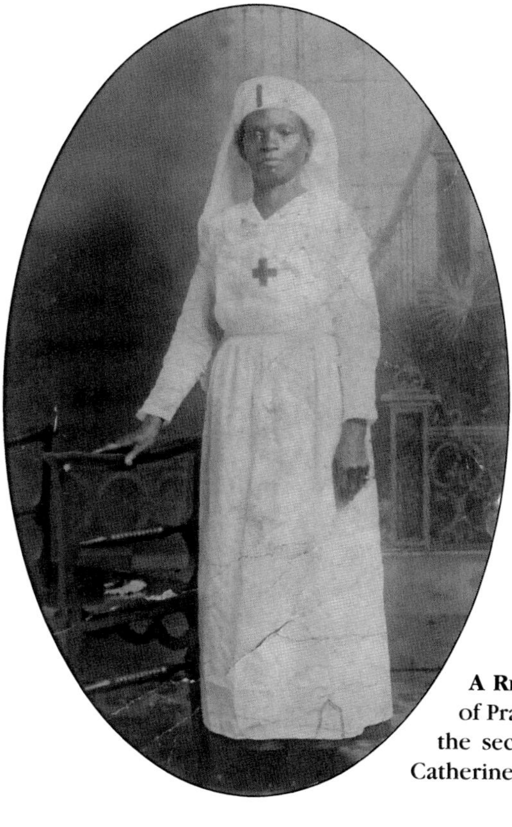

A Red Cross Nurse. Mary Anderson, then a resident of Prall Street, is pictured here in her uniform during the second decade of the 20th century. (Courtesy of Catherine Lewis.)

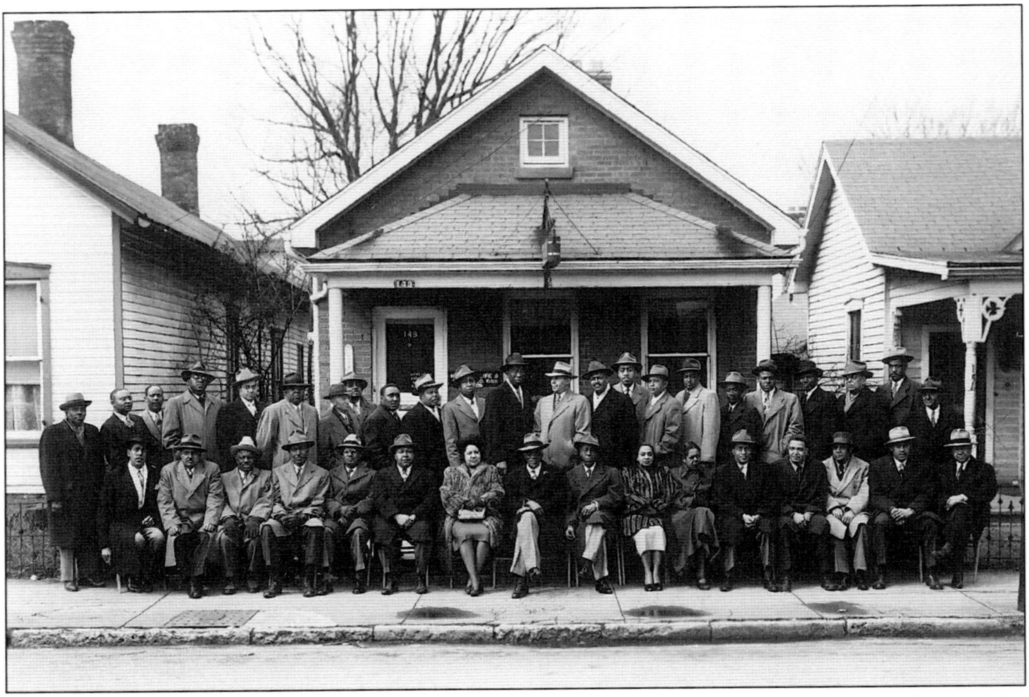

Mammoth Life Insurance Company. In this picture, associates with the company pose in front of the district office located at 149 Deweese Street in February 1949. (Courtesy of Lafayette Collection, Special Collections, University of Kentucky.)

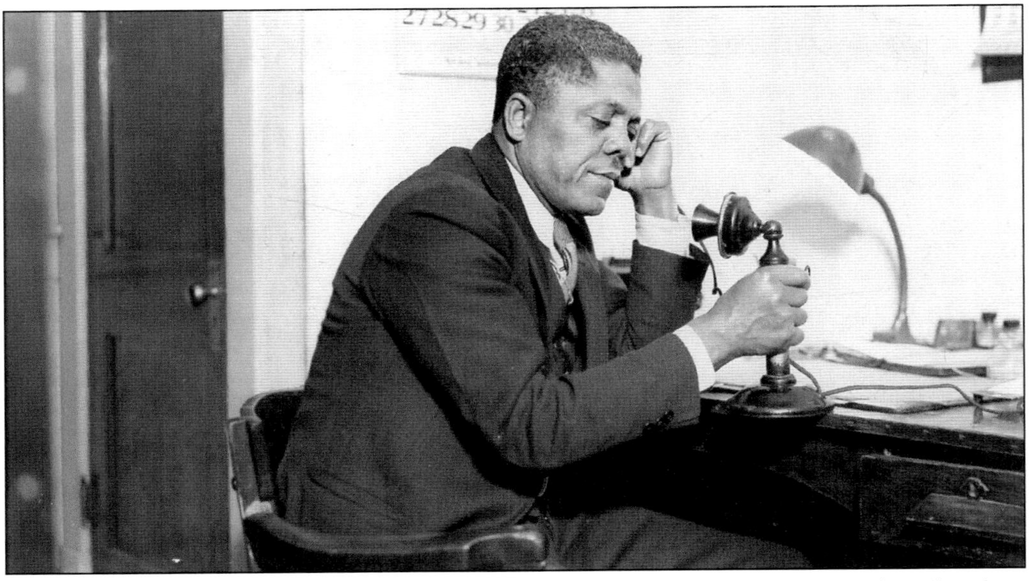

John T. Hawkins. On September 14, 1905, the Kentucky Colored Embalmers and Undertakers Association met at the U.B.F. Hall on North Limestone Street. An article in the *Lexington Herald* reported that the group was the first African-American association for embalmers in the country. Pictured at his desk is John T. Hawkins. A graduate of the Cincinnati College of Embalming, Hawkins operated a funeral home in the city from the 1920s until his death in 1949. (Courtesy of Dwight Hughes.)

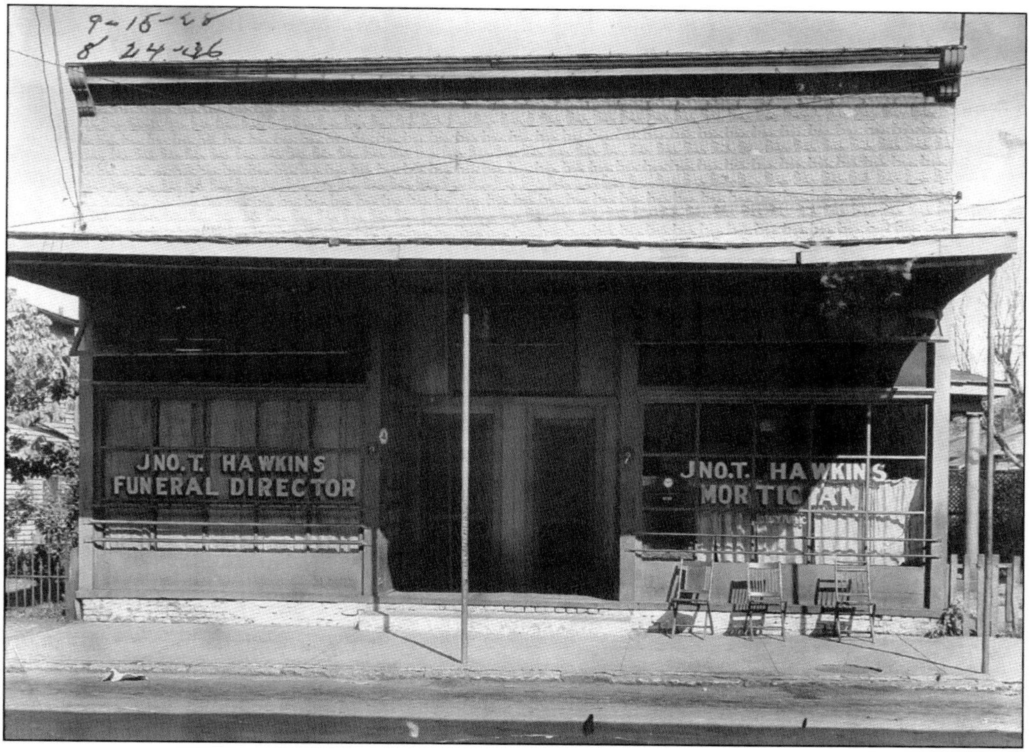

Hawkins Funeral Home at 409 Patterson Street. Pictured in the early 1930s is Hawkins's second building. In 1936, he built a first-class funeral home at 632 Pine Street. (Courtesy of Dwight Hughes.)

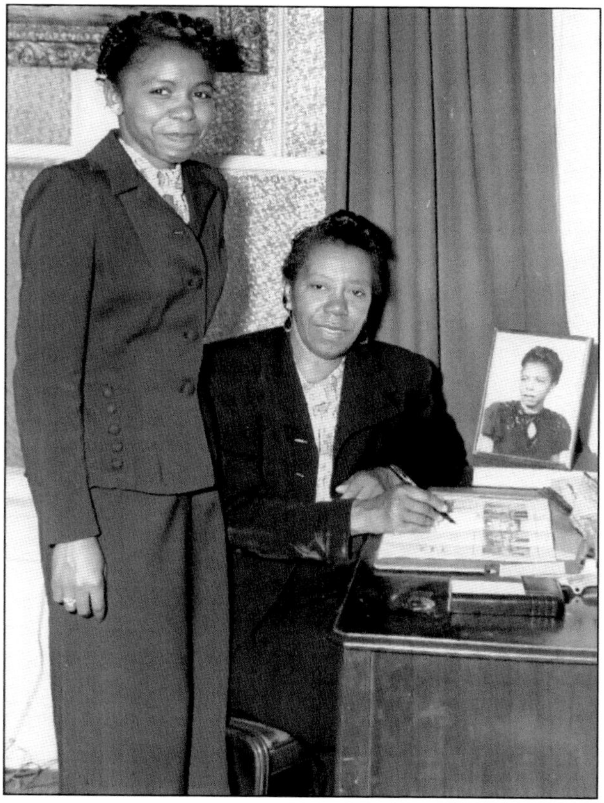

Funeral Home Owners. After his death, Hawkins's wife and daughter continued to operate the funeral business he had established. Pictured from left to right are his daughter, Ann Hawkins Taylor, and her mother, Vina Mae Hawkins. (Courtesy of Dwight Hughes.)

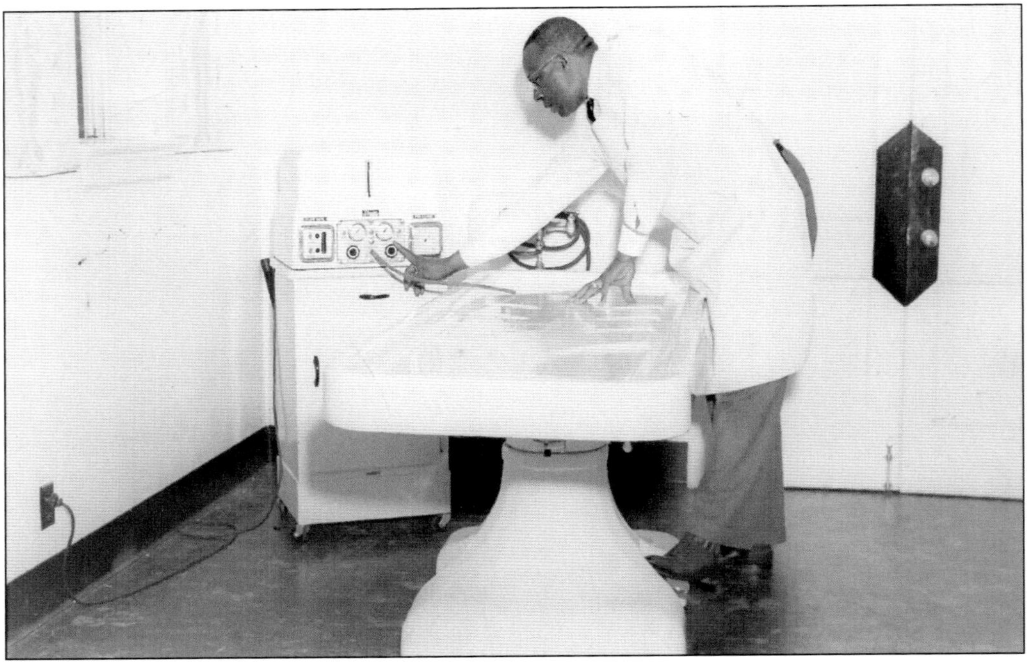

Charles Haggard. Through the years, Lexington has had several African-American funeral homes. They have included Cunningham, Claughton-Brown, H.L. Stewart, Porter and Jackson, and Smith and Smith. Pictured is Charles Haggard at work in his funeral home at 370 East Second Street. (Courtesy of Dwight Hughes.)

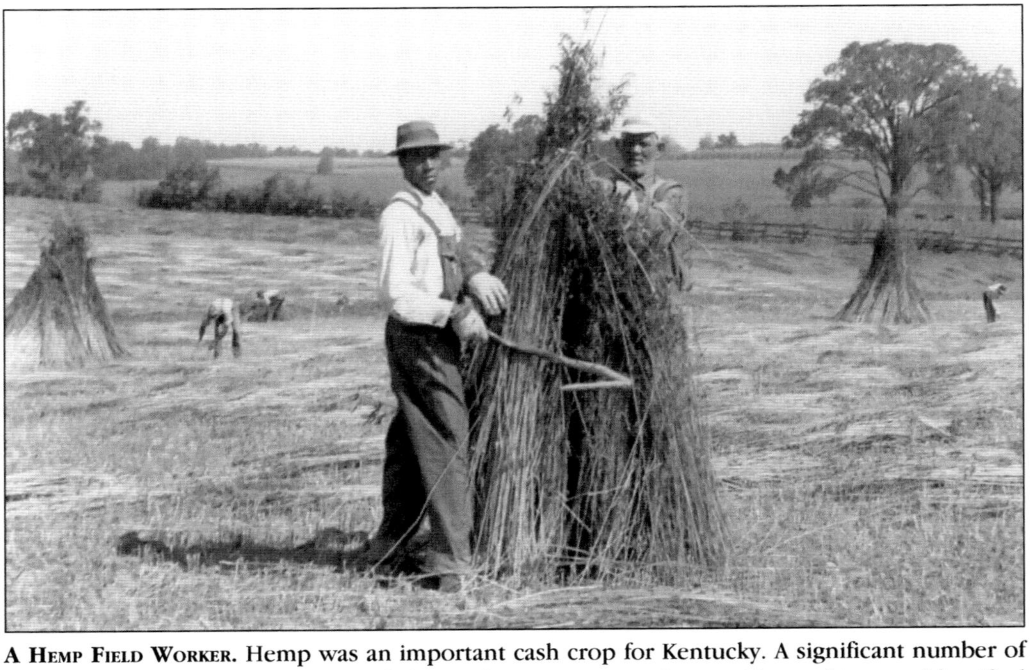

A Hemp Field Worker. Hemp was an important cash crop for Kentucky. A significant number of African Americans worked in hemp fields on farms in Fayette County. Pictured is an unidentified worker on J. Winston Coleman's Winburn farm on Russell Cave Road in August 1941. (Courtesy of Coleman Collection, Transylvania University.)

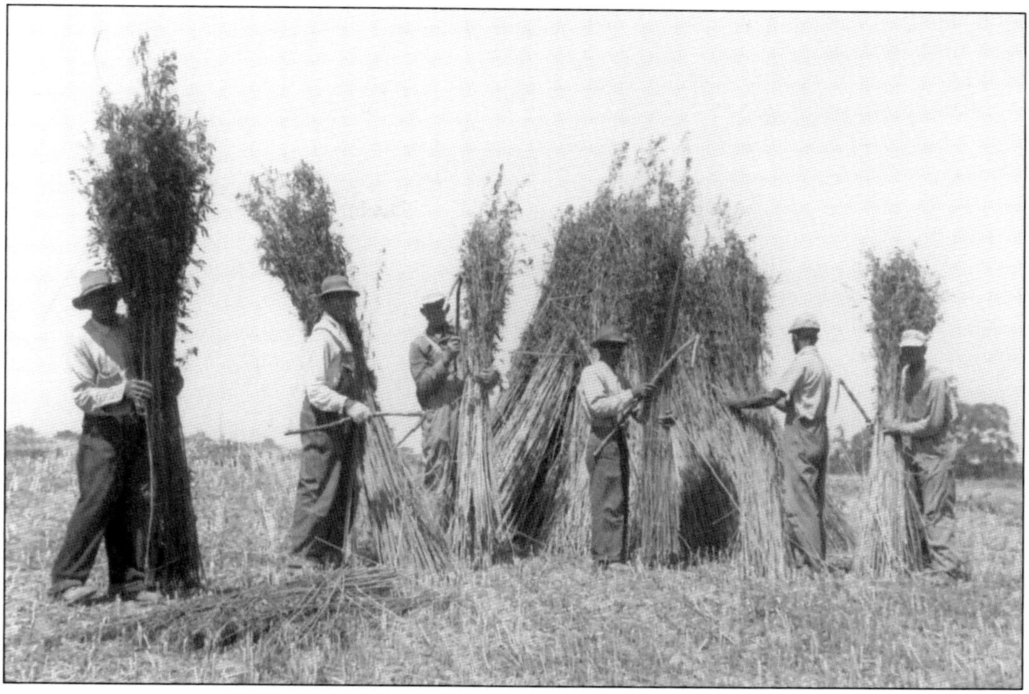

Workers on Winburn Farm. Hemp crop fibers were used to make cloth and rope. The outbreak of World War II led to an increase in the production of hemp. Pictured are workers in the field during the fall of 1942. (Courtesy of Coleman Collection, Transylvania University.)

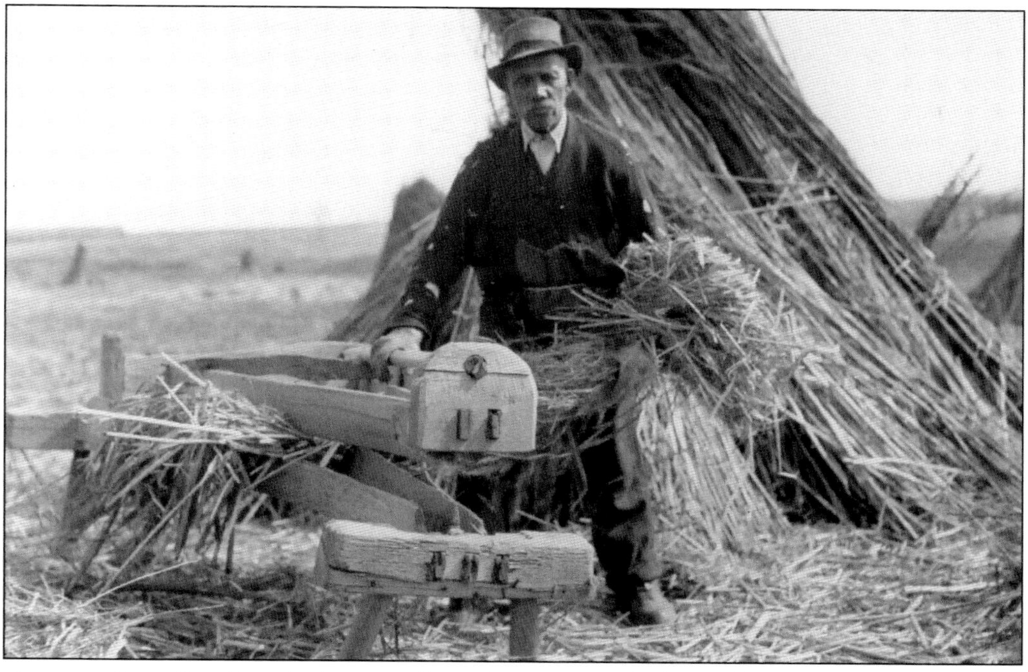

Castleton Farm. Breaking the hemp stalks and separating the hemp fiber was an important part of the production of hemp. Pictured here is an unidentified worker at a hemp brake, *c.* 1940. (Courtesy of Coleman Collection, Transylvania University.)

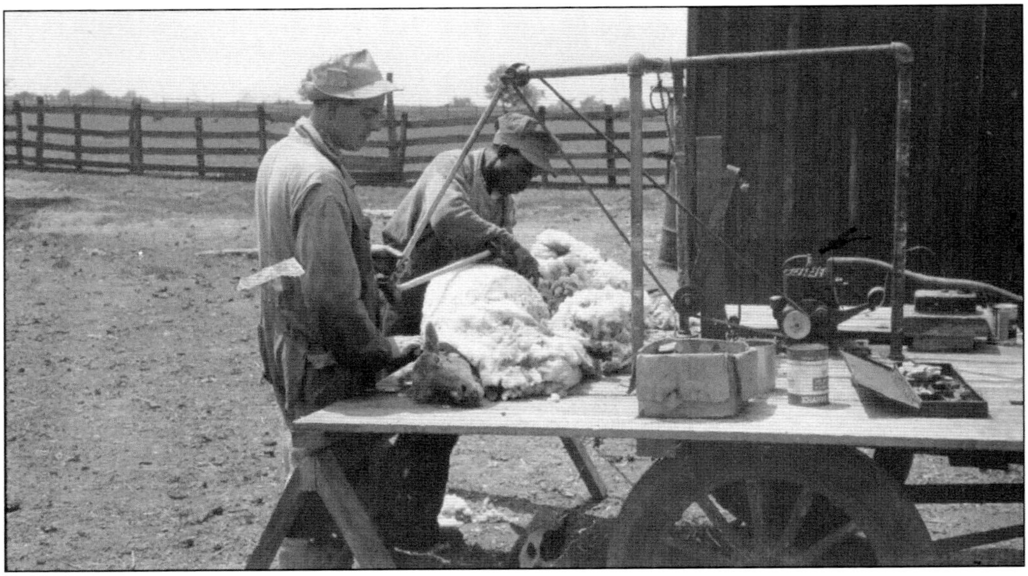

Shearing Sheep. African Americans did a variety of jobs in rural Fayette County. Pictured is William Yates Sr. at work on Tom Nash's farm on May 11, 1944. (Courtesy of Betty Smithers.)

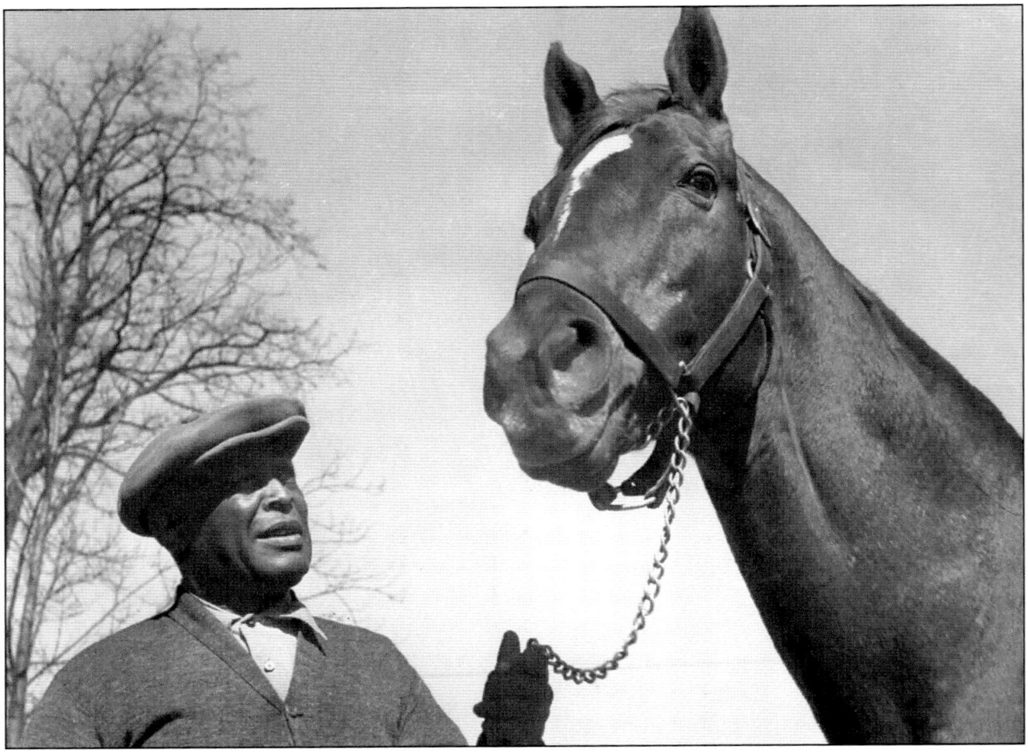

Will Harbut. Will Harbut groomed the famous local racehorse Man O'War for more than 15 years and developed a strong attachment to the horse. Harbut died October 3, 1947, and was buried in the Maddoxtown Baptist Church Cemetery. Less than a month later, on November 1, 1947, the famed race horse Man O'War died in his stall at the Faraway Farm. Pictured is Harbut and Man O'War. (Courtesy of Barton Battaile Collection, Lexington Public Library.)

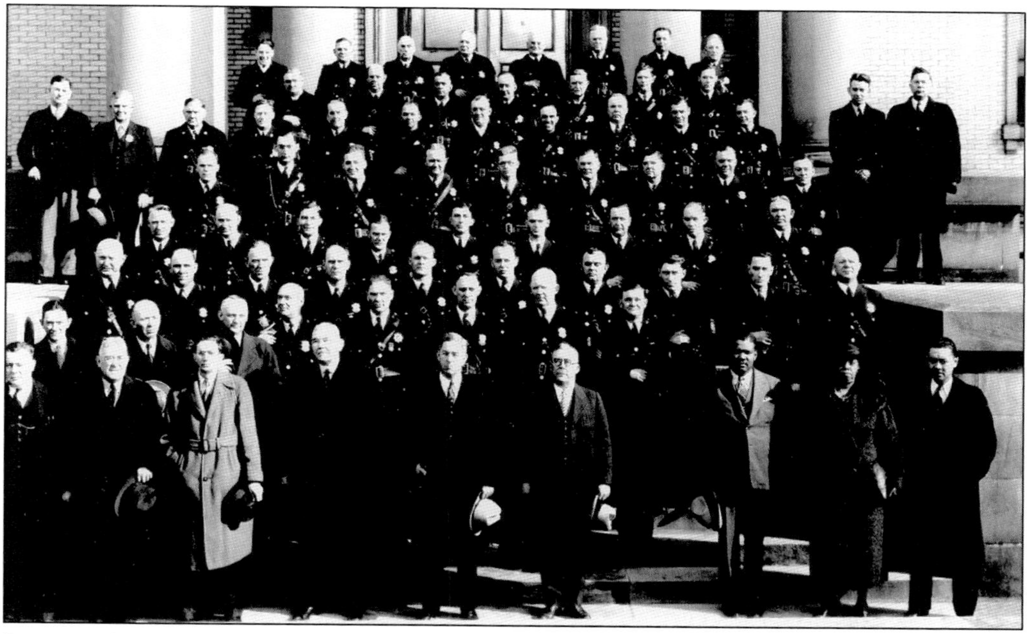

Lexington Police Department. In 1895, local African Americans appealed to the mayor of Lexington to appoint an African-American patrolman. In July 1918, R.F. Bell was selected as the policeman and Mrs. Lee Christie was selected as the matron at Douglass Park. By the mid-1920s, Susan Lynn Tabb, a member of First African Baptist Church, was serving as police matron. Pictured standing off to the side, from left to right, are Prather Walker, Tabb, and James Paige in 1937. (Courtesy of Lafayette Collection, University of Kentucky.)

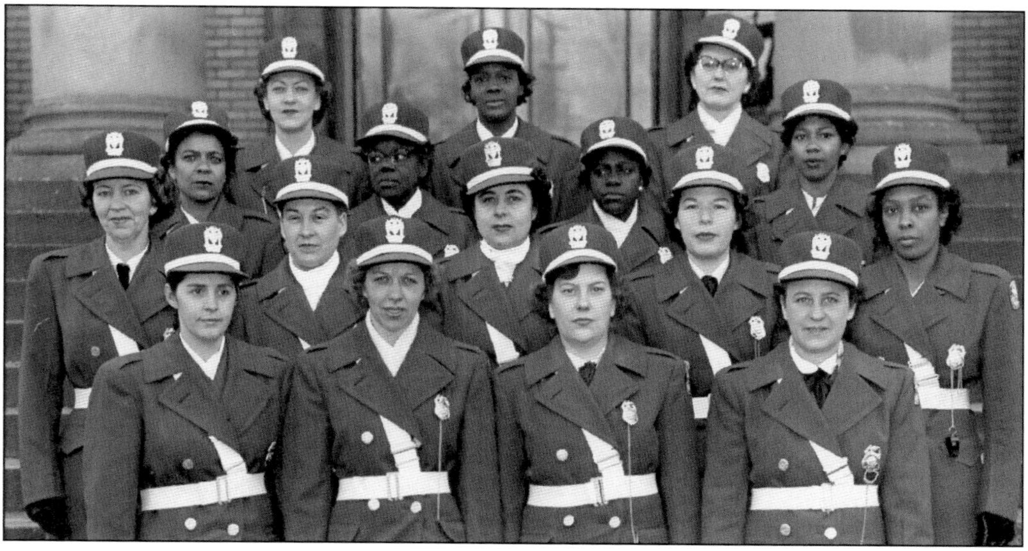

Crossing Guards. In 1952, several African-American women were hired as crossing guards. These women also worked major citywide social events. The African-American women pictured above, from left to right starting from the first person on the third row, are Jane Drake Hawthorne, Virginia Henderson, Margaret Thornton, Florence Smallwood Mitchell, and Josephine Jackson Hatchett. Amanda Cooper Elliott is pictured in the second row on the right. (Courtesy of Amanda Elliott.)

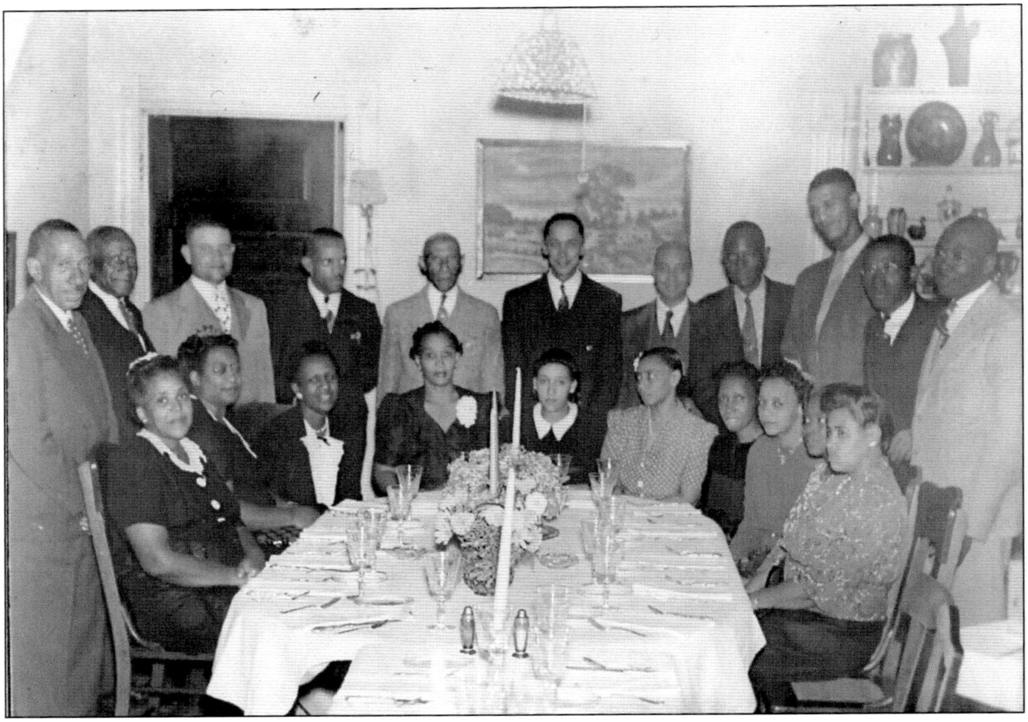

University of Kentucky Janitors. Abbie's Food Shoppe on East Third Street entertained a dinner for University of Kentucky (UK) janitors, *c.* 1945. The principal of Booker T. Washington Elementary School, Lucy Harth Smith, was the speaker for the occasion. (Courtesy of Phaon Patton and Lawrence Williams.)

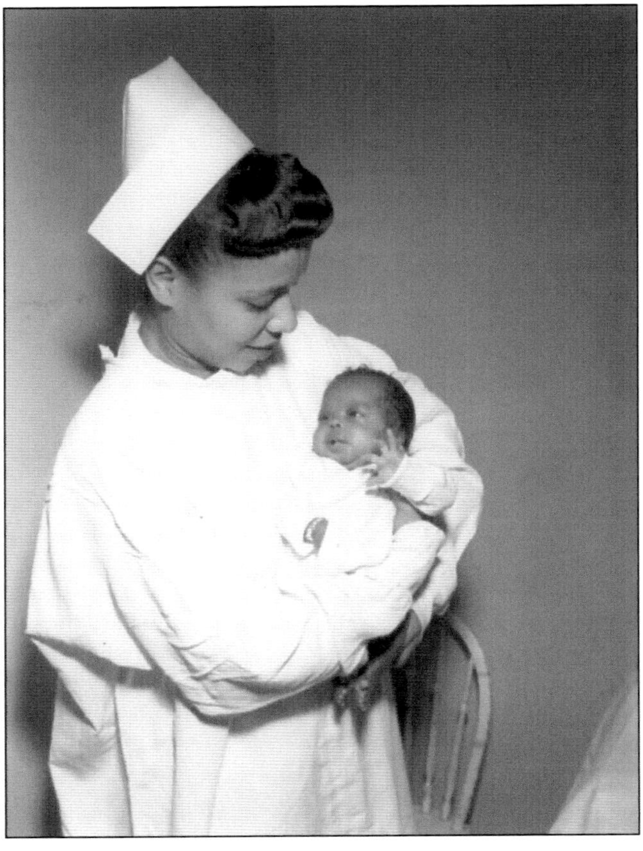

Thelma Merchant. Thelma Merchant was a registered nurse at St. Joseph Hospital for 37 years. In this June 22, 1949 photo, she holds a baby that had been delivered on May 4, 12 minutes after the mother's death. (Courtesy of *Lexington Herald Leader*.)

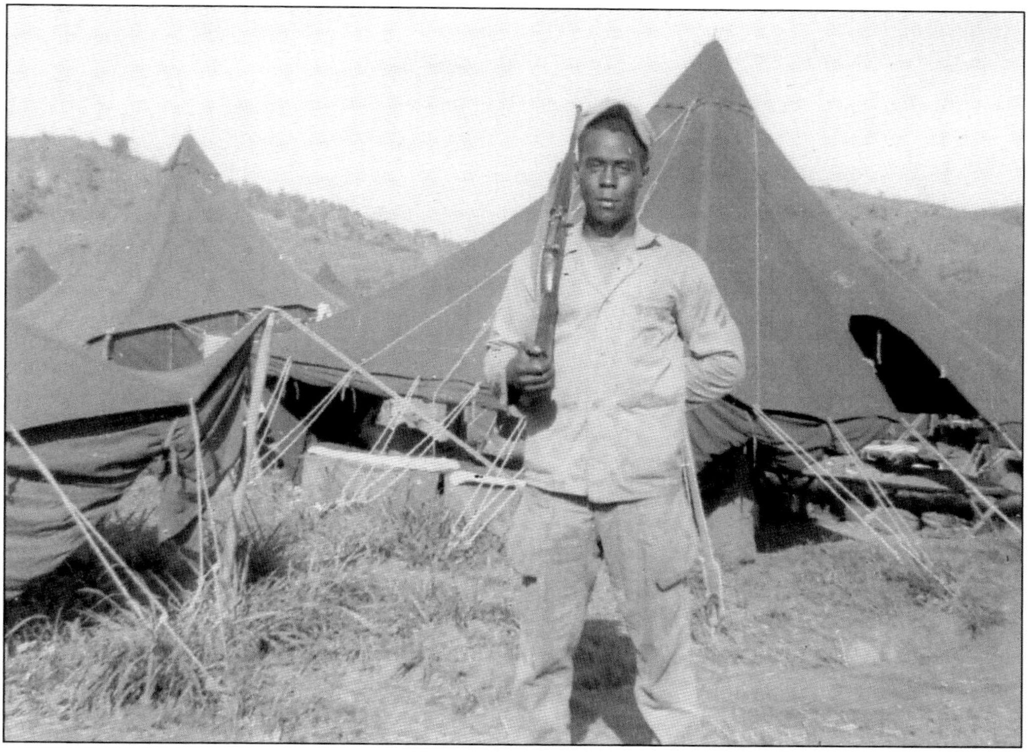

A Soldier Serving the Nation During Wartime. Since the Civil War, Kentucky African Americans have served in the armed forces. Pictured here is United States marine Richard Owens during the Korean War. Owens spent more than 20 years in the marines, and he became a first sergeant at the Marine Corps Reserve Center. (Courtesy of Laura Tompkins Owens.)

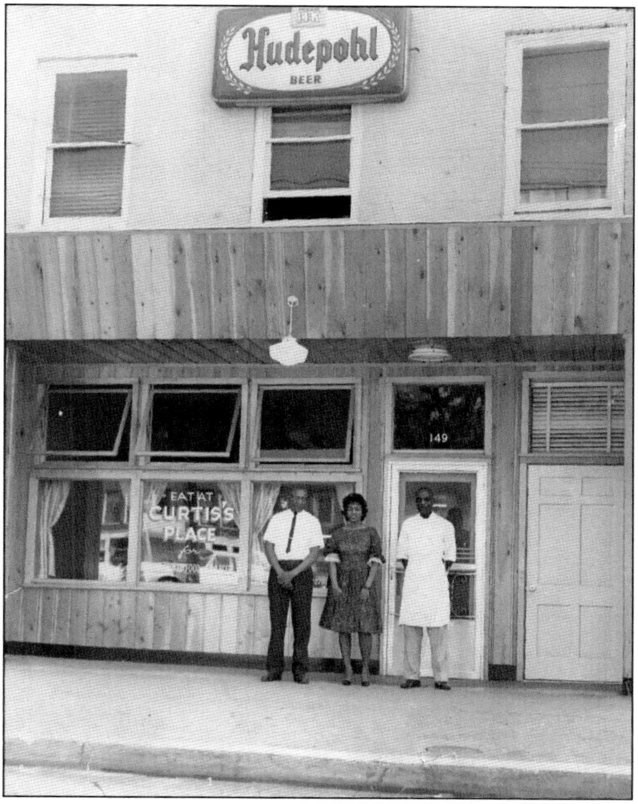

Curtis's Place. Located at 149 Water Street near North Upper Street, Curtis Shores operated a poplar downtown restaurant. Fats Domino and Stepin Fetchit were among the celebrities who visited his establishment. Shores's widow, Ella S. Bosley, owned the store until 1968. She is pictured here with employees Taylor Ballew on her left and Lester Watson on her right. (Courtesy of Ella S. Bosley.)

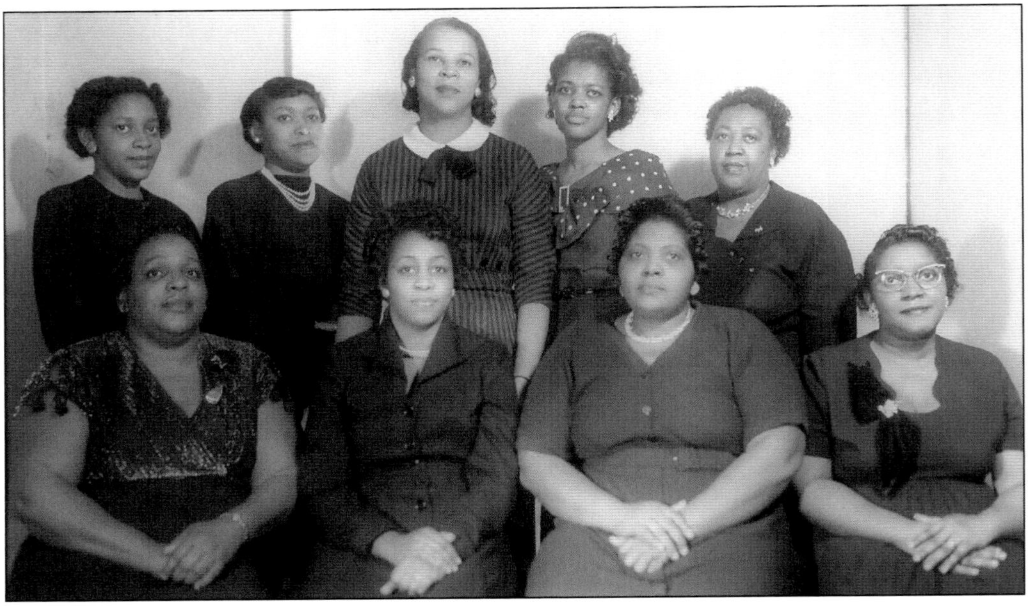

Beauticians. The Kentucky Congress of Barbers and Beauticians Inc. was an African-American organization that held its 20th annual state convention in Lexington in 1957. The souvenir booklet included this photo of Unit 4 of Lexington. Sitting, from left to right, are Jane Etta Moore, Ella S. Bosley, Martha Cobb (state president), and Audrey Coleman. Standing, from left to right, are Emma L. Mitchell, Jessie Latimer, Majorie Johnson, Mary L Rice, and Ollie Lewis. (Souvenir Program for Kentucky Congress of Barber and Beauticians, 1957, Courtesy of Winston Powell.)

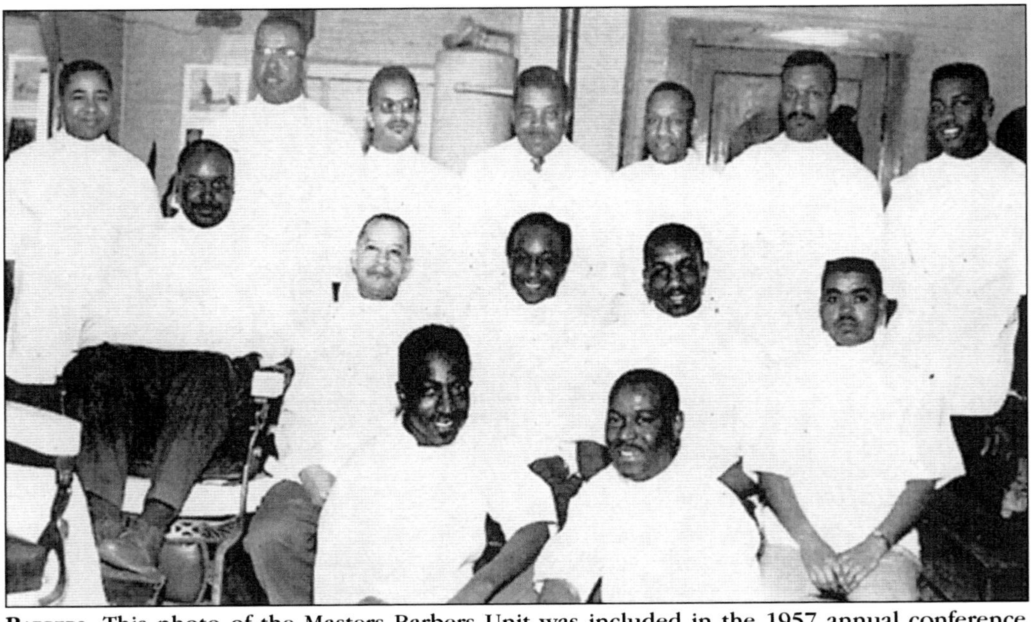

Barbers. This photo of the Masters Barbers Unit was included in the 1957 annual conference souvenir booklet. In the front row, left and kneeling, is Vincent Black. Seated in the barber chair is George Tarrance. In the back row and to the left of Tarrance, standing, is Johnnie H. Jackson. (Courtesy of Souvenir Program for Kentucky Congress of Barber and Beauticians, 1957, Courtesy of Winston Powell.)

Three

Spiritual Forces

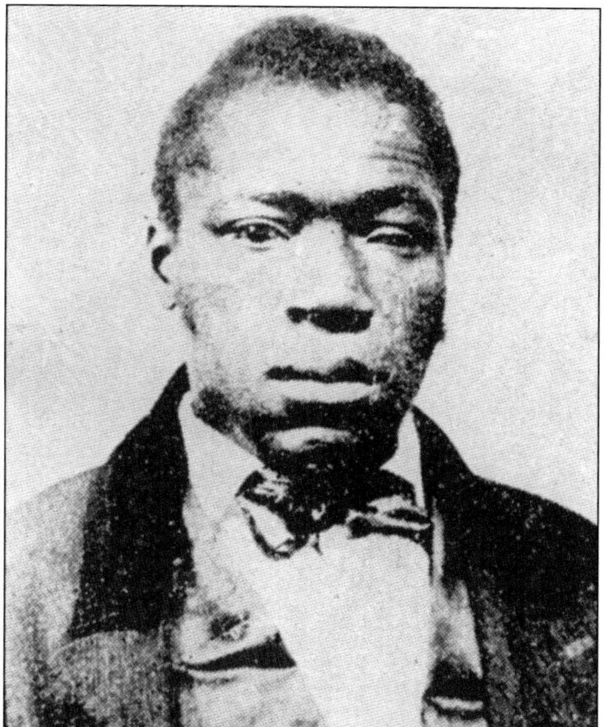

Rev. Frederick Braxton. African-American churches were founded in Lexington before the Civil War. Peter "Old Captain" Duerett and London Ferrill were the two most instrumental African-American preachers during this period. In 1854, Reverend Braxton was the pastor of First Baptist Church (now First African Baptist). Eight years later, he organized Main Street Baptist Church and served as pastor of that church until his death in 1876. While at Main Street he opened a school for African-American children in 1867. (Courtesy of the Sallie Price Collection, First Baptist Church Souvenir Bulletin, 1940, UK Special Collections.)

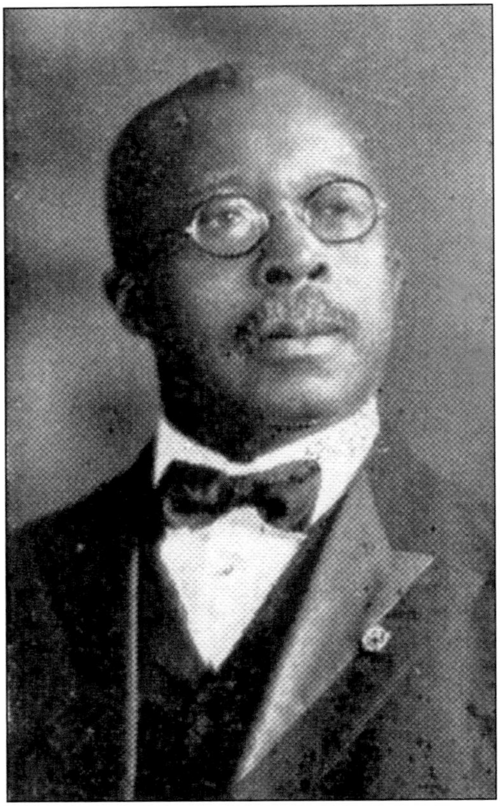

Charles H. Parrish. Born a slave in Lexington in 1859, Parrish attended public schools after slavery. He served as church clerk at First African Baptist Church before moving to Louisville in 1880. He later graduated from State University (renamed Simmons), accepted the pastorate of Calvary Baptist Church in Louisville, and presided over Eckstein Norton Institute in Cane Springs, Kentucky. From 1913 to 1918, he served as president of Simmons University. (Courtesy of the Sallie Price Collection, First Baptist Church Souvenir Bulletin, 1940, UK Special Collections.)

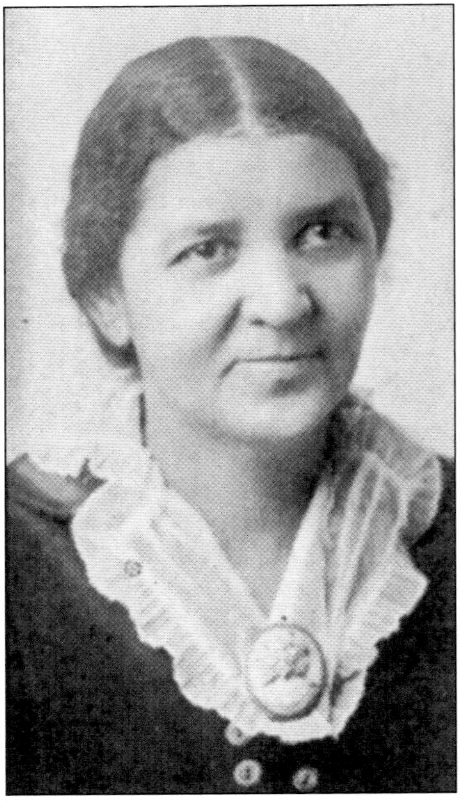

Mamie E. Steward. Recognized as the first organist at First African Baptist Church, Steward was a strong advocate for expanding the role of women in the church. Steward once held the position of president of the Baptist Educational Convention. (Courtesy of the Sallie Price Collection, First Baptist Church Souvenir Bulletin, 1940, UK Special Collections.)

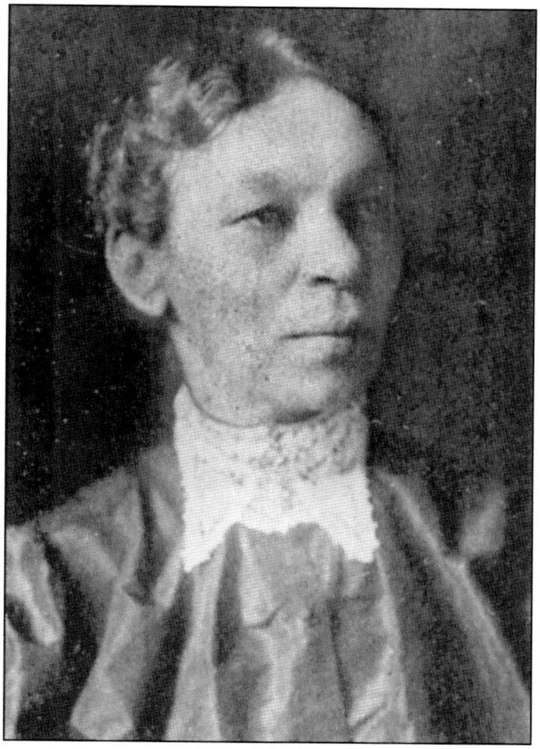

Amanda Nelson. A member of First African Baptist, Nelson served as the statistical secretary of the American National Baptist Convention in 1887. She also served as the first president of the State Baptist Women's Educational Convention. (Courtesy of the Sallie Price Collection, First Baptist Church Souvenir Bulletin, 1940, UK Special Collections.)

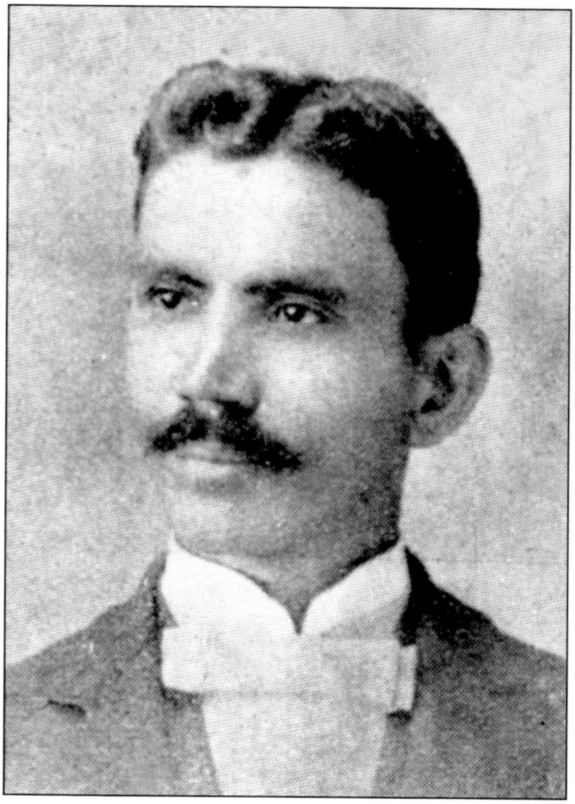

Rev. W.L. Johnson. Throughout segregation, Baptist was the largest denomination in the city. Other denominations in the city included Episcopalian and Methodist. Pictured is the pastor of the First Congregational Church, which was located on Short Street in 1907. (Courtesy of Negro Population of Lexington, 1907.)

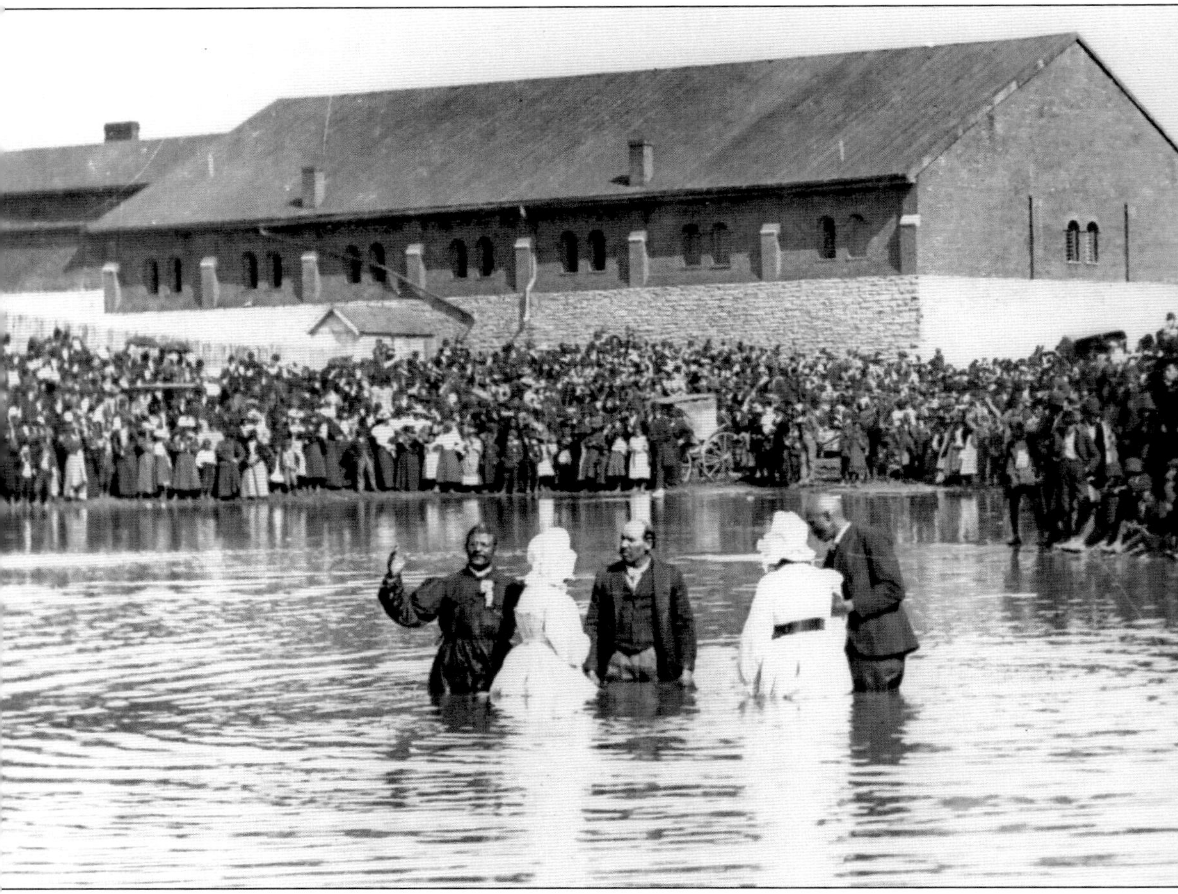

Historic Pleasant Green Missionary Baptist Church Baptismal. It was common in Lexington to baptize in nearby ponds. This photograph was taken at the limestone quarry pond between Bolivar and Scott Streets, *c.* 1898. (Courtesy of the Barton Battaile Collection, Lexington Public Library.)

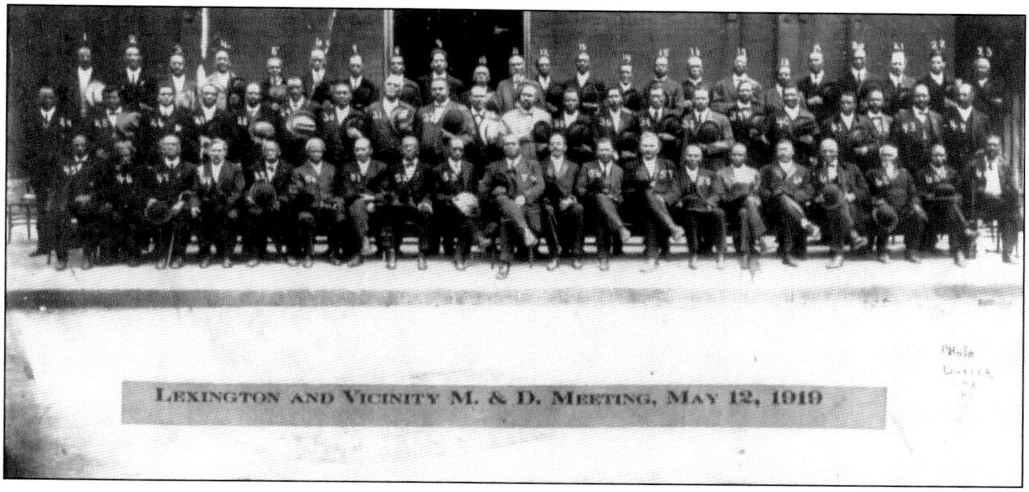

MEETING OF THE LEXINGTON MINISTERS AND DEACONS. This group of 64 ministers includes several local pastors. (Courtesy of Lilla Bentley.)

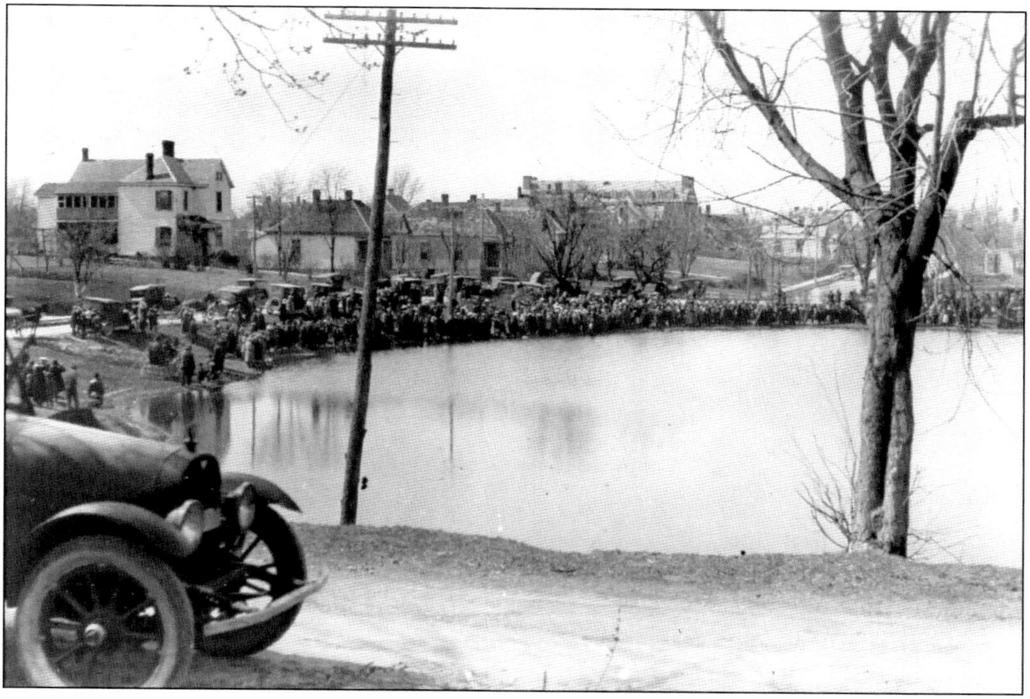

CONSOLIDATED BAPTIST CHURCH BAPTIZING AT CLIFTON POND. Organized at a prayer meeting on Adams Street in 1884, Consolidated Baptist Church was located on Winslow Street before moving to Upper Street in the 1920s. William Ray Allen, a professor of zoology at the University of Kentucky, captured this scene from his front porch steps, *c.* 1923. The University of Kentucky W.T. Young Library now stands next where the pond once existed. (Courtesy of Ellen Allen.)

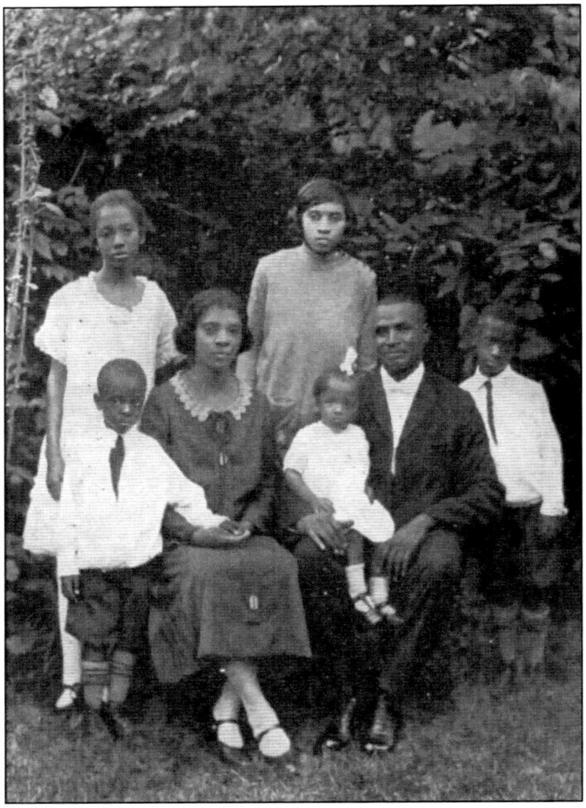

Rev. Thomas Horace Smith and Family. In January 1932, Reverend Smith became the third pastor of the Shiloh Baptist Church and served there until 1961. This picture was taken when Reverend Smith was pastor of Zion Baptist Church in Georgetown. Seated, from left to right, are Helen E. Ray Smith, Rev. T.H. Smith, and Rose Anna Smith (child in lap). Standing, from left to right, are Gloster Maceo Smith, Minnie Smith, Mary Smith, and John Thomas Smith. Gloster Smith, now Rev. Gloster Smith, has served as pastor of the Evergreen Baptist Church on Florida Street for over 50 years. (Courtesy of Amanda Elliott.)

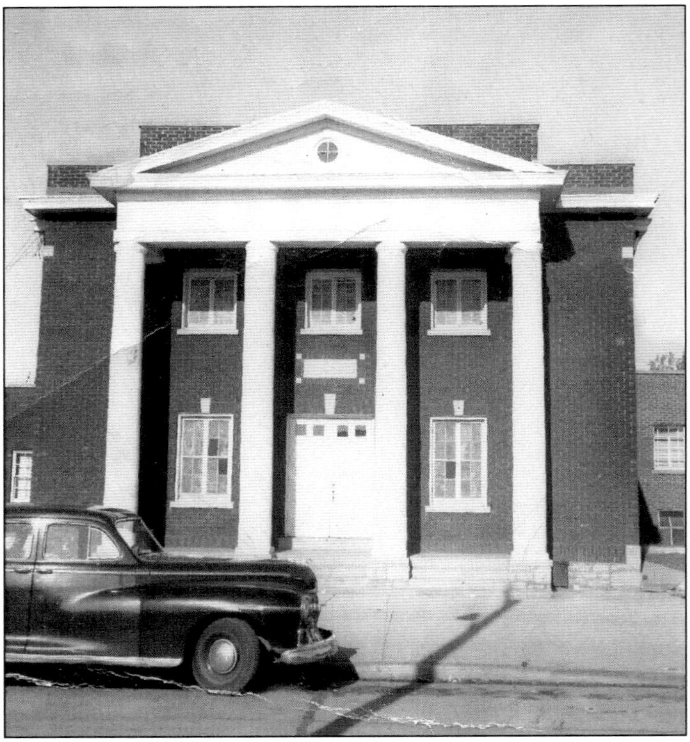

Shiloh Baptist Church. In April 1896, members from Main Street and Liberty Baptist Churches began worshipping together and formed Shiloh. This is a picture of Shiloh at 57 1/2 Thomas Street. The church moved to 237 East Fifth Street in 1963. (Courtesy of Calvert McCann.)

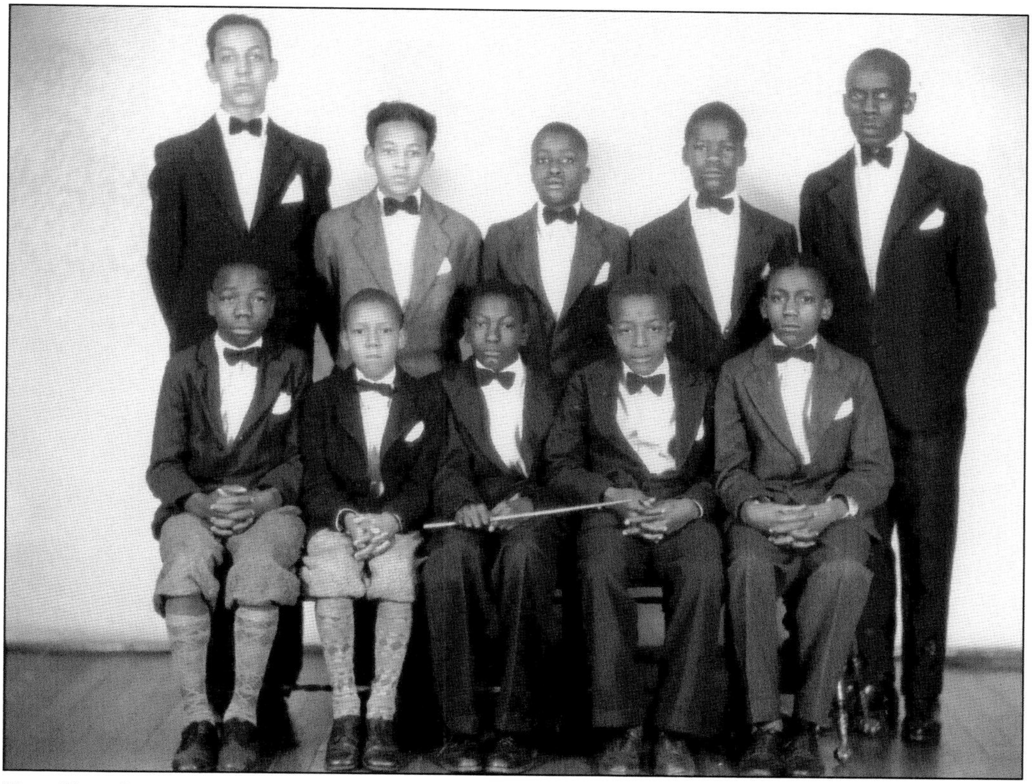

Nine Keys Chorus at Historic Pleasant Green Missionary Baptist Church. Standing, from left to right, are John Wallace (lead singer), Alex Williams, James Lee, John Polk, and George Smith (director). Sitting, from left to right, are James Sinclair, Robert Burbage, Hiram Brown, John Will "Scoop" Brown, and James Young. The group performed at the Lafayette Hotel and local churches. (Courtesy of the Lafayette Collection, UK Special Collections.)

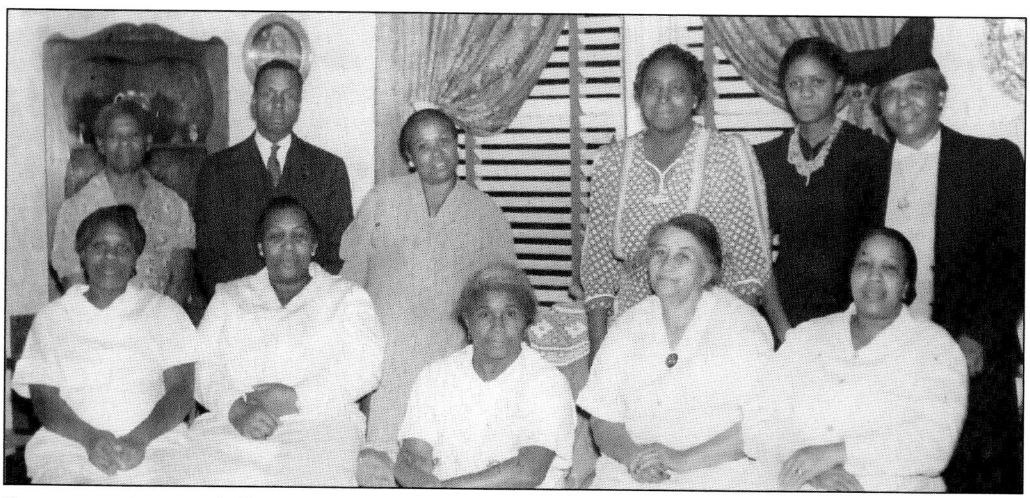

Stewardess Board. Phillips Memorial C.M.E Church was organized in Davis Bottom at the home of Edward and Mary Haggard and their daughter Dora Lacey Doty in 1900. The church was later located on Corral Street. Pictured is the stewardess board of the church at the home of Sally Duncan in the late 1940s. (Courtesy of Henrietta Fender.)

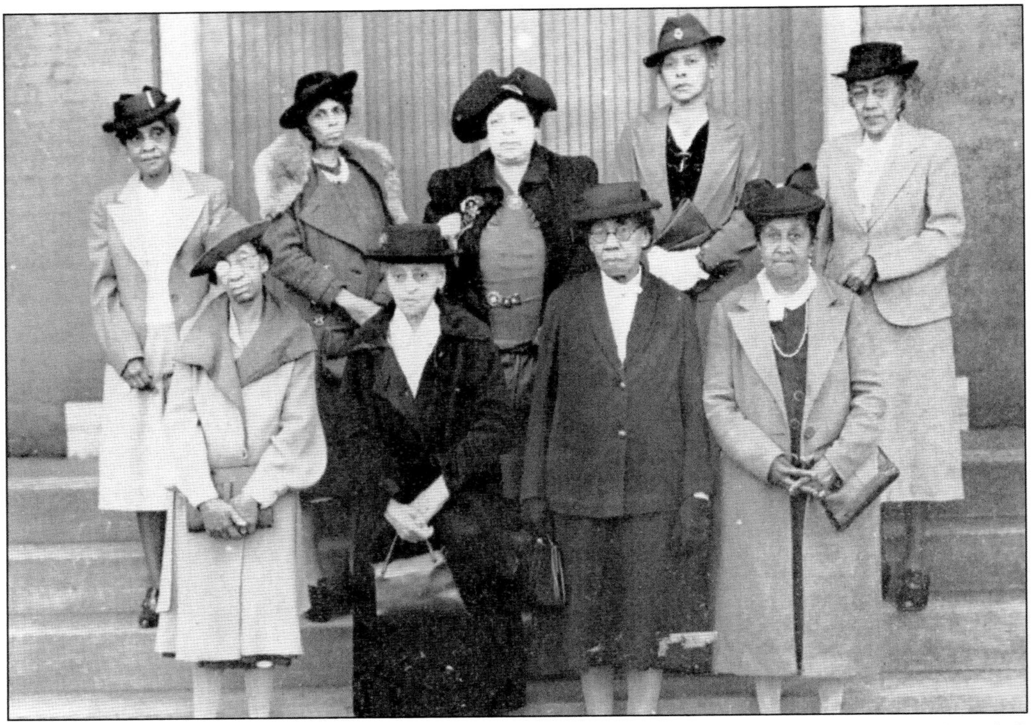

First African Baptist Church Pastor's Aid Society. Members of the Pastor's Aid Society, from left to right, are (front row) Lena Evans, Maggie Dry, Annie Shropshire, and Julia Tyler; (back row) Sarah Dupee, Fannie Brown, Lizzie Woodson, Emma Price, and Emma Rowe. (Courtesy of Sallie Price Collection, First Baptist Church Souvenir Booklet, 1940, UK Special Collections.)

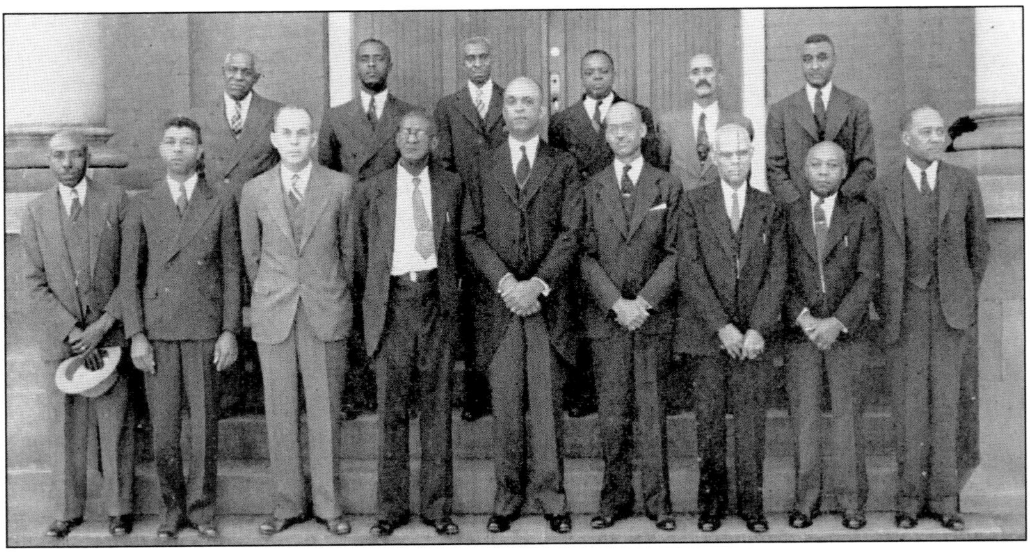

Deacons and Trustees. The First African Baptist Church deacons and trustees, from left to right, are (front row) William Thomas, Clarence Starling, George L.J. Johnson, J.B. Caulder, Pastor H.E. Nutter, R.H. Hogan, F.J. Wilson, N.S. Smith, and J.P. Black; (back row) Henry Keys, James Owens, George H. Lee, James H. Taylor, Henry Poynter, and J.W. Taylor. (Courtesy of Sallie Price Collection, First Baptist Church Souvenir Booklet, 1940, UK Special Collections.)

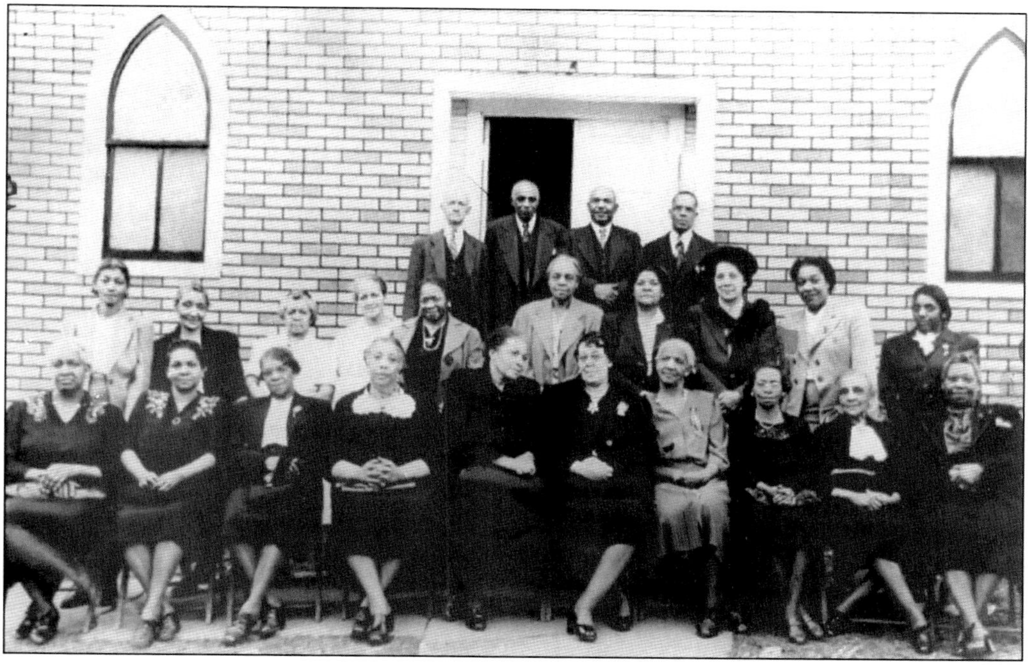

Baptist Women's Educational Institute Meeting. Lexington-Fayette County includes several African-American hamlets such as Bracktown, Cadentown, Jimtown, Jonestown, Fort Springs, Little Georgetown, and Maddoxtown. This photo was taken at the Utteringtown Baptist Church on Royster Road on March 24, 1949. (Courtesy of Amanda Elliott.)

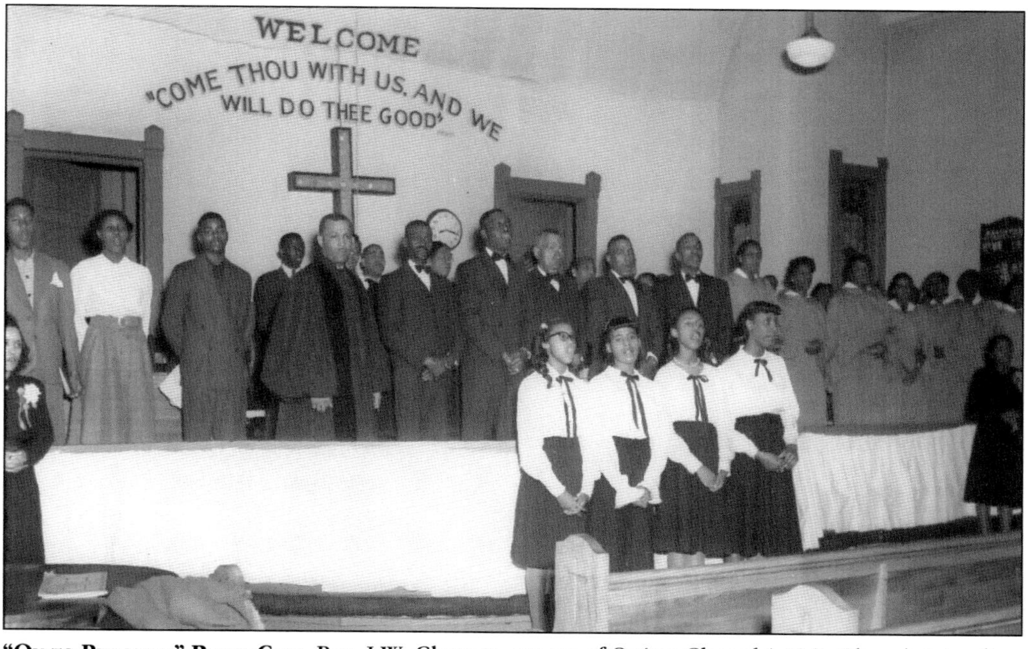

"On to Progress" Radio Cast. Rev. J.W. Chavers, pastor of Quinn Chapel A.M.E. Church (standing in front on the second row), organized a 90-voice choir at his church. The choir was heard on the regularly scheduled Sunday night radio program "On to Progress" for the first time on June 15, 1947. (Courtesy of *Lexington Herald Leader*.)

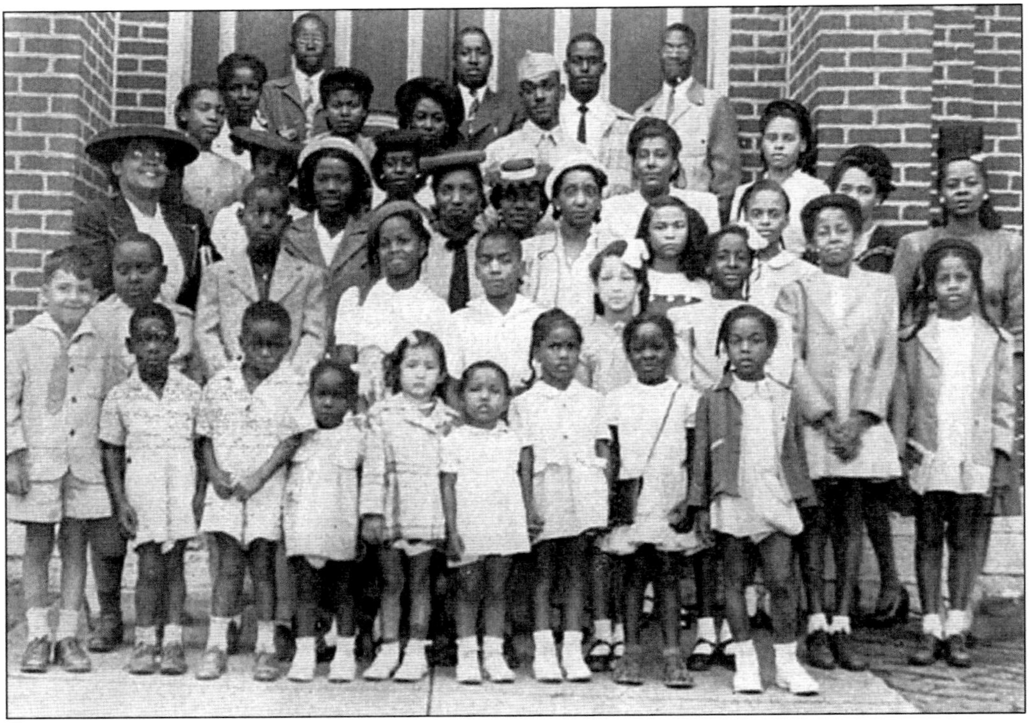

Sunday School. Members of the East Second Street Christian Church Sunday School posed for this picture in 1945. (Courtesy of the Sallie Price Collection, East Second Street Christian Church 94th Anniversary Program, 1945, UK Special Collections.)

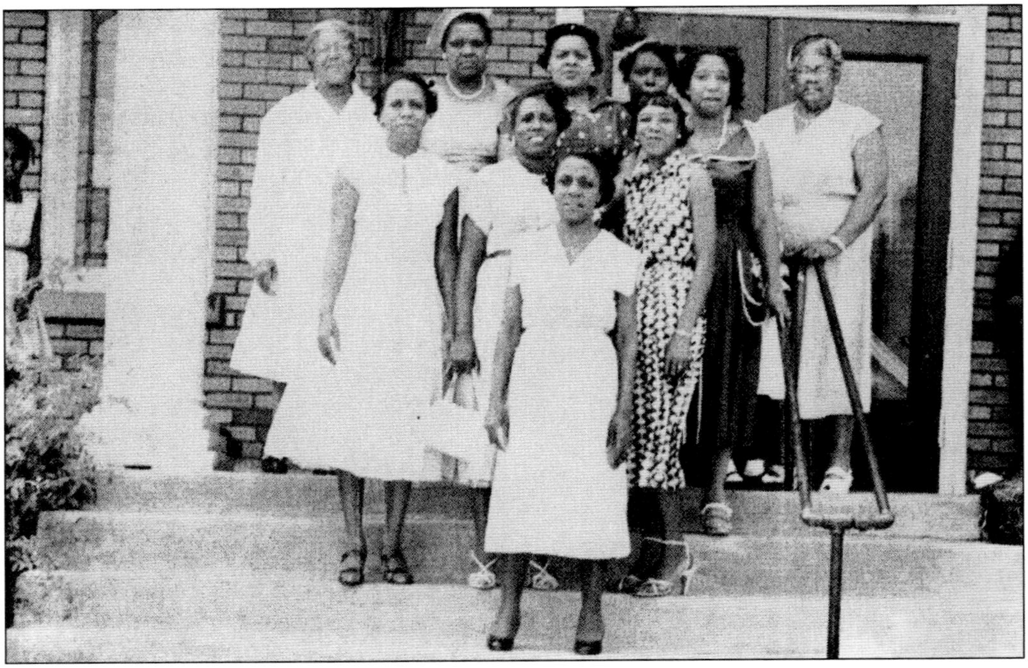

Church Members. Pictured here are church members standing in front of Quinn Chapel A.M.E. Church at 744 Charles Avenue. (Courtesy of Lutisha Coleman.)

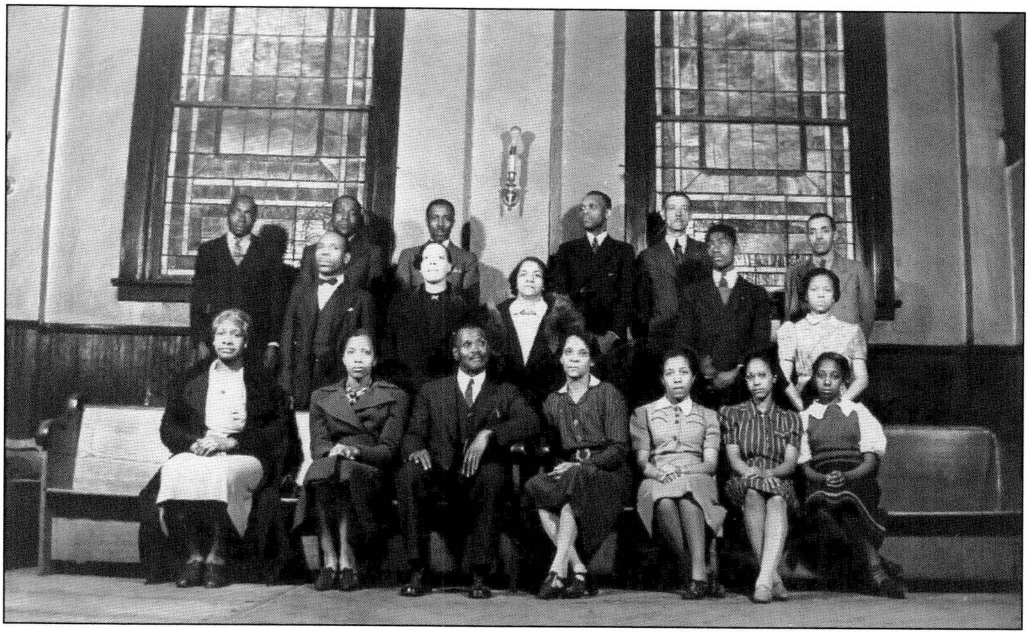

Shiloh Baptist Church Members. Shiloh members are pictured here with their pastor, Thomas H. Smith, who is seated in the center. (Courtesy of Amanda Elliott.)

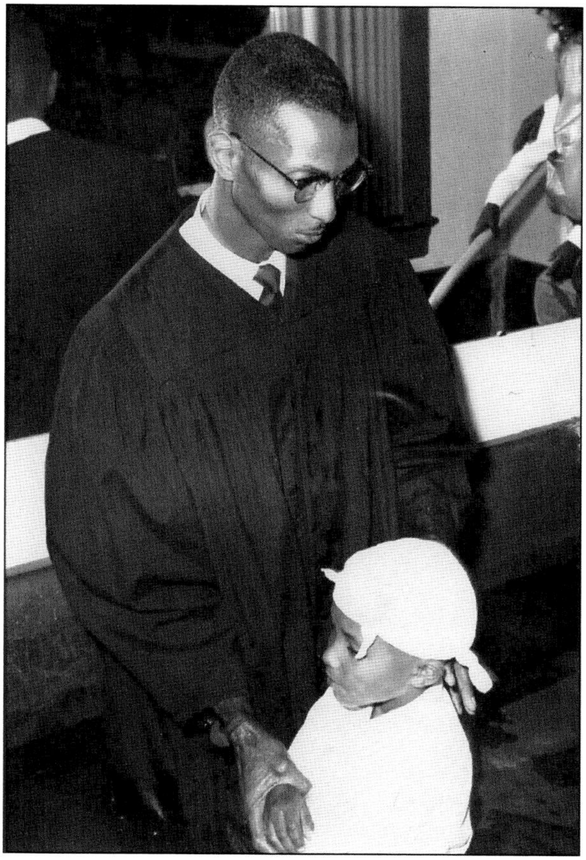

Baptizing. Rev. Horace Smith baptizes a child at Shiloh Baptist Church on Thomas Street. Reverend Smith has been the pastor of the Pilgrim Baptist Church on Jefferson Street for over 50 years. (Courtesy of Calvert McCann.)

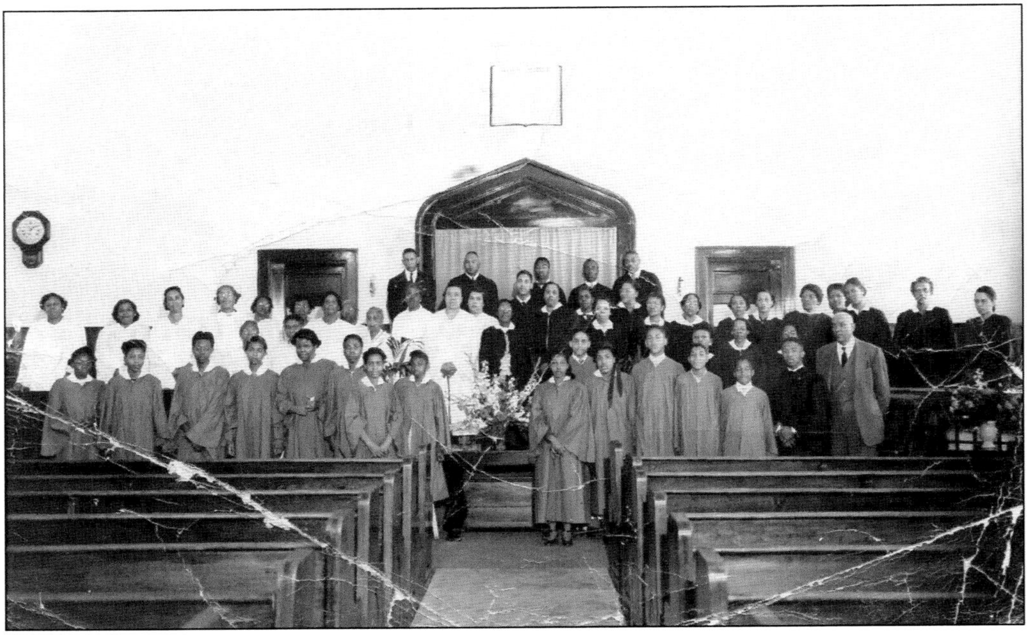

Rev. W.H. Howard. Reverend Howard served as pastor of Consolidated Baptist Church from 1944 to 1974 and is pictured on the front row, right, with the choir in the Consolidated sanctuary in the 1940s. The church was located on South Upper Street. (Courtesy of Henrietta Fischer.)

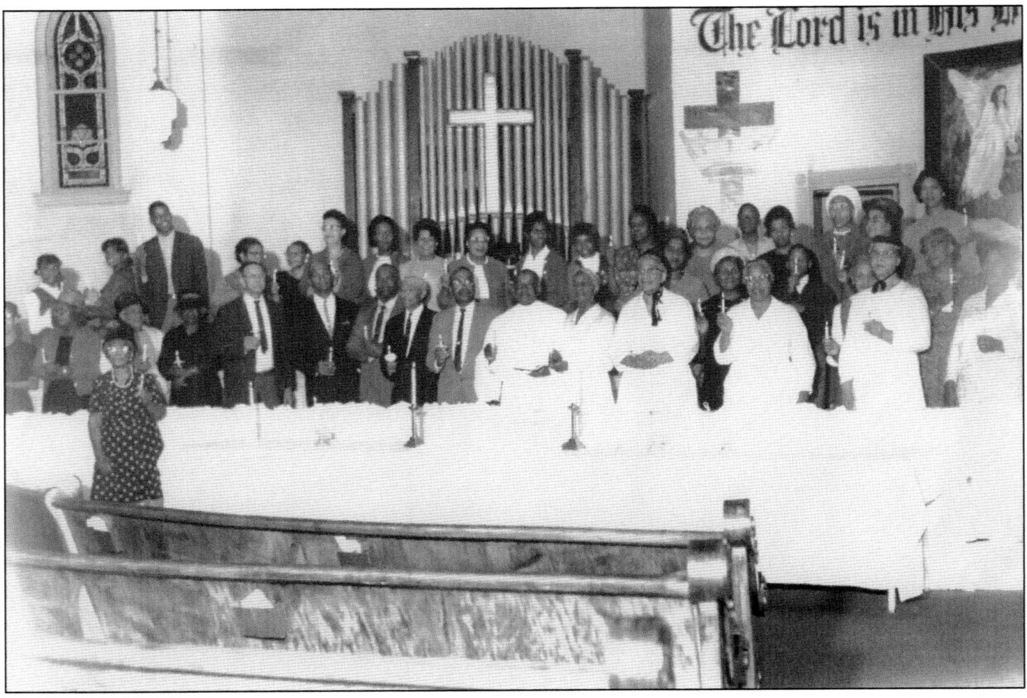

St. Paul A.M.E. Church. Established during the antebellum period, St. Paul is one of the oldest churches in the community. On June 22, 1892, a statewide convention of African Americans met at the church to discuss and protest Kentucky's Separate Coach Bill. Pictured are members assembled in the church in the 1950s. (Courtesy of Doris Coffey.)

Four

School Days

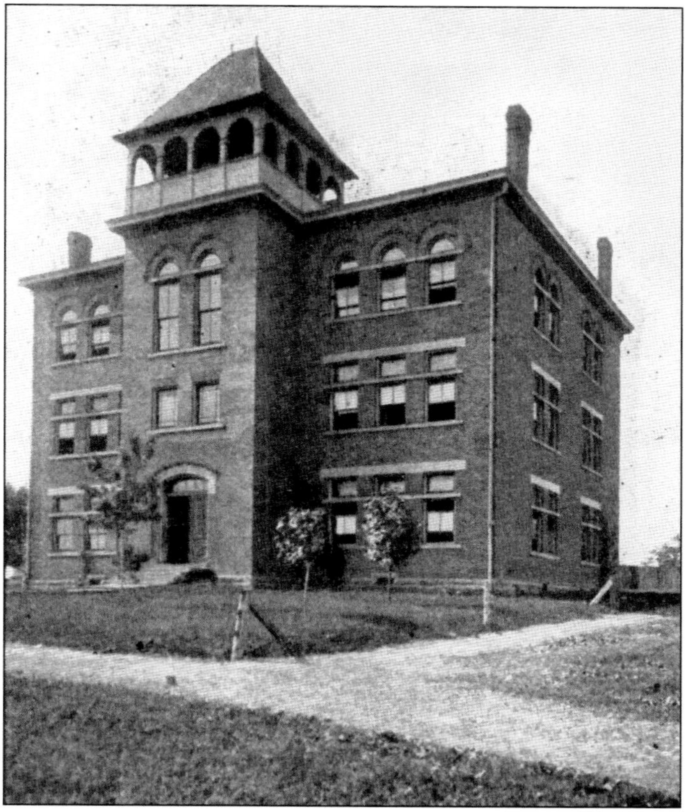

Chandler Normal School. Phoebe Chandler, a New England philanthropist, donated funds for the establishment of this school, which was dedicated on February 10, 1890. The school was located at 548 Georgetown Street. (Courtesy of Negro Population of Lexington, 1907.)

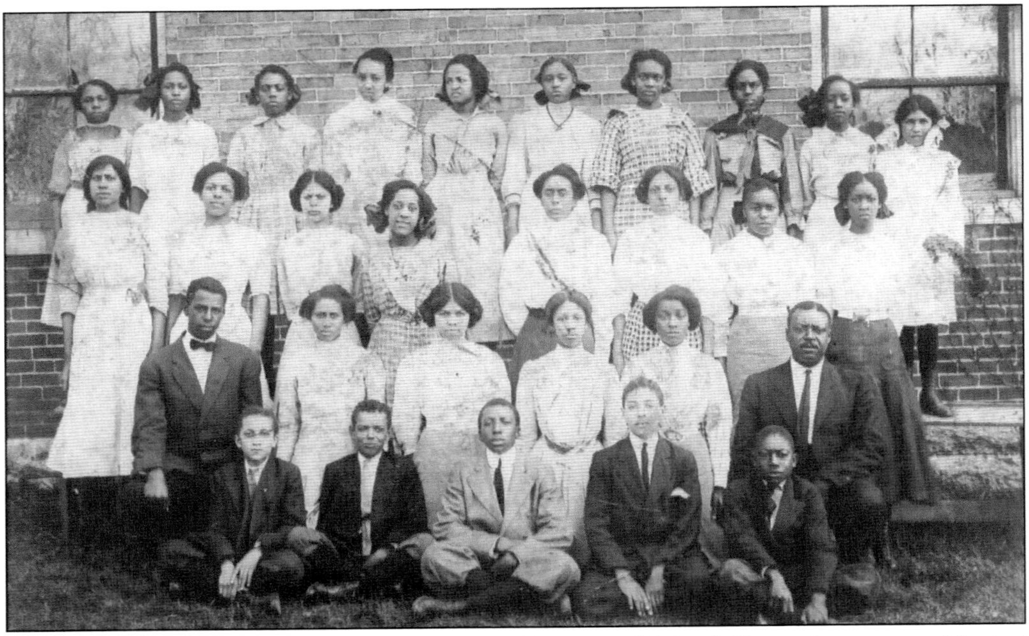

Whitney M. Young Sr. A former student of Chandler Normal School, Young became president of the Lincoln Institute in Simpsonville, Kentucky, in 1935. His son, Whitney M. Young Jr., was the executive director of the National Urban League in the 1960s. Young Sr. is shown in this 1910 photograph on the far left of the second row with other Chandler students. (Courtesy of Whitney M. Young Sr. Collection, Kentucky State University Archives and Special Collections.)

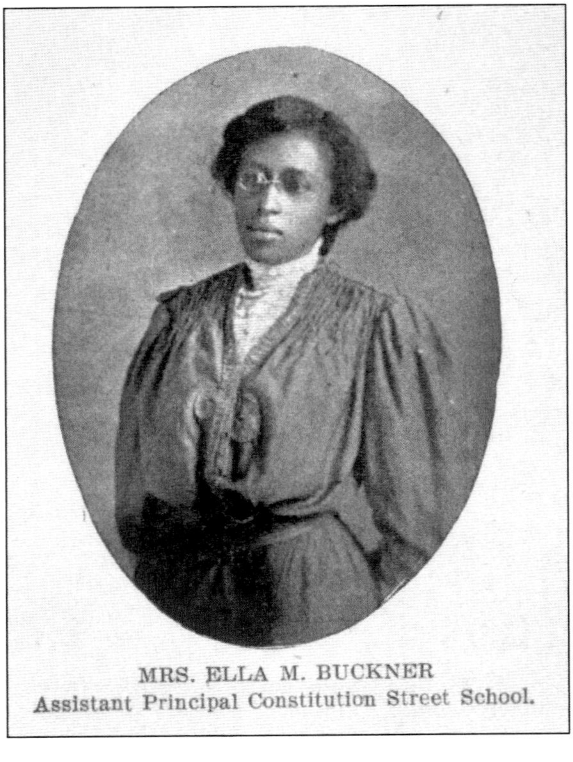

MRS. ELLA M. BUCKNER
Assistant Principal Constitution Street School.

Ella M. Buckner. Constitution Street School opened in 1883 with 100 students. Pictured is Ella M. Buckner, the school's assistant principal in 1907. (Courtesy of Negro Population of Lexington, 1907.)

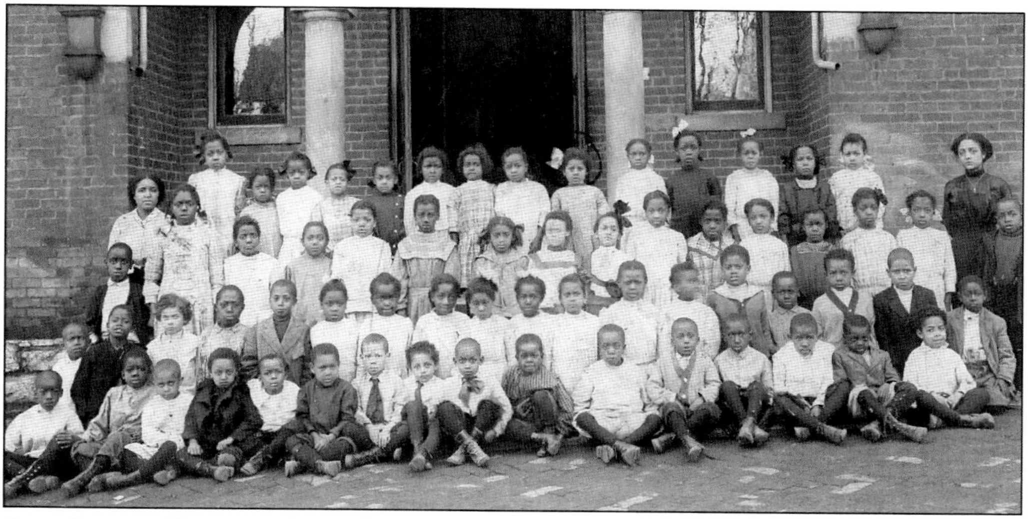

Class Picture. Shown in this early 1900s photograph, on the back row, nine students over, is Jennie V. Wendell. She is among other first grade students at Constitution Street School. (Courtesy of Thomas Tolliver.)

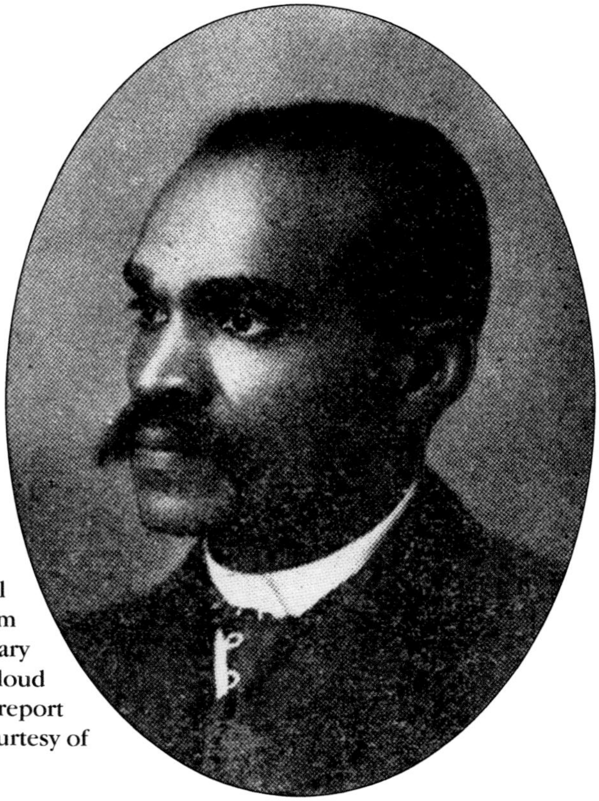

Green P. Russell. Born in Logan County, Kentucky, and a graduate of Berea College, Russell served as principal of Lexington High School from 1890 to 1894. He was appointed supervisor of the Lexington City African-American schools, and in 1895, the high school was named in his honor. Russell served as president of the Kentucky Normal and Industrial Institute (KNII) in Frankfort from 1912 to 1923 and from 1924 to February 20, 1929. He left KNII under a cloud of controversy after an auditor's report questioned his use of school funds. (Courtesy of Negro Population of Lexington, 1907.)

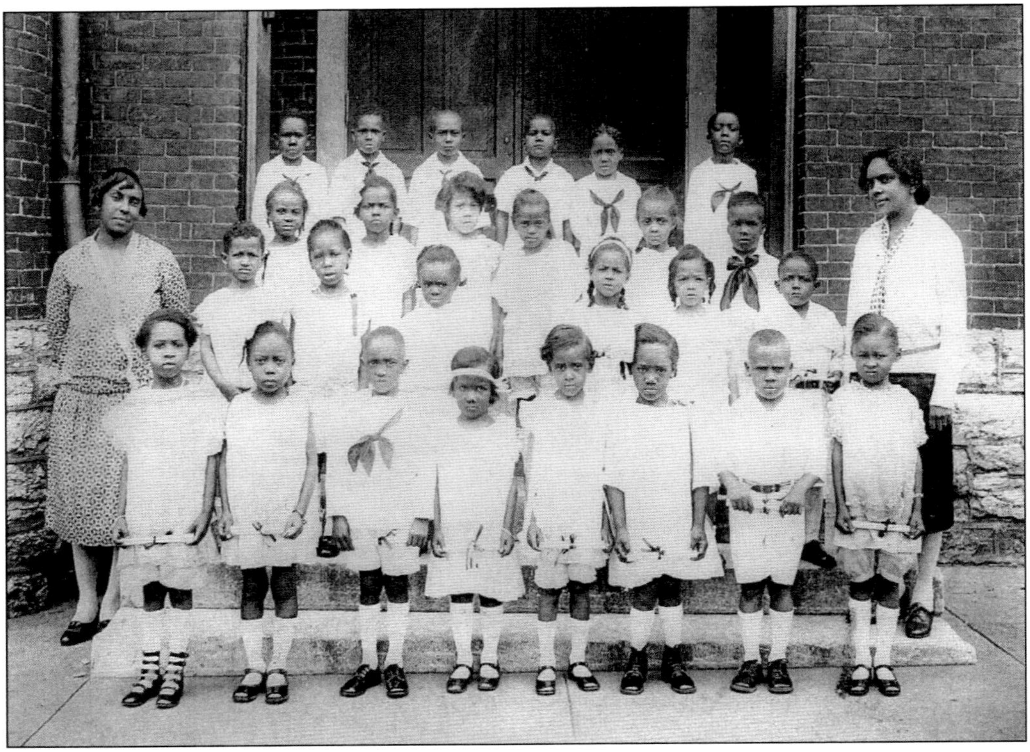

Russell School. This is a picture of the kindergarten class in June 1927. On the left is assistant teacher Emma Livisay and on the right is teacher Margaret Jackson. (Courtesy of Amanda Elliott.)

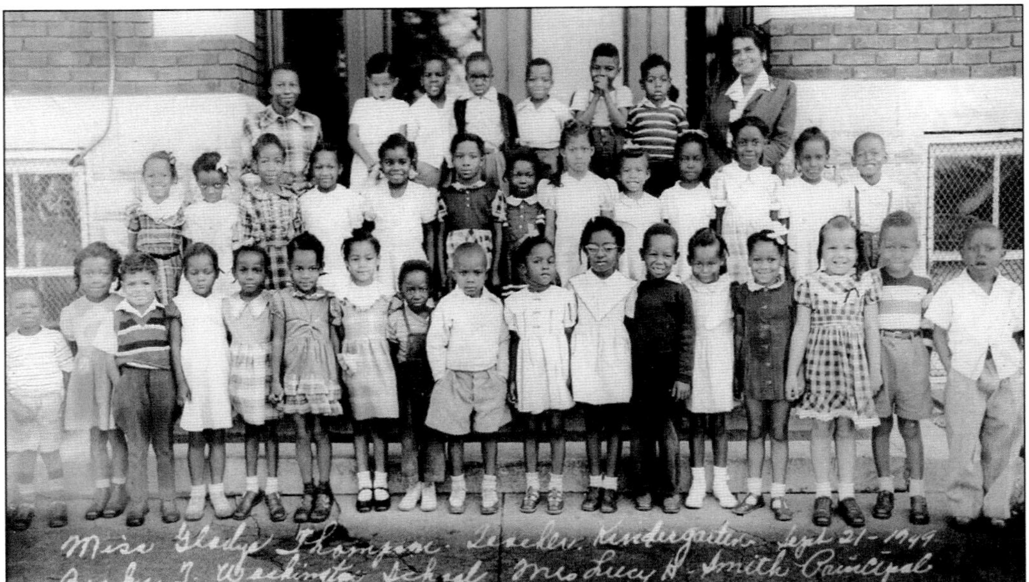

Booker T. Washington Elementary School. The kindergarten students in this class picture, taken on September 21, 1949, attended Booker T. Washington Elementary School , which was located at 498 Georgetown Street. Gladys Thompson, back row, left, was the teacher. Lucy Harth Smith, back row, right, was the principal. (Courtesy of Amanda Elliott.)

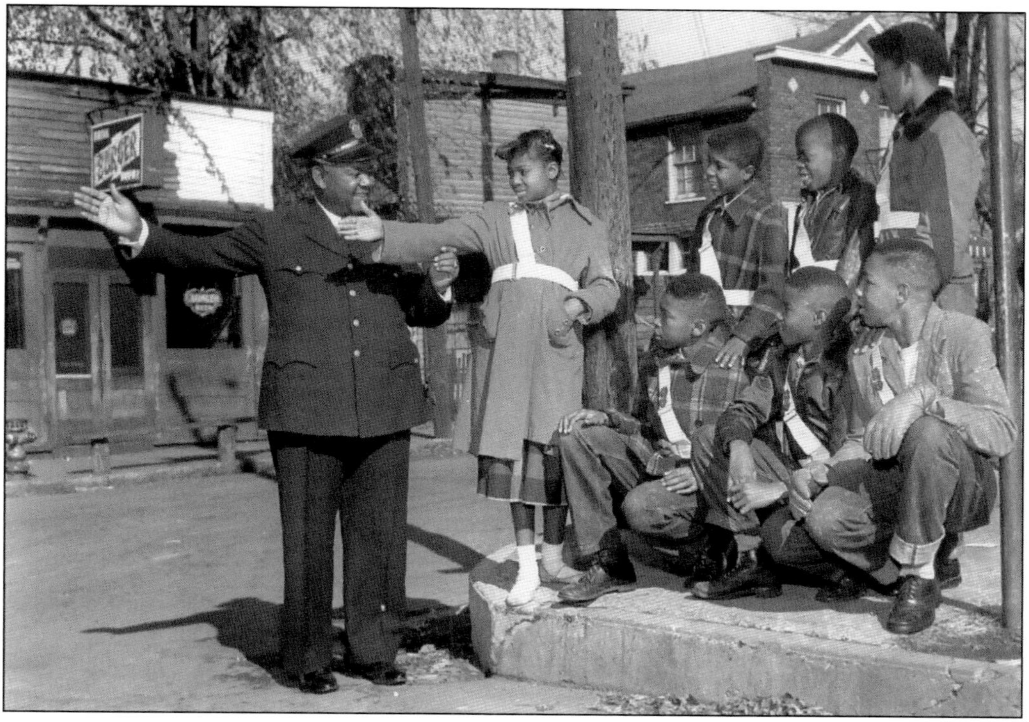

Patrolman Prather Walker. The new safety patrol at George Washington Carver School on 522 Patterson Street receives instructions from Walker in this photo that was published November 10, 1951. (Courtesy of *Lexington Herald Leader*.)

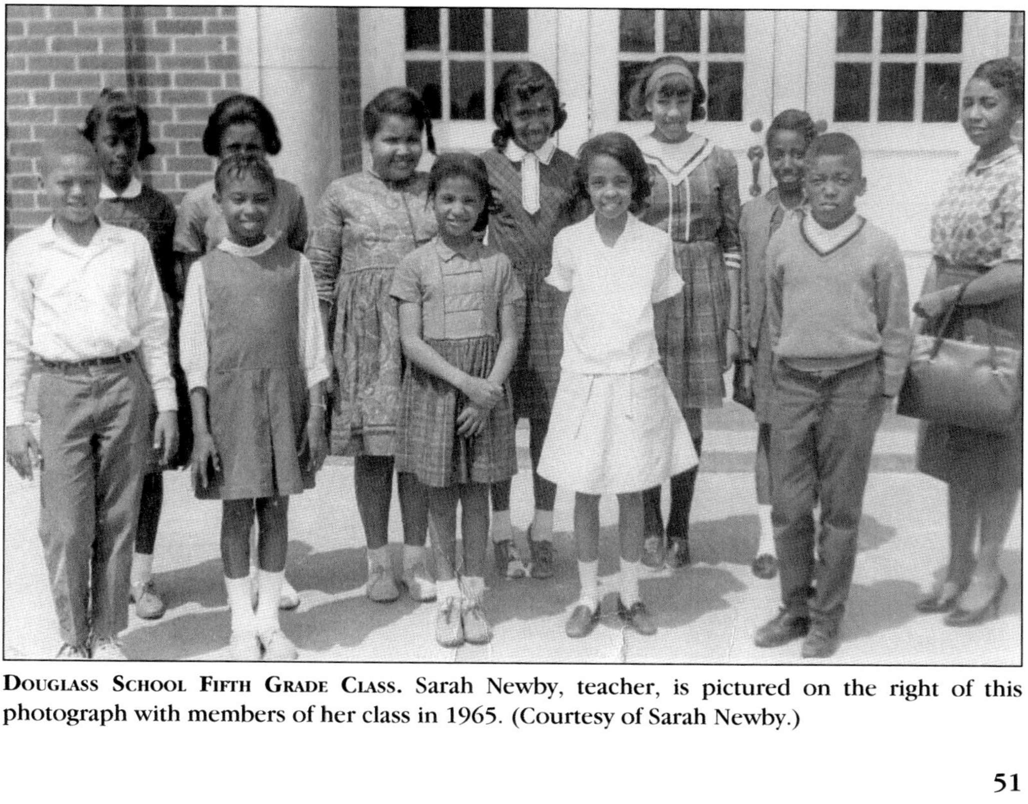

Douglass School Fifth Grade Class. Sarah Newby, teacher, is pictured on the right of this photograph with members of her class in 1965. (Courtesy of Sarah Newby.)

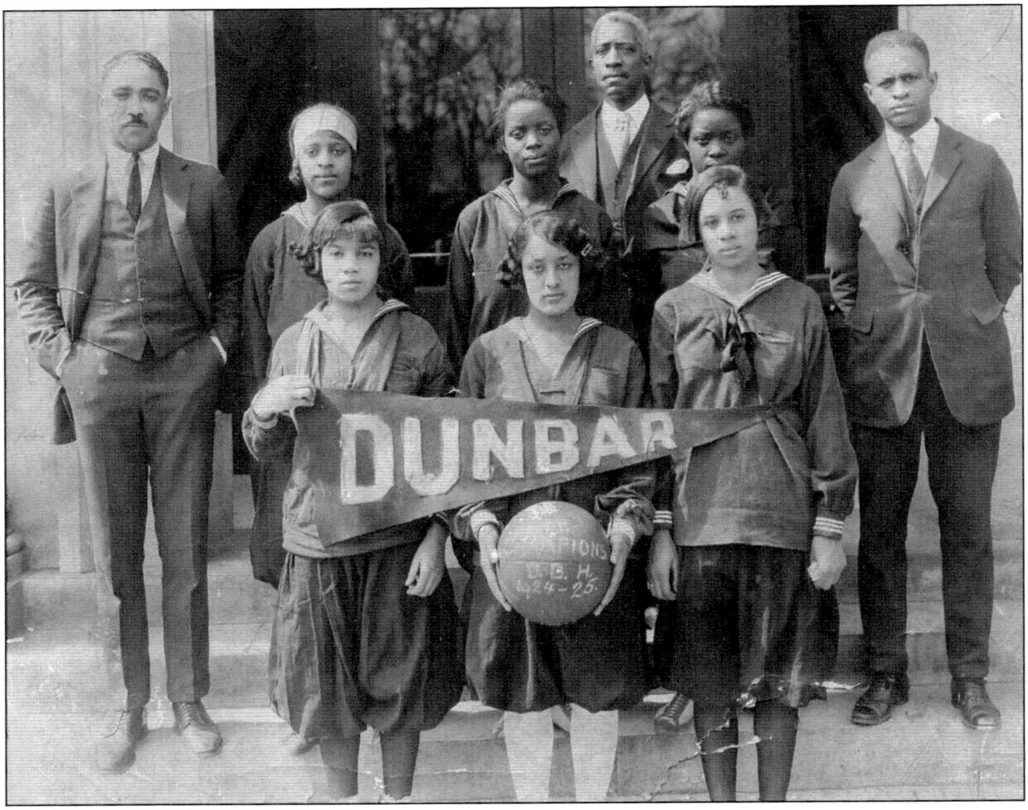

The Original Dunbar 1924–1925 Girl's Basketball Team. Standing in the first row and holding the ball is Sally Row. Her sister, Lucy Rowe Estill, is standing to her right. (Courtesy of Lucy Estill Papers, Lexington Fayette County Urban Government [LFUCG] Archives.)

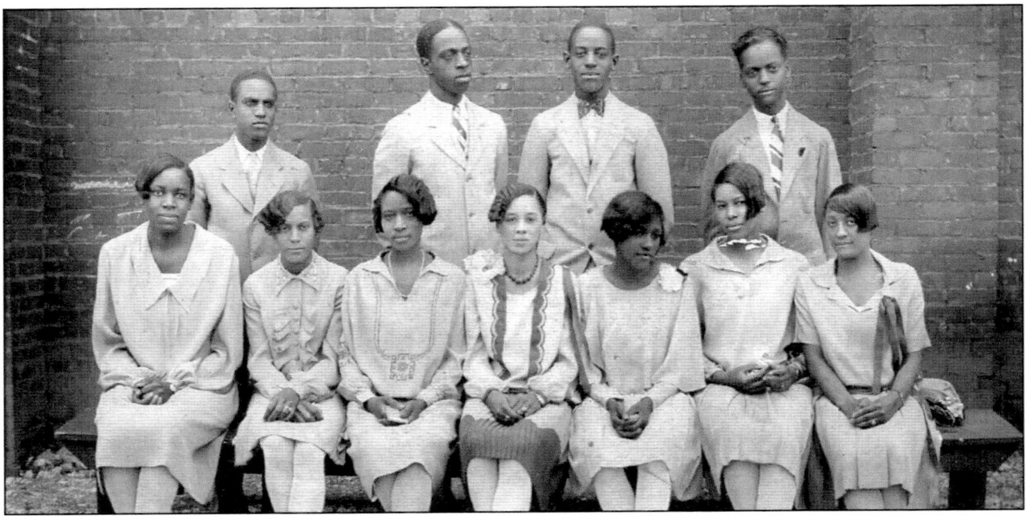

Original Dunbar High School in the Early Years. Pictured here are students from the class of in 1926 1/2. Seated in the center and fourth from the left is Lucy Rowe Estill, valedictorian of her class. (Courtesy of Lucy Estill Papers, Lexington Fayette Urban County Government [LFUCG] Archives.)

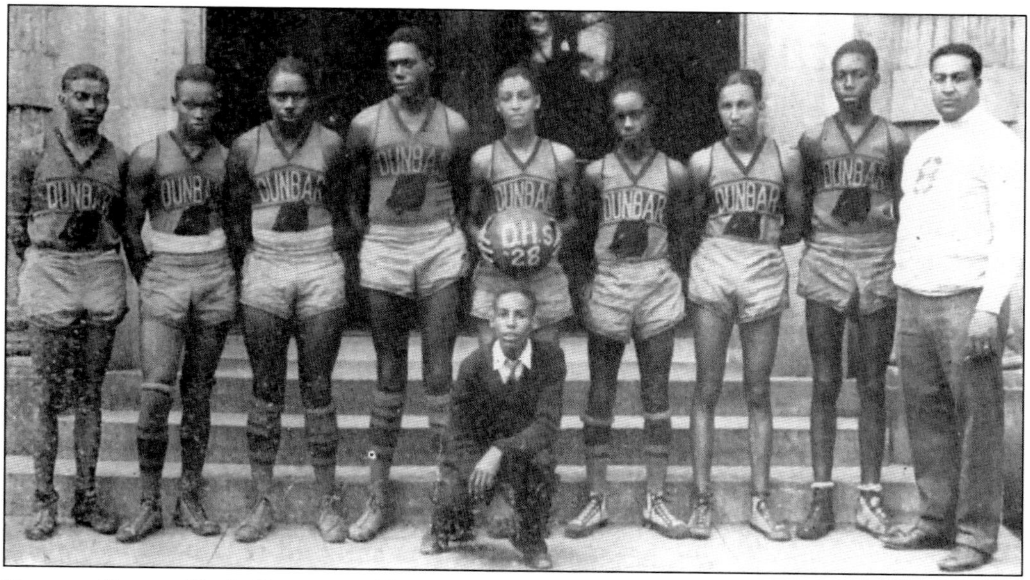

Original Dunbar Boy's Basketball Team in 1928. Team members, from left to right, are Leon Shiddell, William Livisay, Samuel Smallwood, Anderson Smallwood, Virgil Worsham, Joseph Kavanaugh, Julian Mealy, Cecil Posey, and Coach A.W. Wade. Kneeling in front is Raleigh Worsham, the mascot. (*Dunbar Echo*, Courtesy of Winston Powell.)

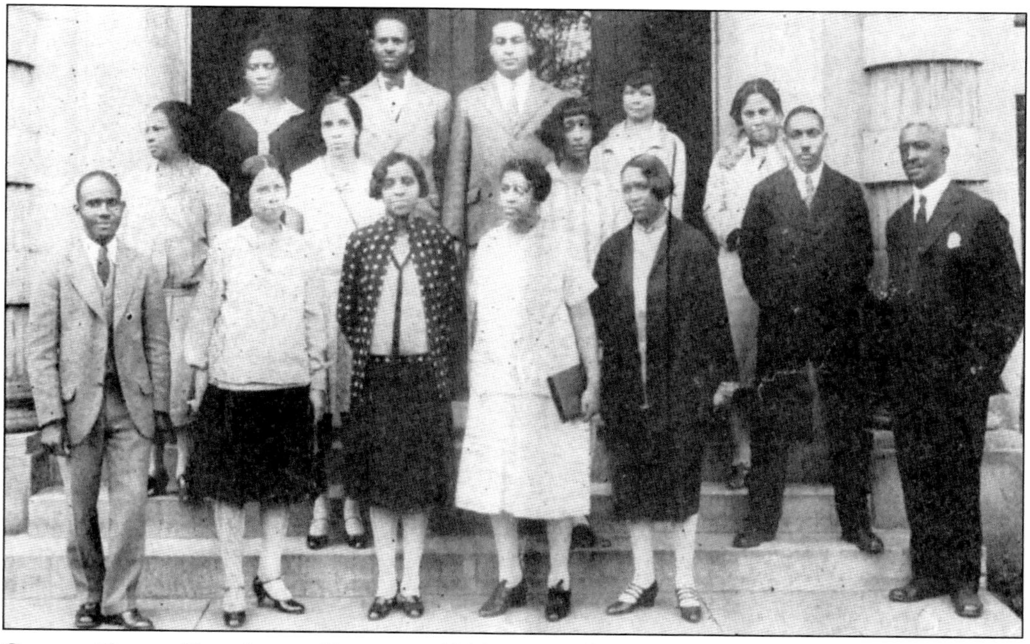

Original Dunbar High School Faculty in 1929. Pictured on the far right, wearing a handkerchief in his pocket, is Principal William Henry Fouse. Fouse was one of Kentucky's most respected educators. He served as president of the Kentucky Negro Education in 1938. He died at his home on North Upper Street June 1, 1944. (*Dunbar Echo*, Courtesy of Winston Powell.)

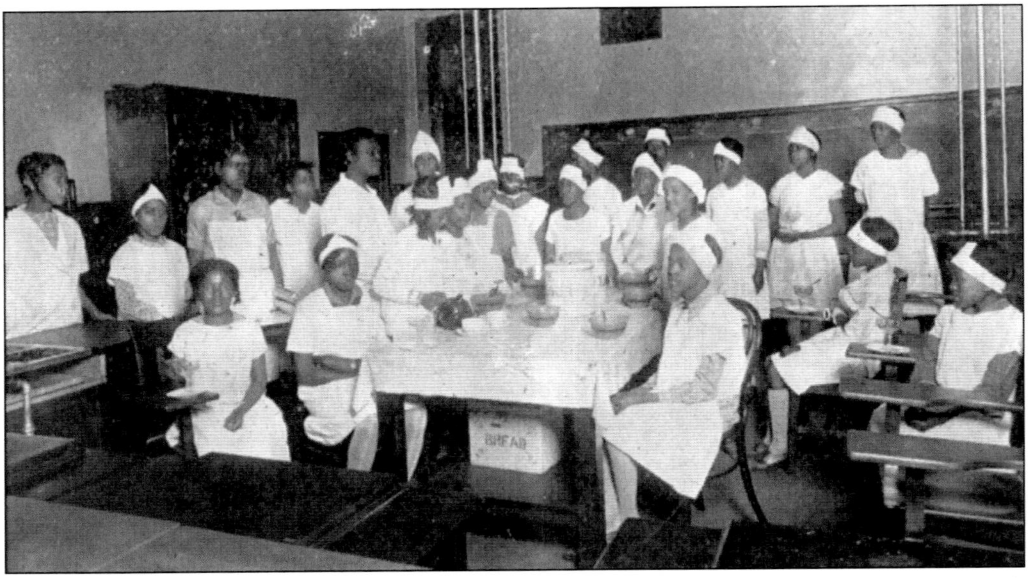

Dunbar Cooking Class in 1929. The original Dunbar High School was constructed on North Upper Street in 1922. It had 28 classrooms, 4 science labs, 2 music rooms, 2 home economics classrooms, 2 industrial arts rooms, an auditorium, a library, a gymnasium, and a cafeteria. The school was razed in 1974. A new Paul Laurence Dunbar High School opened in August 1990 off Man O' War Boulevard. Pictured are students in one of the original Dunbar classrooms. (*Dunbar Echo*, Courtesy of Winston Powell.)

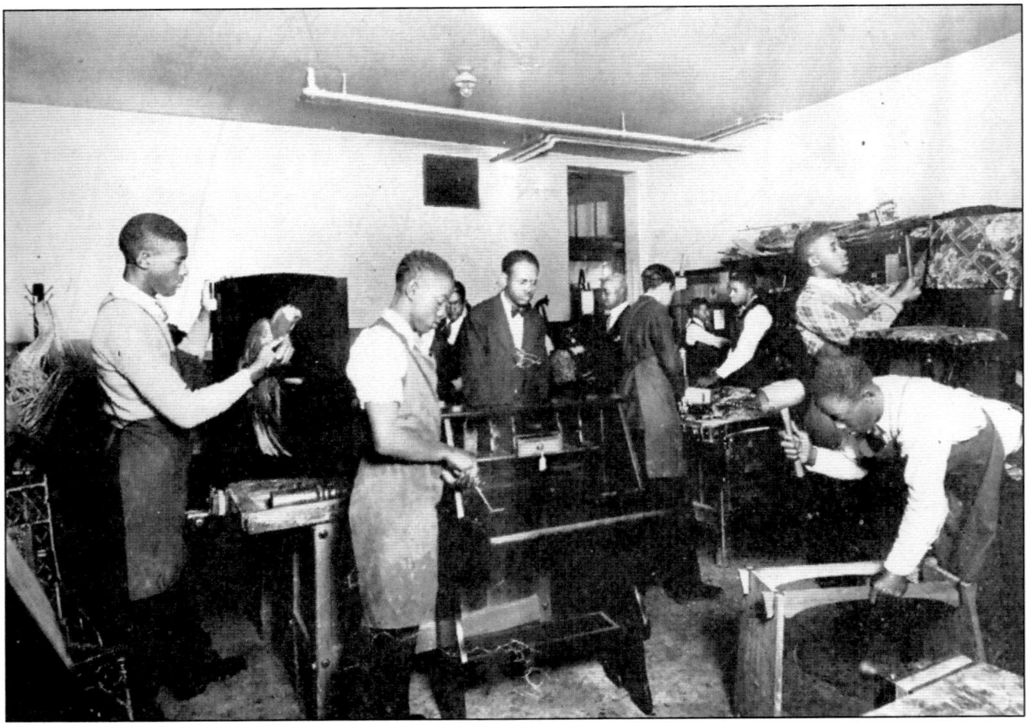

Original Dunbar Manual Training Department. Students enrolled in this department learned furniture making skills. (*Dunbar Echo*, Courtesy of Winston Powell.)

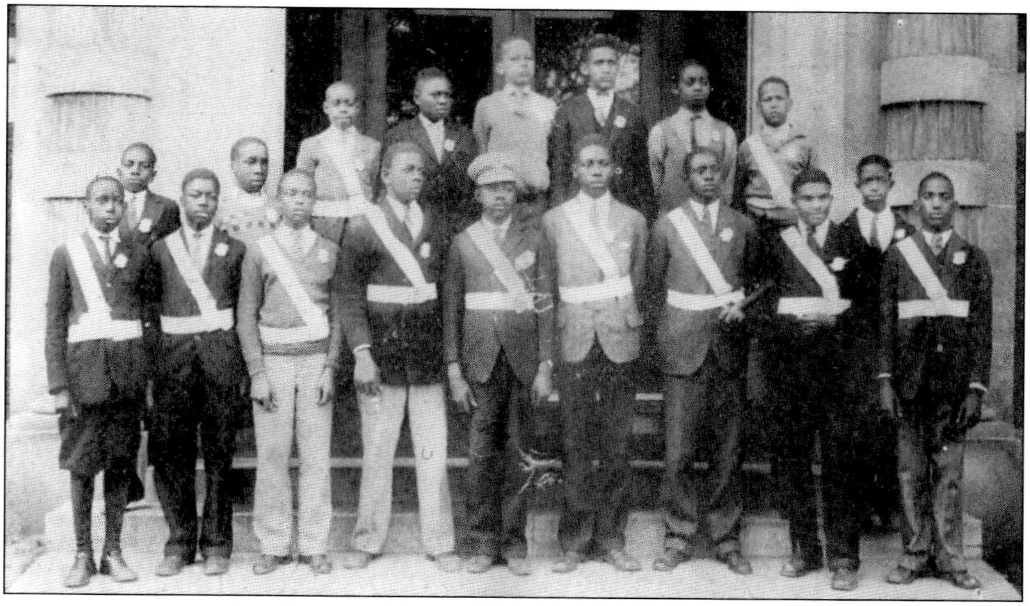

"LEXINGTON COLORED SAFETY PATROL." First row, standing fifth from the left wearing a hat, is Maurice W. Strider, the major of the patrol. This is a 1929 photograph. (*Dunbar Echo*, Courtesy of Winston Powell.)

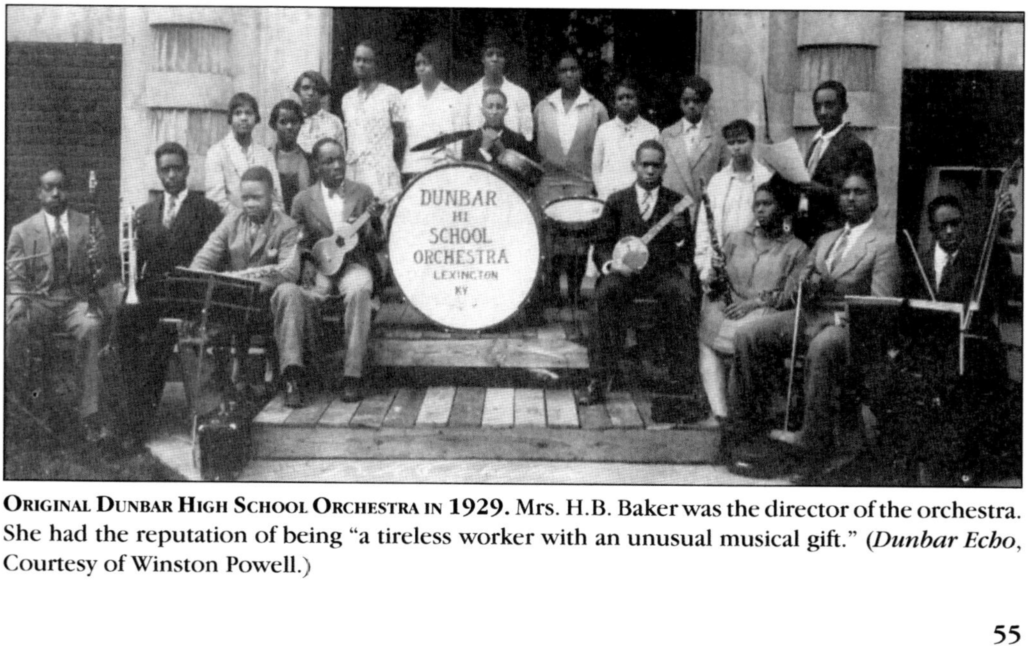

ORIGINAL DUNBAR HIGH SCHOOL ORCHESTRA IN 1929. Mrs. H.B. Baker was the director of the orchestra. She had the reputation of being "a tireless worker with an unusual musical gift." (*Dunbar Echo*, Courtesy of Winston Powell.)

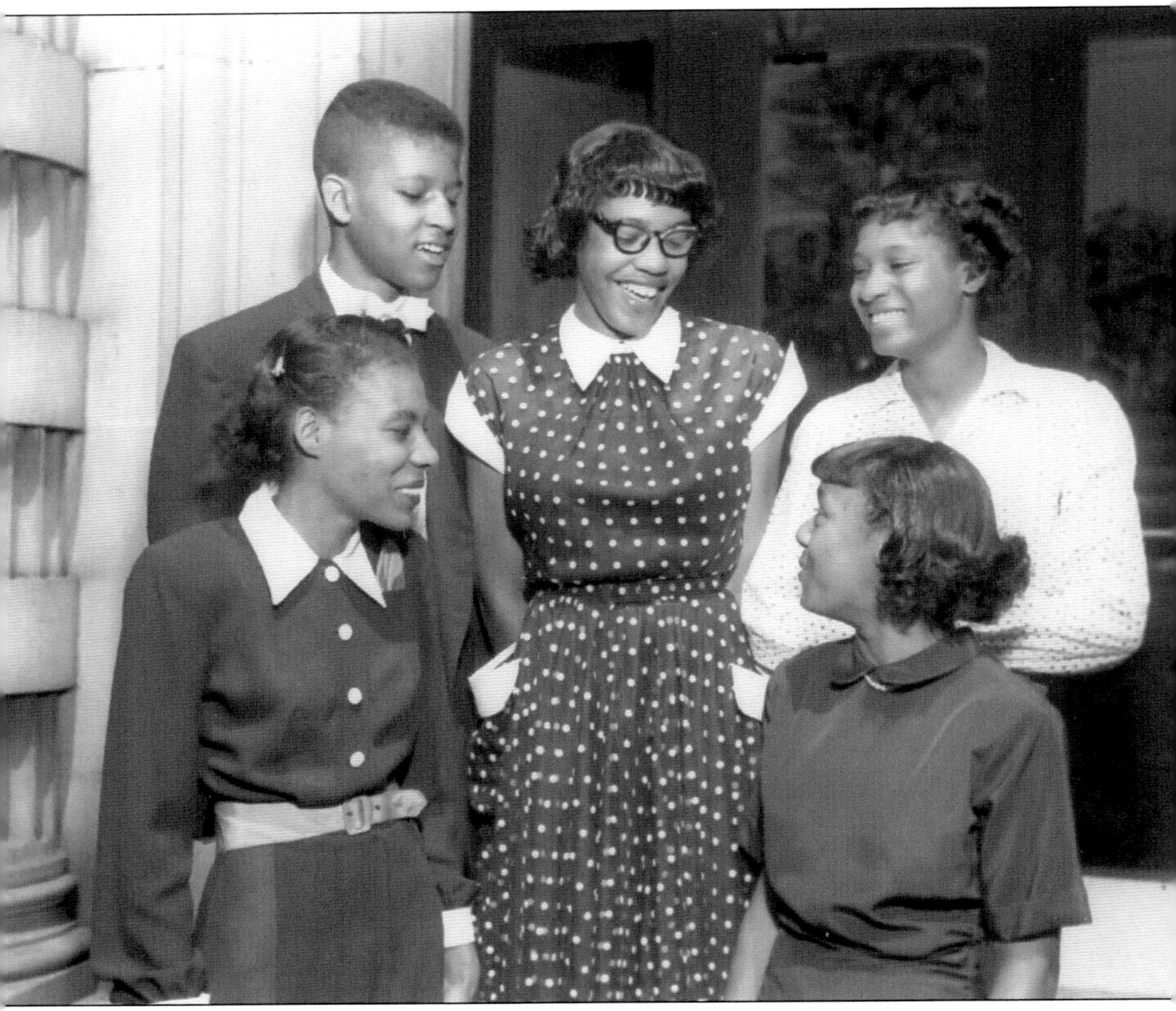

ORIGINAL DUNBAR HONOR STUDENTS, 1950. Pictured, from left to right, are (front row) Hazel Williams and Emily Mills; (back row) William Cooper, Joan Neal, and Kathryn Smith. Principal P.L. Guthrie presented the students their Honor Society memberships. (Courtesy of *Lexington Herald Leader*.)

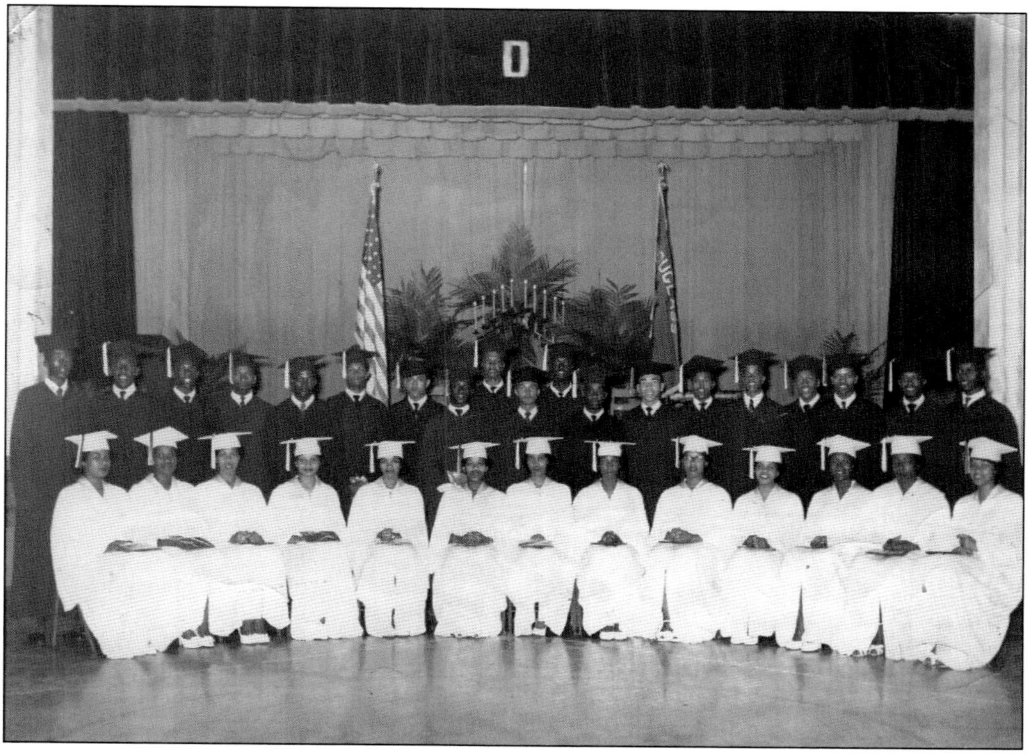

Douglass High School Class of 1954. Originally located on the corner of Price Road and Chiles Avenue, the school moved to 475 Price Avenue in 1948. (Courtesy of Betty Smithers.)

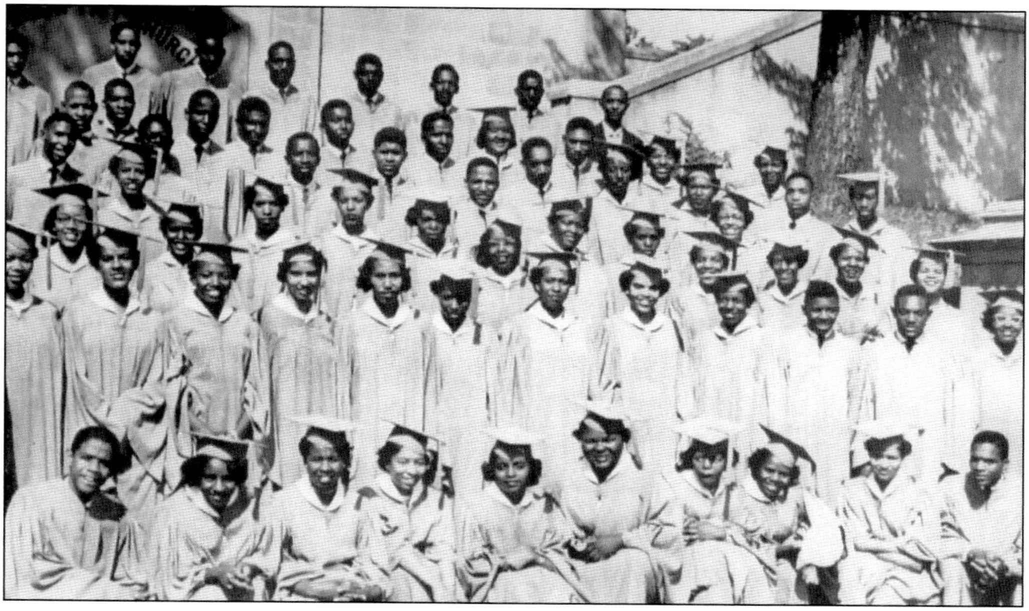

Dunbar High School Class of 1954. On May 17, 1954, the U.S. Supreme Court ruled that separate and unequal education was unconstitutional. This historic decision initiated the process of school desegregation. Students from Douglass and Dunbar were among the first undergraduates to attend the University of Kentucky in the 1950s. (Courtesy of Sarah Newby.)

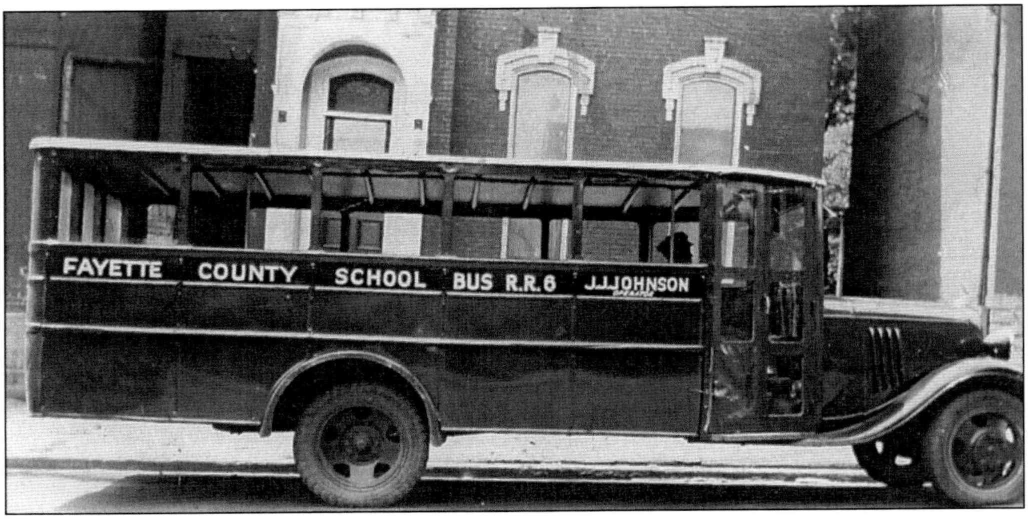

School Bus for African-American Children. J.J. Johnson, an African American, owned this bus in the 1930s. He was hired to transport African-American children from several rural black settlements surrounding Lexington to Douglass and Dunbar. (Courtesy of Ella S. Bosley.)

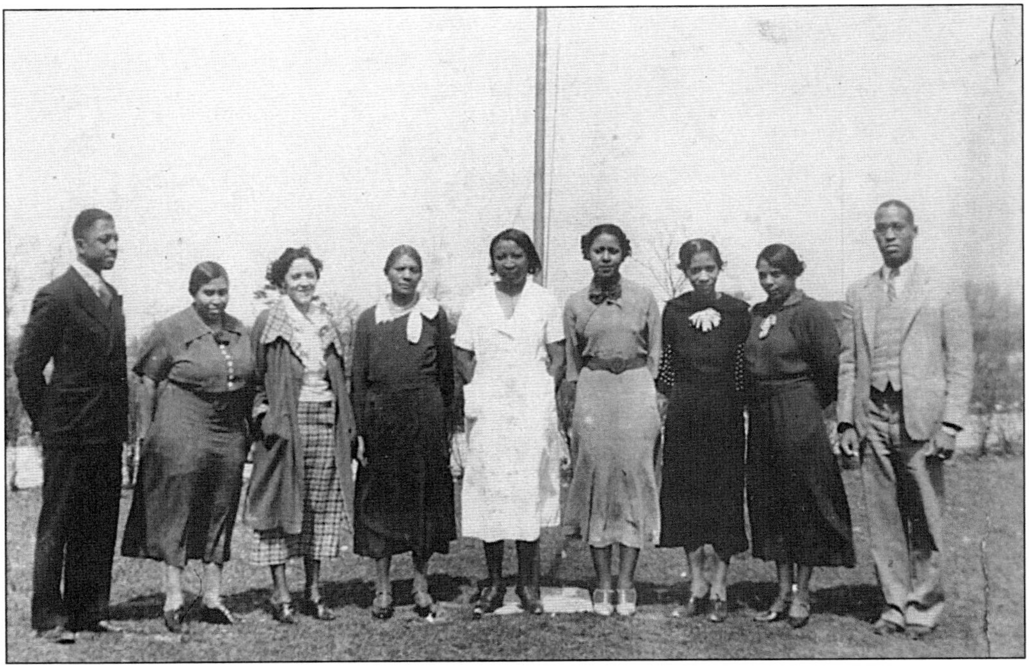

Douglass High School Teachers. This photograph was taken during the 1938–1939 term. (Courtesy of Betty Smithers.)

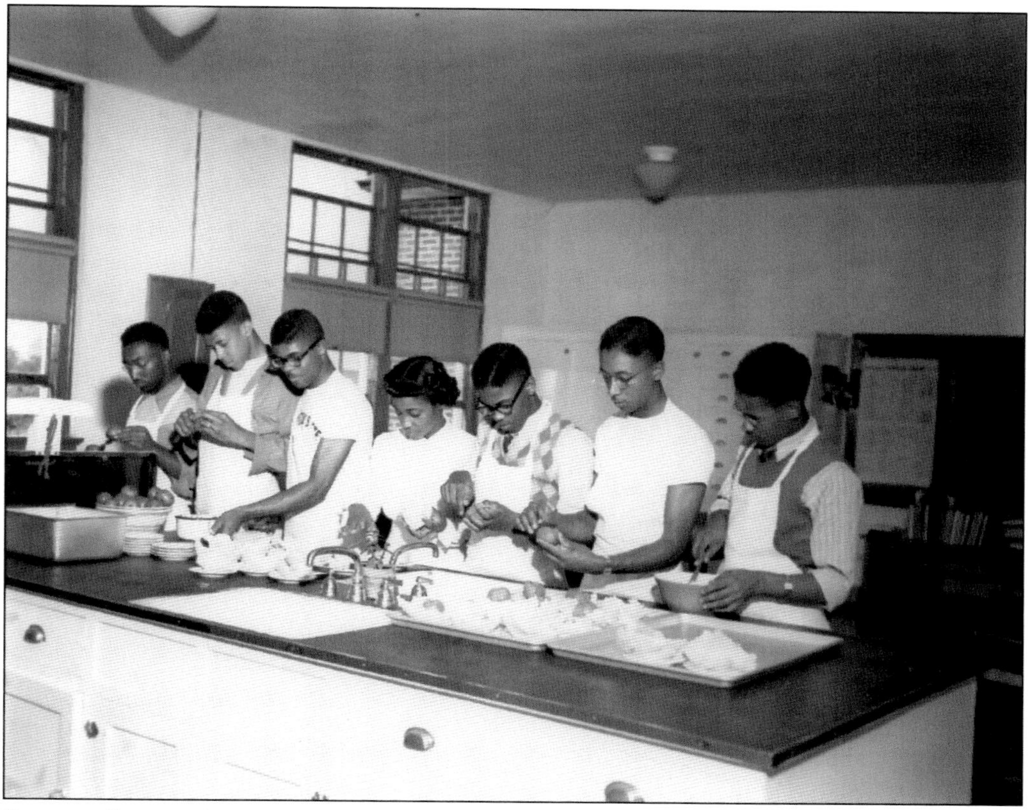

Douglass Students Prepare for Banquet. Twelve students were enrolled in this home economics class. Pictured are six students preparing for a father and son banquet with their teacher, Mattie Ballew, in 1949. From left to right, they are Demosthenes Hunn, August Mack Jr., Rupert Seals, Mattie Ballew, Walker Green, Jesse Yates, and Murray Cruse. (Courtesy of *Lexington Herald Leader*.)

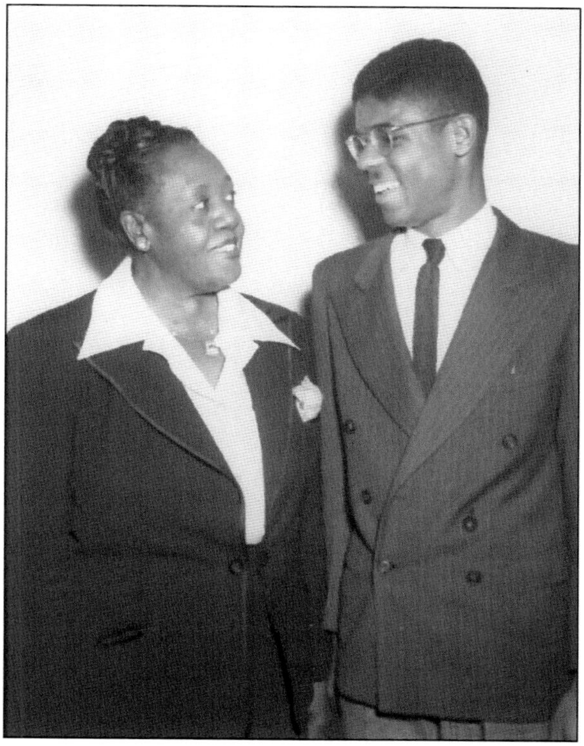

Douglass High School Principal and Student, 1949. In this photo, Principal Theda Van Lowe congratulates Rupert Seals, a senior, after he won a public speaking contest open to Lexington Fayette County High School students. The contest was sponsored by the Lexington Chamber of Commerce in 1949. (Courtesy of *Lexington Herald Leader*.)

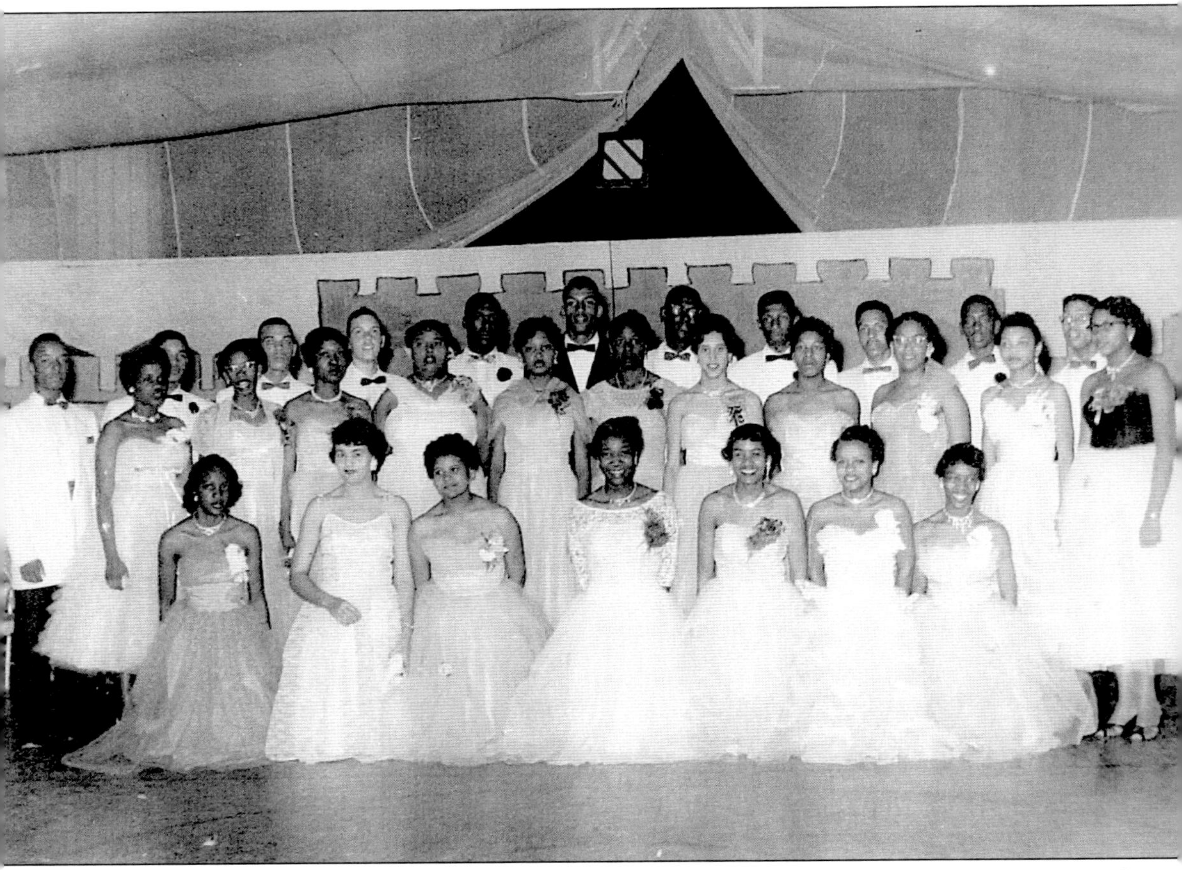

Douglass High School Prom, 1957. The prom was held in the school gymnasium located on Price Road. Pictured, from left to right, are (front row) Rosetta Moore, Francis Sewell, Loretta Beatty, Donaline Ingram, Anita Bledsoe, Helen Carter, and Gladys Haynes; (second row) Mamie James, Mary Laine, Delores Edwards, Gladys Fishback, Anna Logan, Demaris Underwood, Mary Mayfield, Carolyn Fishback, Helen Caise, Joan Miller, and Ann Crutchfield; (third row) James McCann, Joe Hocker, George Bell, Waller Edwards, James Hampton, Paul Price, Deweey Sweat, Robert Shy, Andrew Fisher, Doug Holland, John Higgins, and Donald Demus (Courtesy of Betty Smithers.)

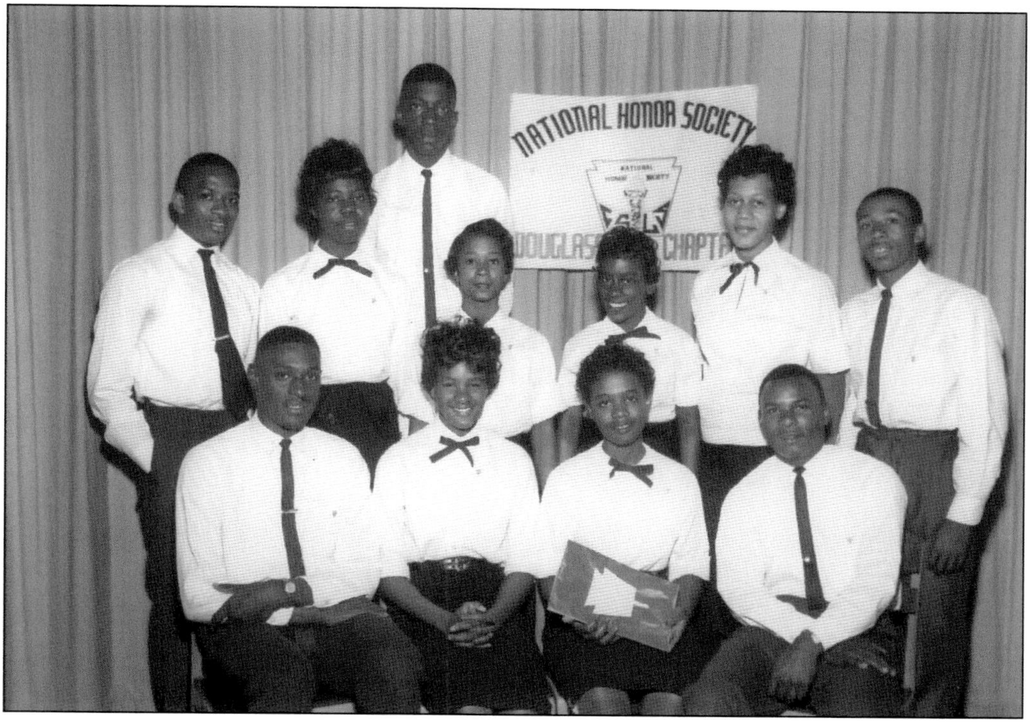

Douglass High School National Honor Society in 1960. The following students were charter members of the school's chapter of the NHS. Pictured, from left to right, are (seated) Robert Morton (president); Henrietta Figgs (vice president), Edna Jackson (secretary), and Wilbur Lewis (treasurer); (standing) F.D. Talbert Jr., Wanda Ross, Lawrence Mason, Anna Belle Jackson, Harrieta Greene, Elizabeth Barlow, and Charles Wilson. (Courtesy of *Lexington Herald Leader*.)

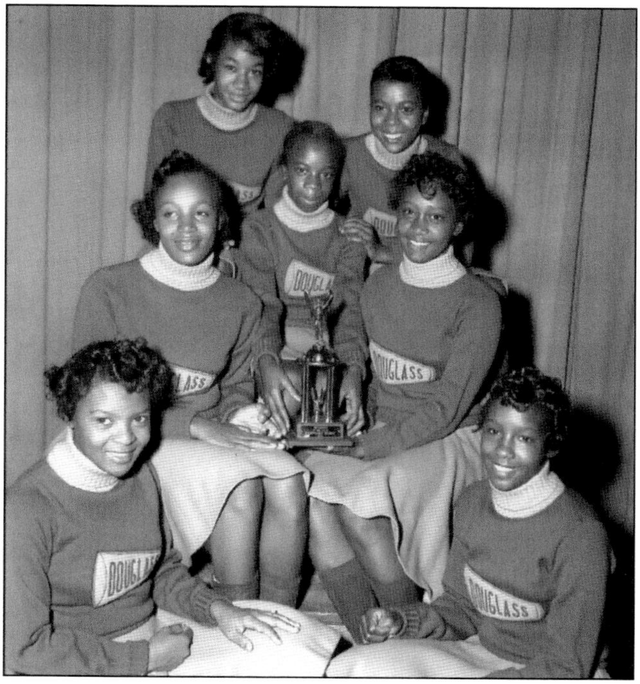

The 1957 Winners of the Statewide Cheerleader Clinic in Frankfort. Douglass High School cheerleaders surround their winning trophy. From left to right, they are Mamie Newman, Gloria Brown, Barbara Clay, Betty Buckner (center), Wilma Smith, Sarah Bowles, and Virginia James. (Courtesy of *Lexington Herald Leader*.)

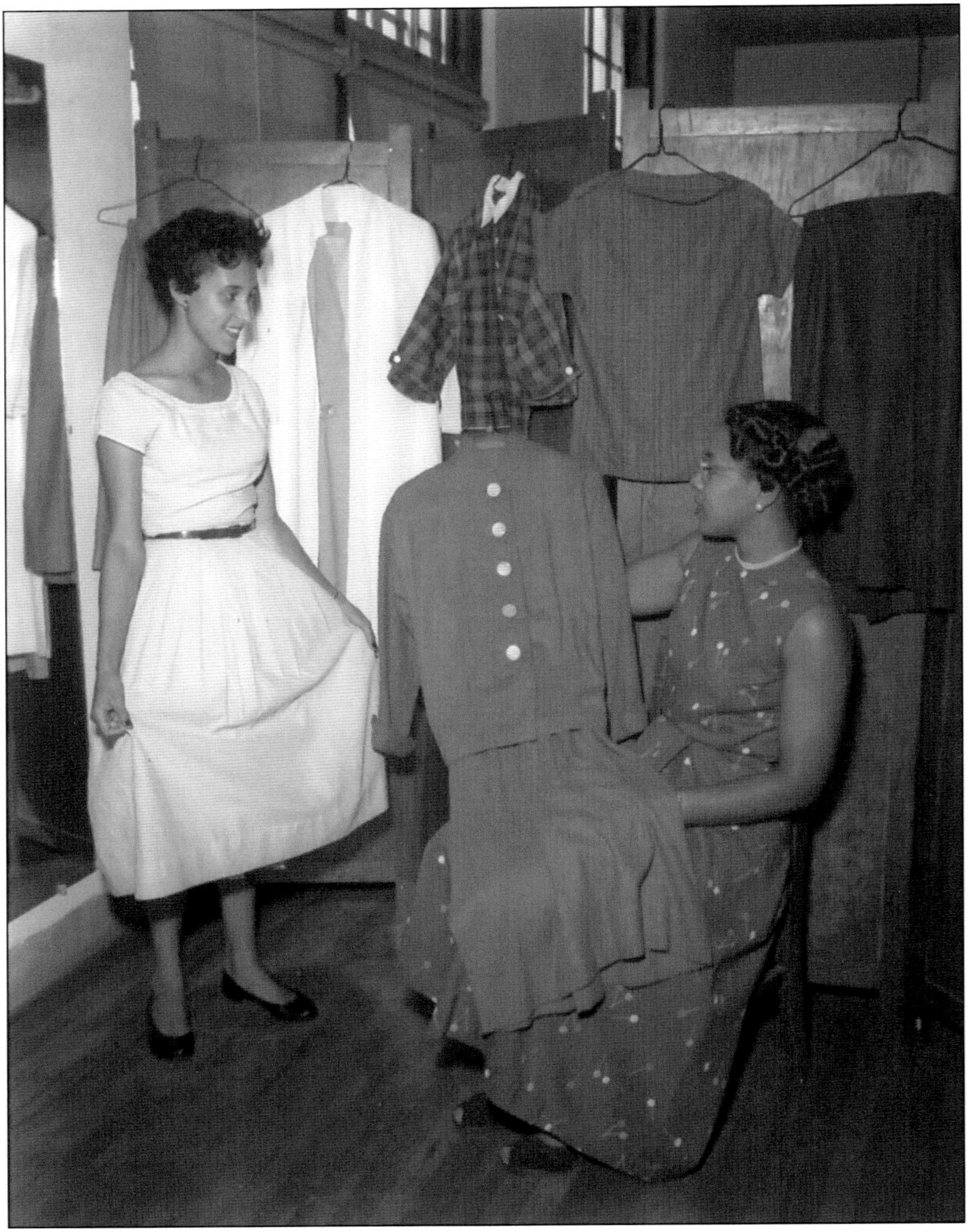

MARY ELIZABETH MAYFIELD CRAWFORD, CHOSEN FOR MCCALL'S PATTERN TEEN FASHION BOARD, 1957. Crawford learned to sew on her grandmother's sewing machine at age 11. In this picture, she models one of the dresses she made for her home economics teacher, Lila Rankin. Crawford graduated from Douglass in 1957. (Courtesy of *Lexington Herald Leader*.)

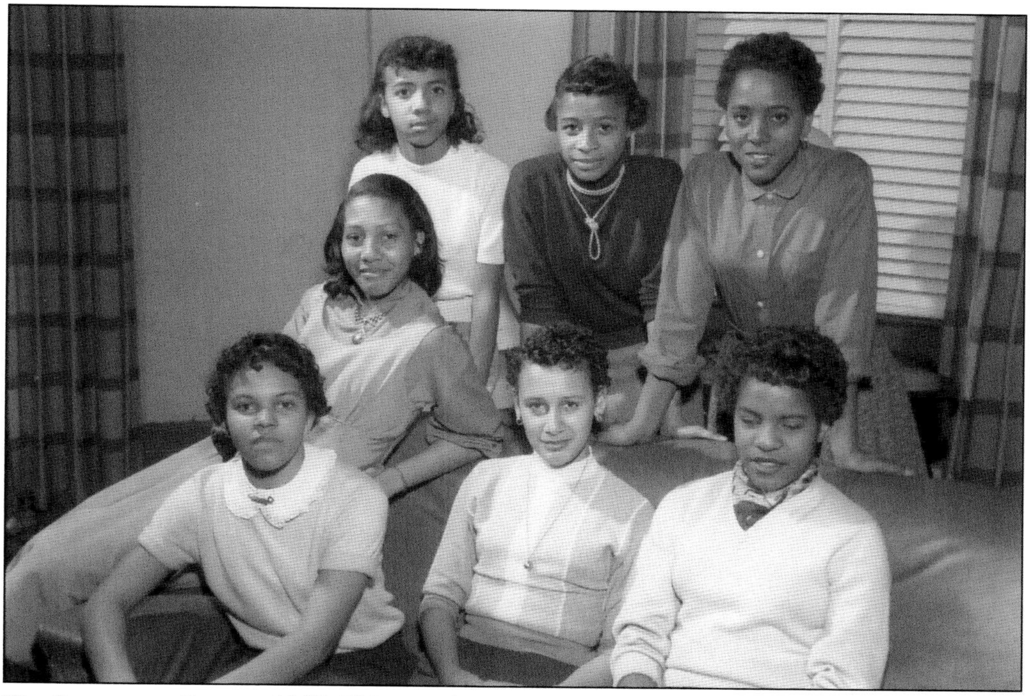

Miss Jabberwock Contest, 1955. This popularity contest was sponsored by the Chi Sigma Chapter of Delta Sigma Theta. The contestants, pictured from left to right, are (front row) Betty Smith, Joan Brown, and Frederick Clay; (second row) Helen Garnett (leaning on couch), Patricia Clayborne, Lizzie Brown, and Mary Evelyn Johnson. (Courtesy of *Lexington Herald Leader*.)

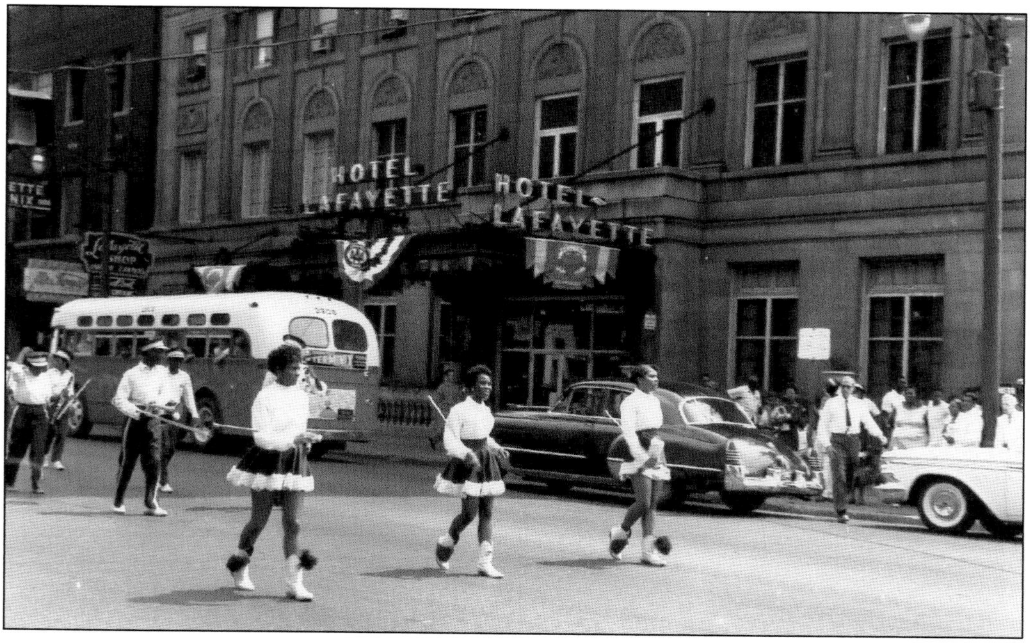

Dunbar Marching Majorettes. The Dunbar Marching Band, led by director Charles Quillings, thrilled the community with their musical performances in downtown parades. Pictured are the three majorettes marching down Main Street in a parade in the early 1960s.

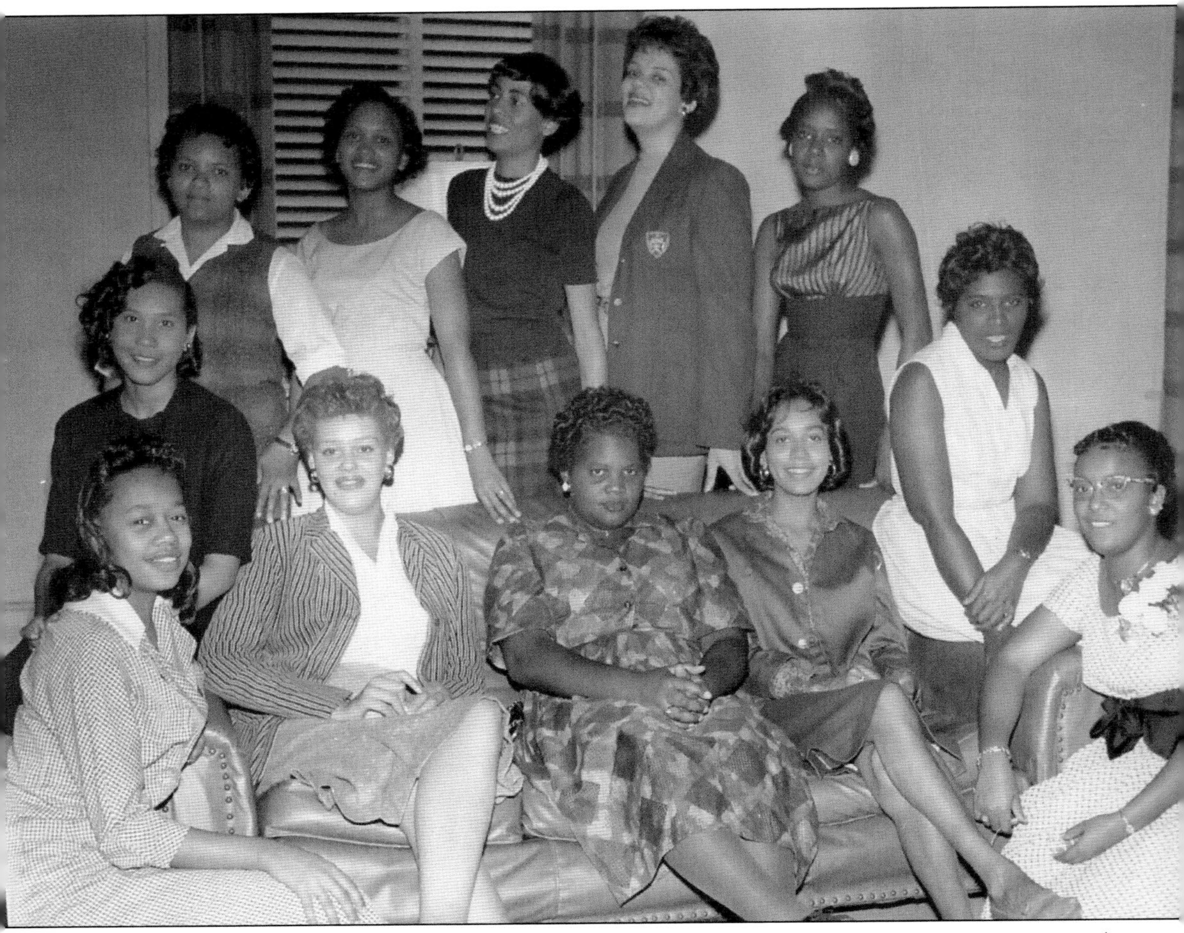

THE UKETTES. A lawsuit forced the University of Kentucky to open its graduate school in 1949. African-American undergraduate students were admitted following the historic *Brown* v. *Board of Education* decision in 1954. There were no social clubs and cultural opportunities for the first black students who attended UK. Doris Wilkinson founded a social club for African-American women and named it the UKettes. The clubmembers pictured in this 1959 photo, from left to right, are (front row) Mary Thomas, Jacqueline Cruse, Henrietta Davis, Barbara Thomas, and Helen Caise; (back row) Nietta Dunn, Joyce Lewis, Carmen McCann, Doris Wilkinson (presently a UK sociology professor), Ruth Cruise Million (presently a UK staff employee), Loretta Jackson Clark (presently a UK staff employee), and Elizabeth Chenault (seated). (Photo Maurice Strider, Courtesy of Doris Wilkinson.)

Five

Community Builders

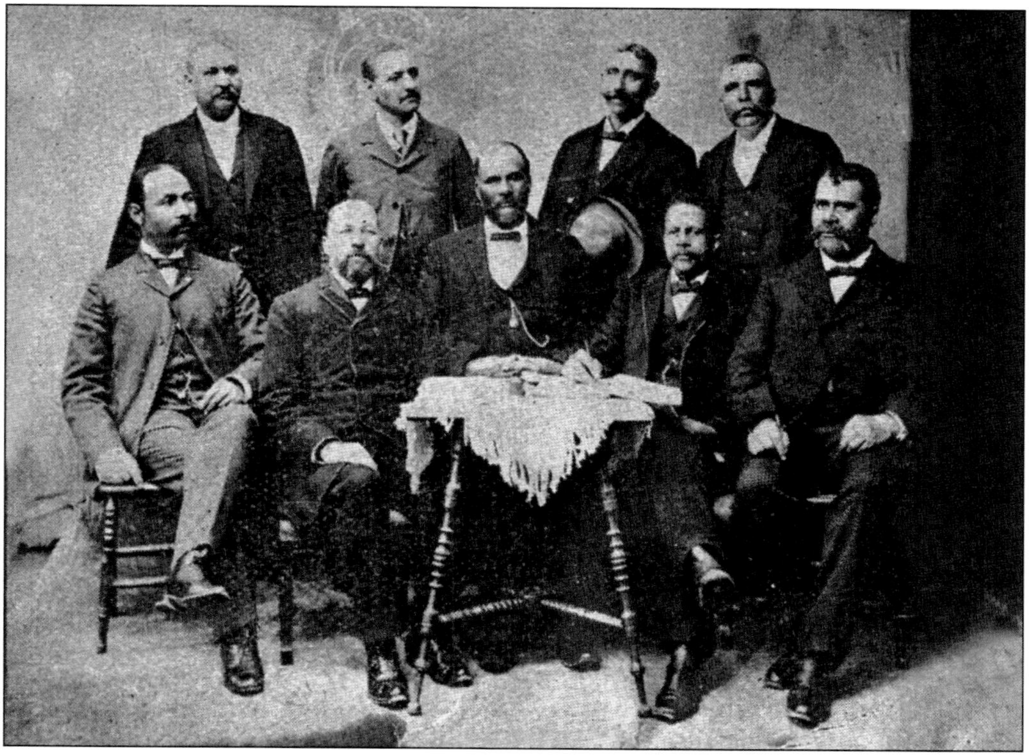

Officers and Board of Directors of the Colored A&M Fair Association in 1899. Founded in 1869, the Fair Association promoted African-American business and entertainment. The association organized the first Lexington "Colored Fair" October 6–9, 1869. About 10,000 African Americans attended the first fair on Georgetown Pike. The fair continued each year into the 1940s. (Courtesy of the Negro Business Directory, 1899.)

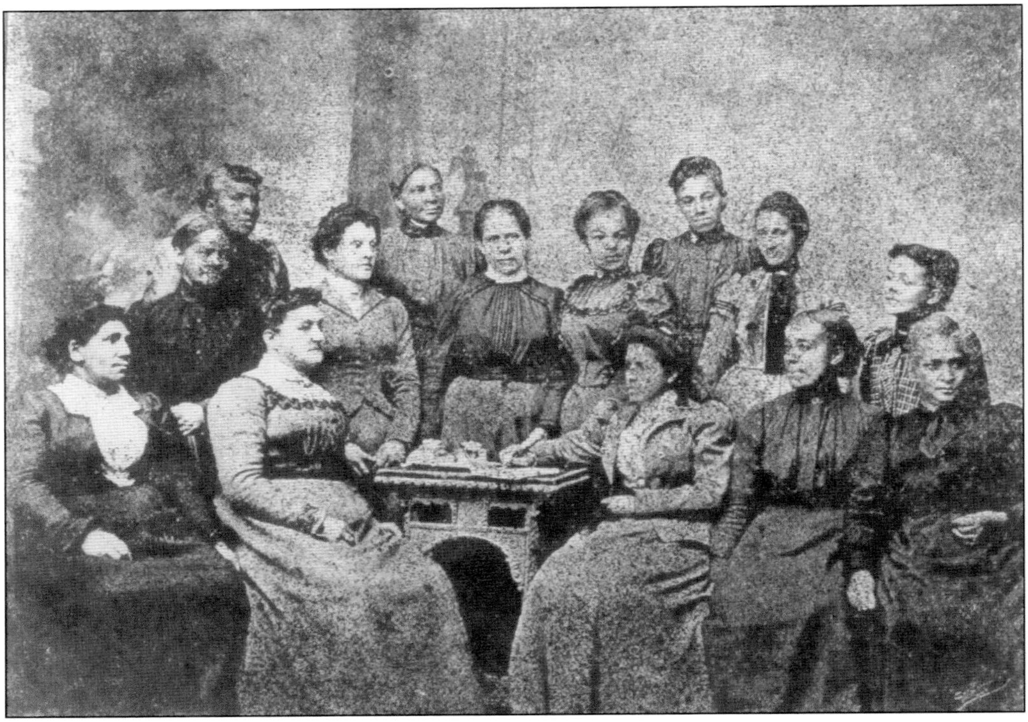

Board of Directors of the Colored Orphan Industrial Home. African-American women played a major role in establishing, developing, and leading important institutions and organizations significant to the African-American community. The Colored Orphan Industrial Home was founded in 1892 and opened November 9, 1894. The mission was revised over the years and the name was changed to Robert H. Williams Cultural Center in 1988. (Courtesy of Julian Jackson.)

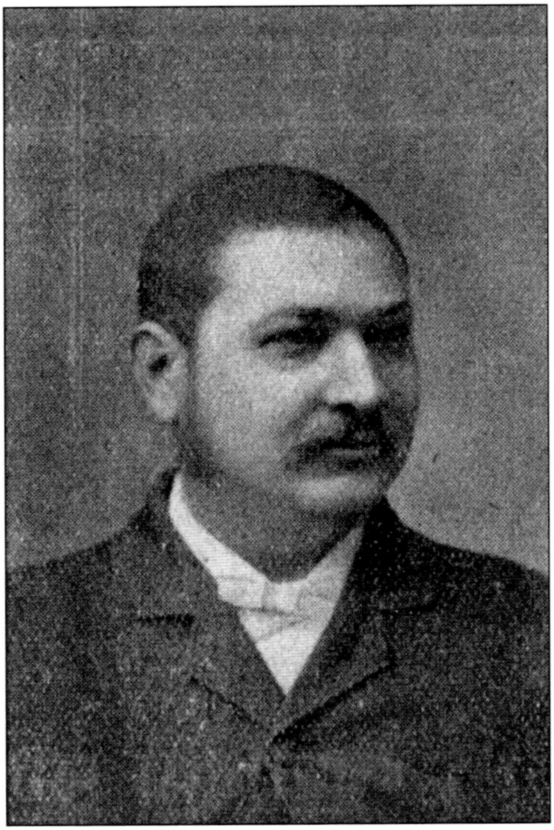

Contractor and Builder. Pictured is H.A. Tandy of the firm Tandy & Byrd. By 1899, the firm had worked on the Merrick Lodge Building, the new courthouse, First National Bank, and buildings on the UK campus. The *Leader* reported on September 29, 1897 that the firm employed between 40 and 50 black and white men. (Courtesy of the Negro Business Directory, 1899.)

E. Belle Jackson. A leader in the community, Jackson was born in Boyle County in 1848. She attended Berea College where she met her husband, J.C. Jackson. She was president of the Colored Orphans Industrial Home and owned a millinery at 9 South Mill Street. (Courtesy of Negro Population of Lexington, 1907.)

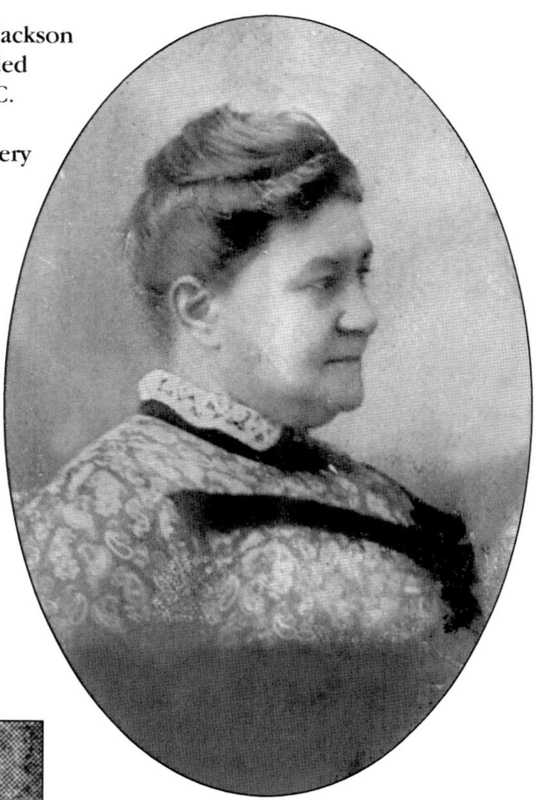

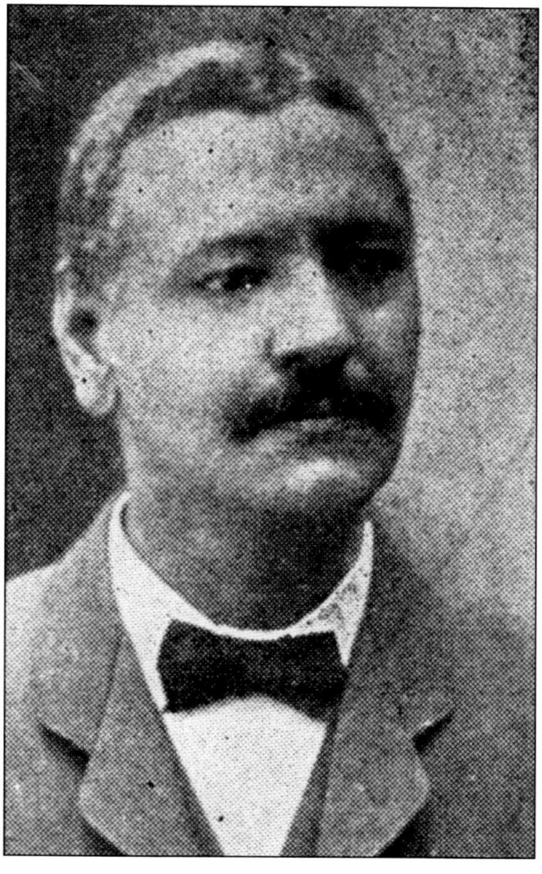

Jordan C. Jackson. Born a slave in Fayette County in 1848, Jackson was a politician and businessman. He was alternate delegate-at-large to the National Republican Convention in 1876 and a delegate in 1892. In October 1912, he won a primary bid for the nomination of commissioner but lost in the general election. The co-owner of an undertaking and livery business, he was a faithful member of the St. Paul A.M.E Church. Jackson died in 1918. (Courtesy of the Negro Population of Lexington, 1907.)

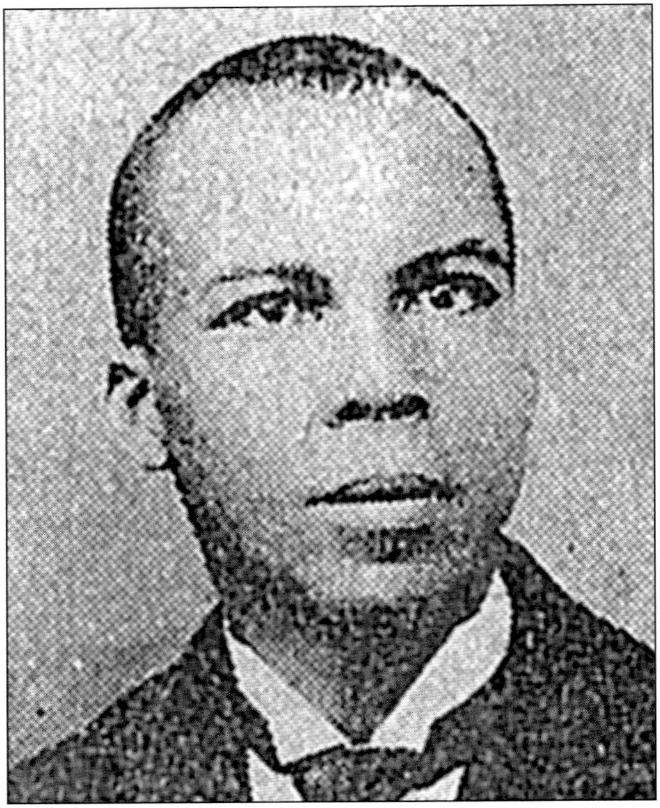

Robert Charles O'Hara Benjamin. Born March 31, 1855, in the West Indies on the island of Kitts, Benjamin was a lawyer, journalist, and author. He edited one of the city's earliest African-American newspapers, the *Lexington Standard*. His efforts to register black voters led to his violent and tragic death on October 2, 1900. (Courtesy of the Negro Business Directory, 1899.)

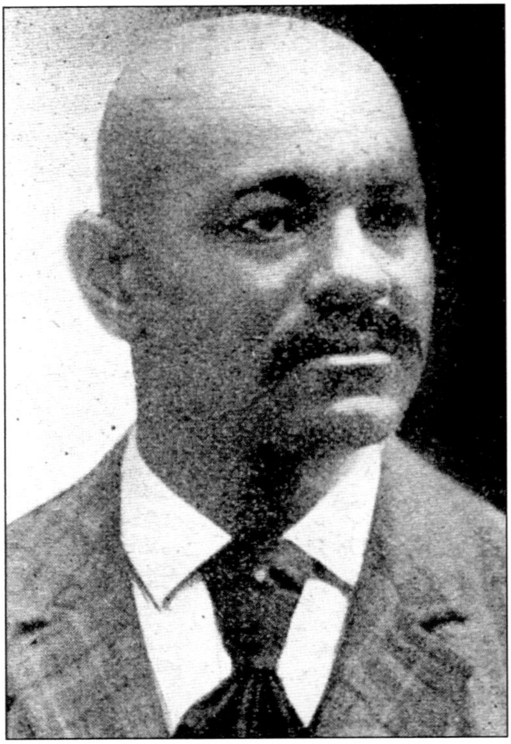

Edward W. Chenault. Born in Mt. Sterling, Kentucky, Chenault was a veteran of the Civil War. He came to Lexington from Helena, Arkansas. A dealer of coal, saloon keeper, active politician, and proponent of equal rights, Chenault served as president of the A&M Fair Association three times by 1897. He died at the age of 88 in 1934. (Courtesy of the Negro Business Directory, 1899.)

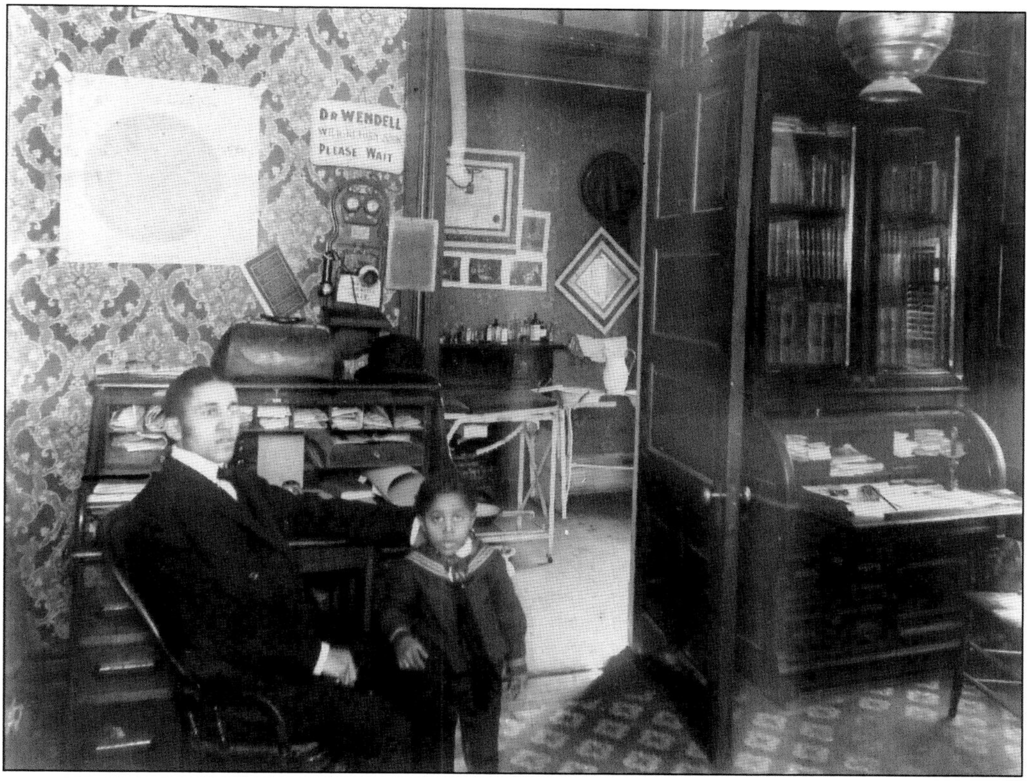

Dr. T.T. Wendell. Pictured in his office with his son John, Wendell earned doctorates of pharmacy and medicine from Meharry Medical College. In 1929, he joined the staff of Eastern State Hospital to work with African-American patients while continuing his medical practice. A building on the Eastern State Hospital grounds was named in his honor in August 1953. A trustee at St. Paul A.M.E. Church for more than 40 years, Wendell died in 1953. (Courtesy of Dr. T.T. Wendell Collection, Kentucky Historical Society, Special Collections and Archives.)

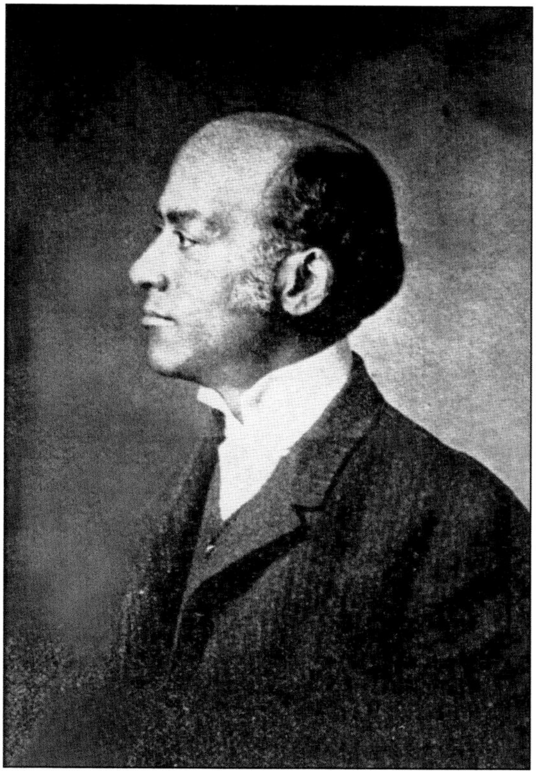

J. Alexander Chiles. Born in Richmond, Virginia, in 1860, Chiles finished school at Lincoln University and law school at the University of Michigan in 1889. Upon the suggestion of local physician Dr. John Hunter, Chiles came to Lexington to live in 1890. In December 1895, he became the first African American to practice before the Court of Appeals of Kentucky. (Courtesy of the Negro Business Directory, 1899.)

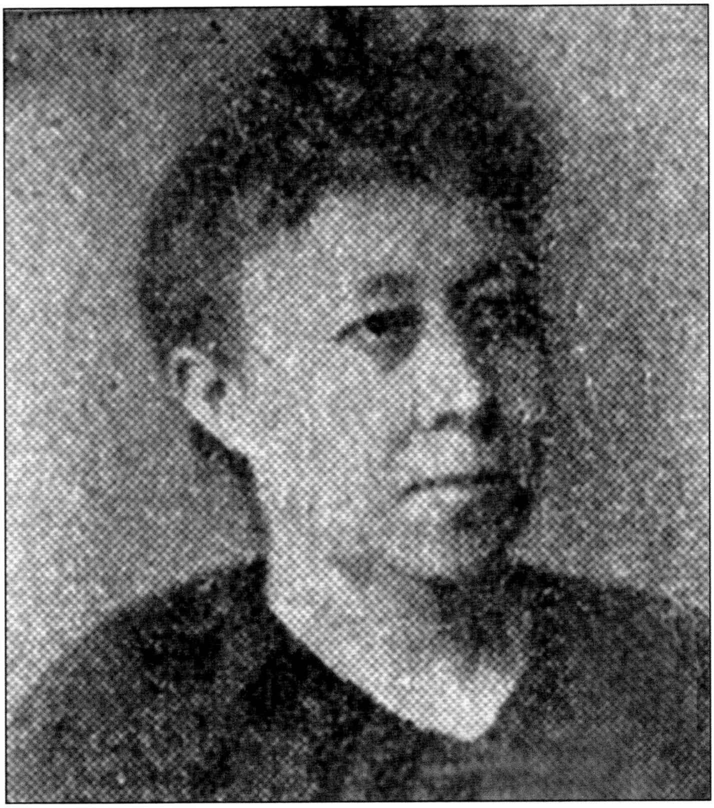

Kittie Phelps Jones. The first female pension notary in Kentucky, Jones was first commissioned on July 20, 1889. Her office was in her residence at 32 Corral Street. (Courtesy of the Negro Business Directory, 1899.)

African-American School Principals. Five African-American schools were in the city in 1929. Professor Fouse is seated in the center with hat in hand. (*Dunbar Echo*, Courtesy of Winston Powell.)

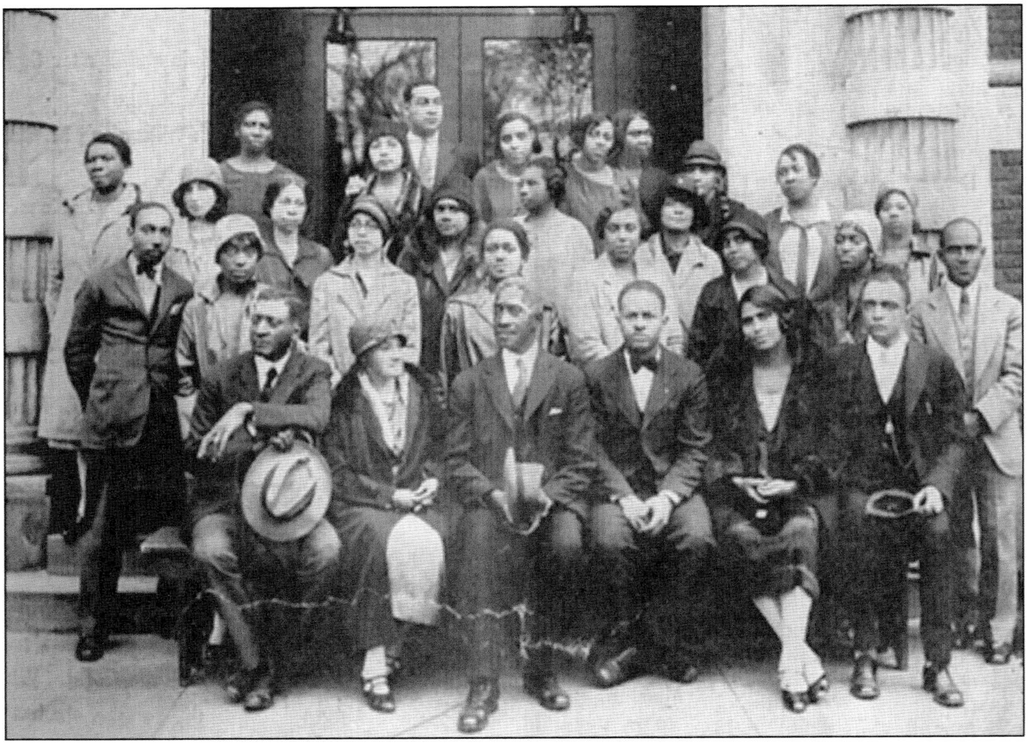

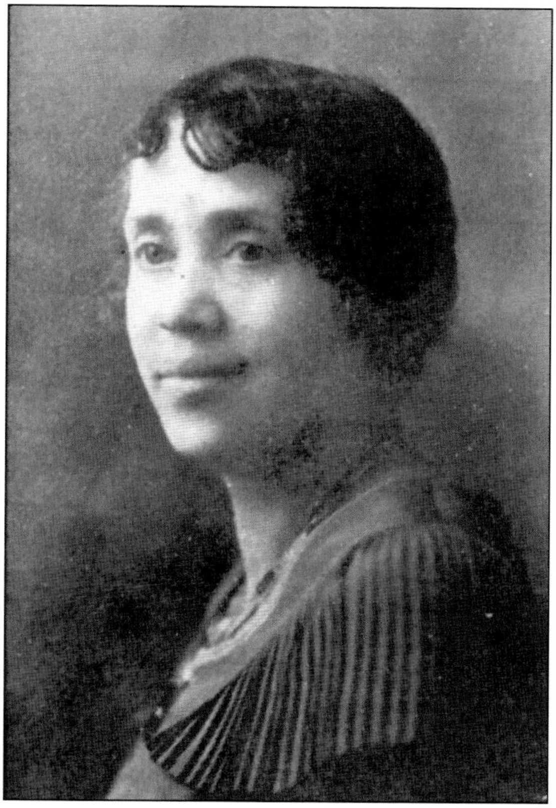

LIZZIE B. FOUSE. Active in numerous religious and civic organizations, Fouse founded the Phillis Wheatley Association in the city in 1920. In 1944, Kentucky governor Simeon Willis appointed her to the Kentucky Commission for the Study of Negro Affairs. A member of First African Baptist Church, Fouse died October 22, 1952. Her tombstone in Cove Haven Cemetery reads "To Live in Hearts We Leave Behind is Not to Die." (Courtesy of Sallie Price Collection, First Baptist Church Souvenir Booklet, 1940, UK Special Collections.)

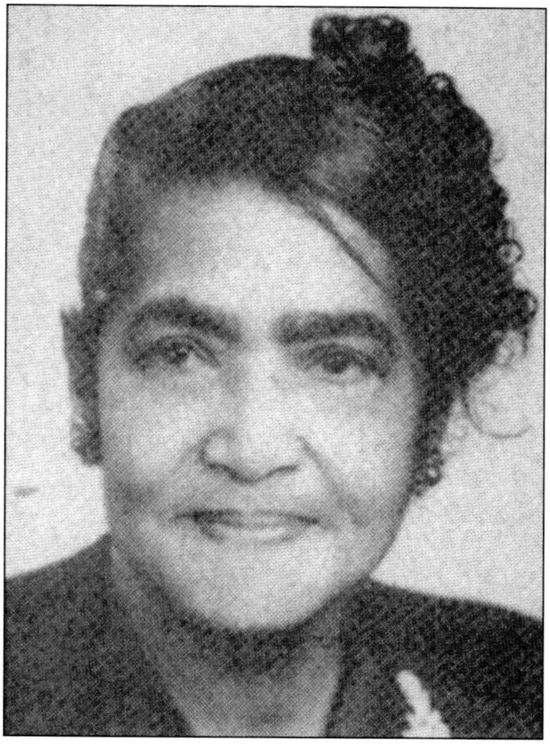

LUCY HARTH SMITH. A longtime principal of Booker T. Washington Elementary School, Smith was a leader in the women's club movement in Kentucky. She was president of the Kentucky Association of Colored Women from 1943 to 1945. She was also a past president of the Kentucky Negro Education Association and a member of the executive council of the Association for the Study of Negro Life and History. Smith died September 21, 1955.

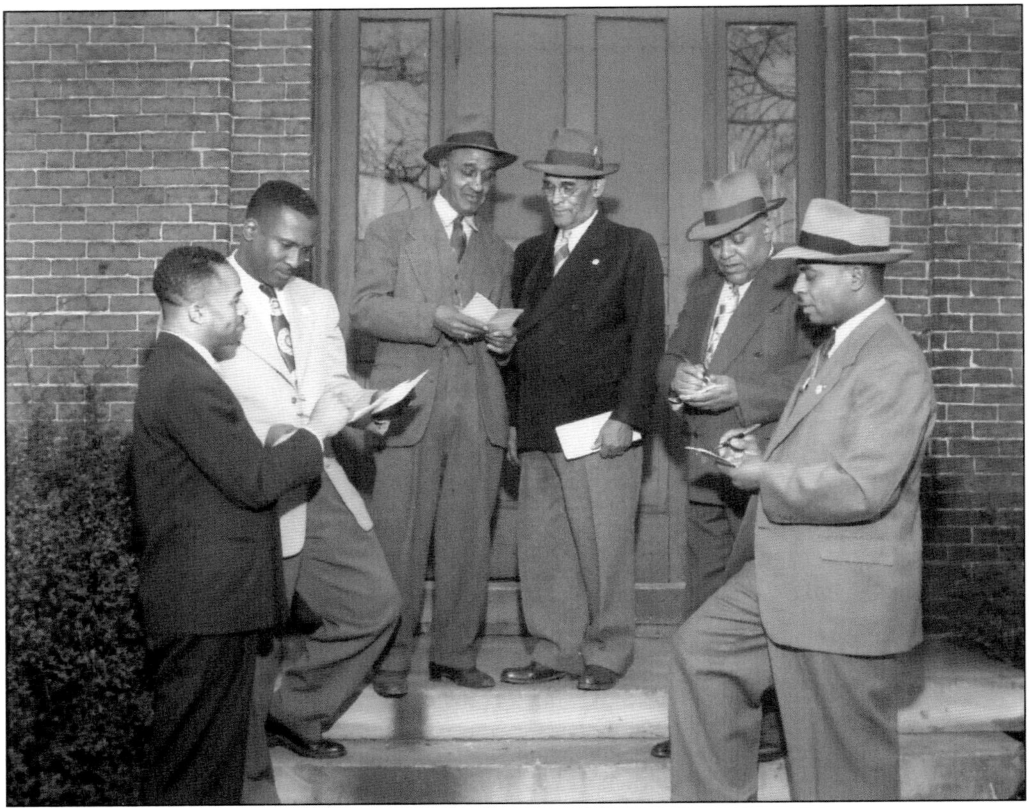

YMCA Board. In April 1951, members of the YMCA inspected the old Chandler School building, which was to be remodeled and used by the Colored YMCA. (Courtesy of Annetta Bibbs.)

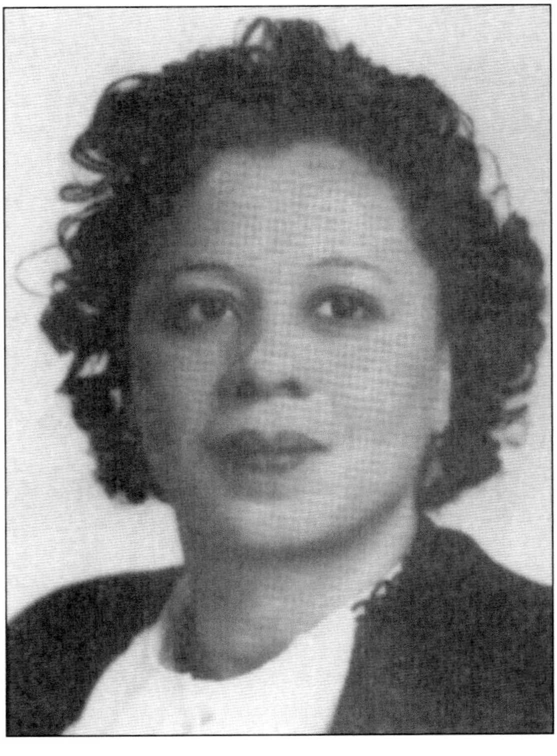

Lucy Rowe Estill. Estill was a city recreation director and a faithful member of Quinn Chapel A.M.E. Church. (Courtesy of Lucy Estill Papers, LFUCG Archives.)

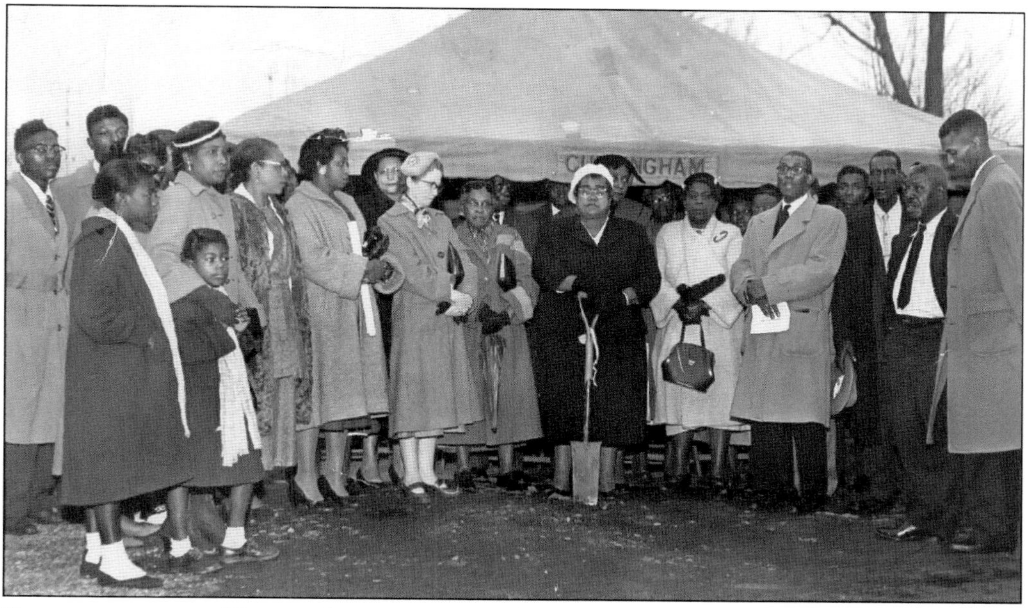

GROUNDBREAKING FOR WILLIAMS SAMARITAN HOME. Florence Williams was a trained beautician with her own business. In 1950, she opened a nursing home at 464 Greenwood Avenue. Pictured in 1956 is Williams, who stands in the center with a shovel during the groundbreaking ceremony for a new nursing home at 444 Glen Arvin Avenue. (Courtesy of Ella S. Bosley.)

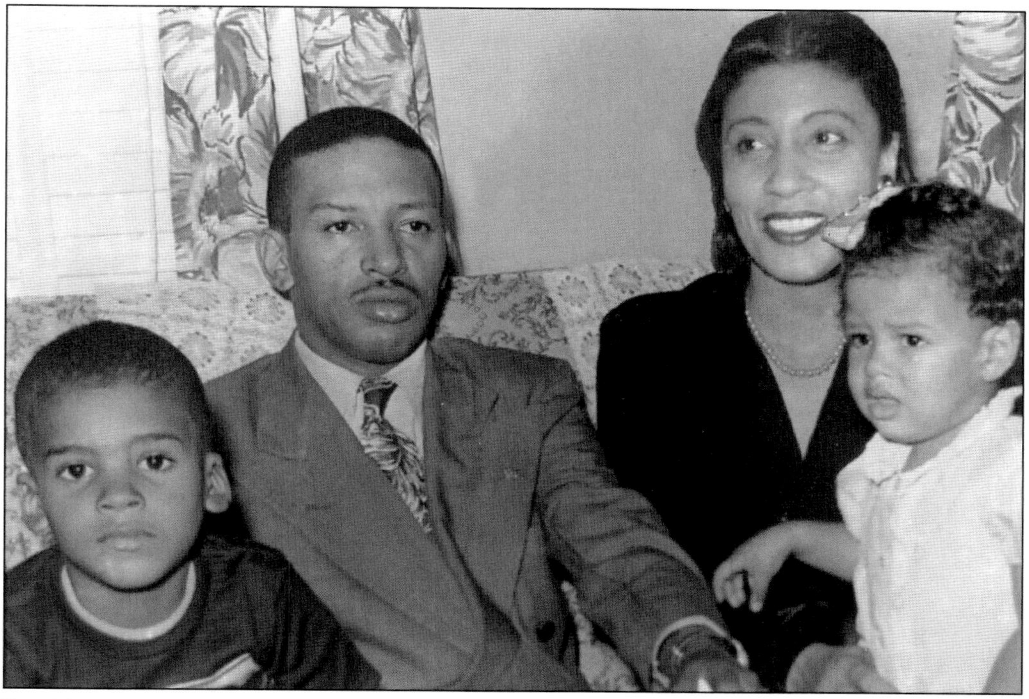

DR. MARSHALL JONES AND FAMILY. A graduate of Dunbar High School, Morehouse College, and Howard University Medical School, Jones was a lieutenant colonel in the army reserve. Jones practiced medicine in the city for nearly 20 years before he died at the age of 48 in 1964. (Courtesy of Doris Wilkinson.)

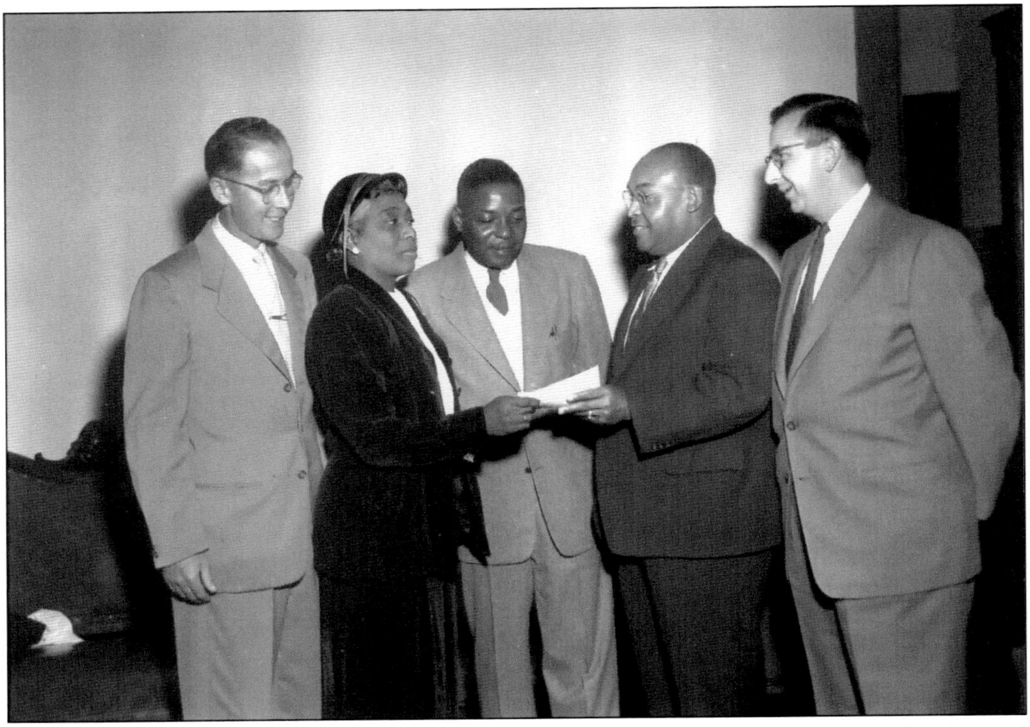

A Donation to the Community Chest Fund Campaign. In this 1953 photo, Mamie Grimsley (second from left) receives a check from Smoke Richardson (second from right) for $135. Grimsley was a Fayette County music teacher and private instructor. Richardson was a delegate of Musicians Union Local No. 635. Standing between Grimsley and Richardson is W.S. Dotson, a civic leader, businessman, and photographer. (Courtesy of *Lexington Herald Leader*.)

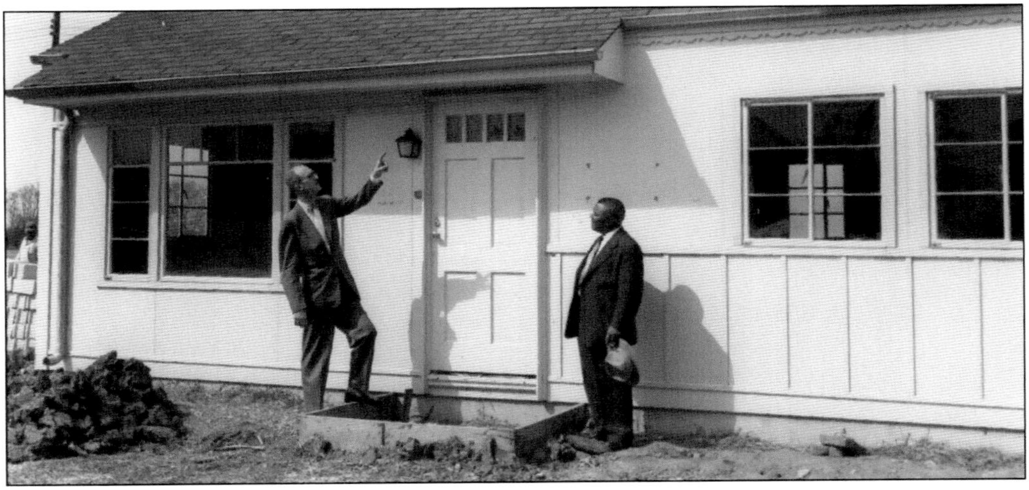

Haskins Drive. In 1948, Ovan Haskins and his wife, Buatha Ramsey Haskins, purchased a seven-and-one-fourth-acre plot of land off Newton Pike. Three years later, the area became the site of the city's first African-American subdivision, Haskins Drive. In a May 13, 1951 interview in the *Lexington Herald Leader*, Haskins credited his wife with the idea. Unfortunately, she did not live to see the first house constructed. Pictured are Mayor Tom Mooney, left, pointing to one of the homes, and Ovan Haskins. (Courtesy of *Lexington Herald Leader*.)

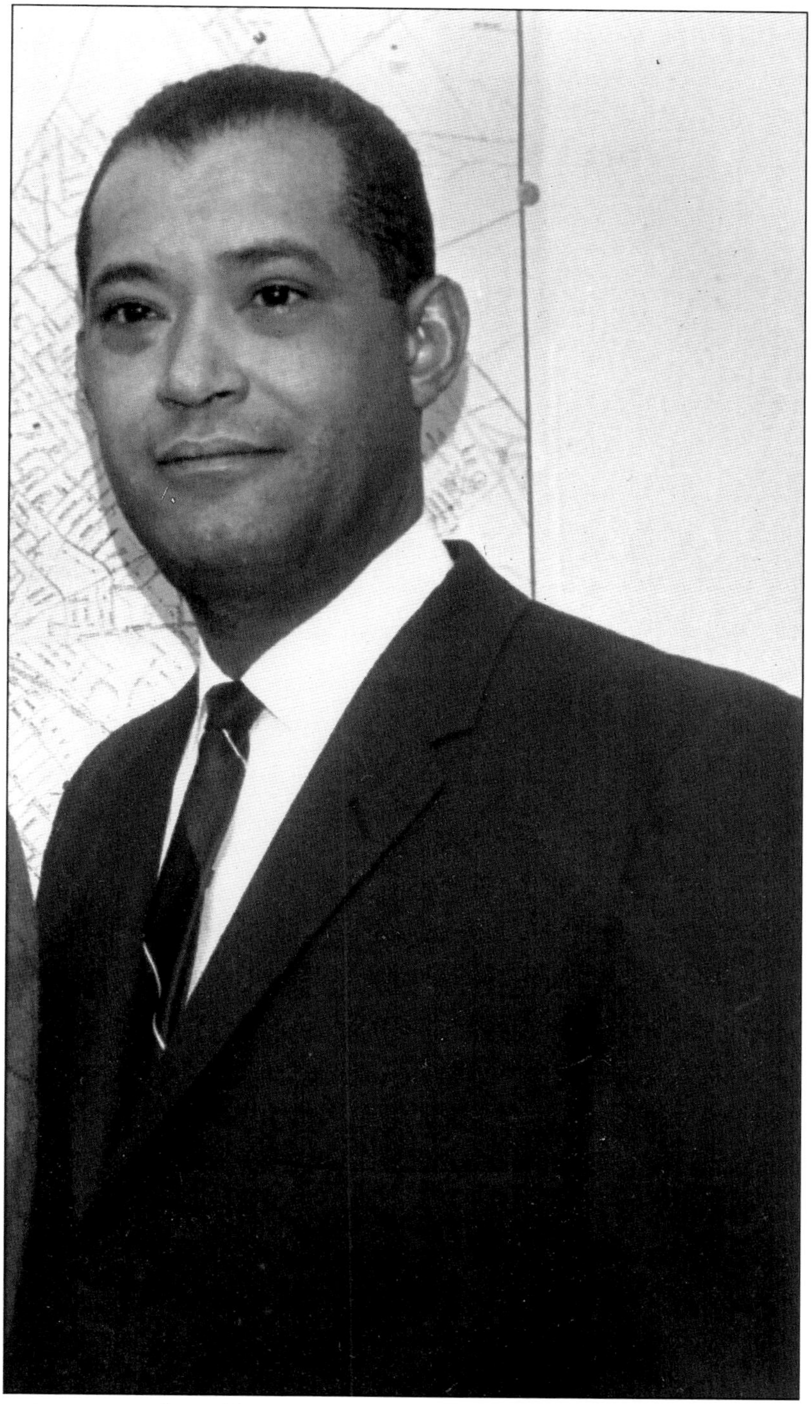

CARL LYNEM. A veteran of World War II and graduate of Kentucky State College, Lynem was employed with Mammoth Life Insurance Company. In November 1964, he became the first African American in Lexington elected to the school board. Lynem was killed in an automobile accident in March 1966 and Rev. H.H. Greene filled the position after his death. (Courtesy of *Lexington Herald Leader*.)

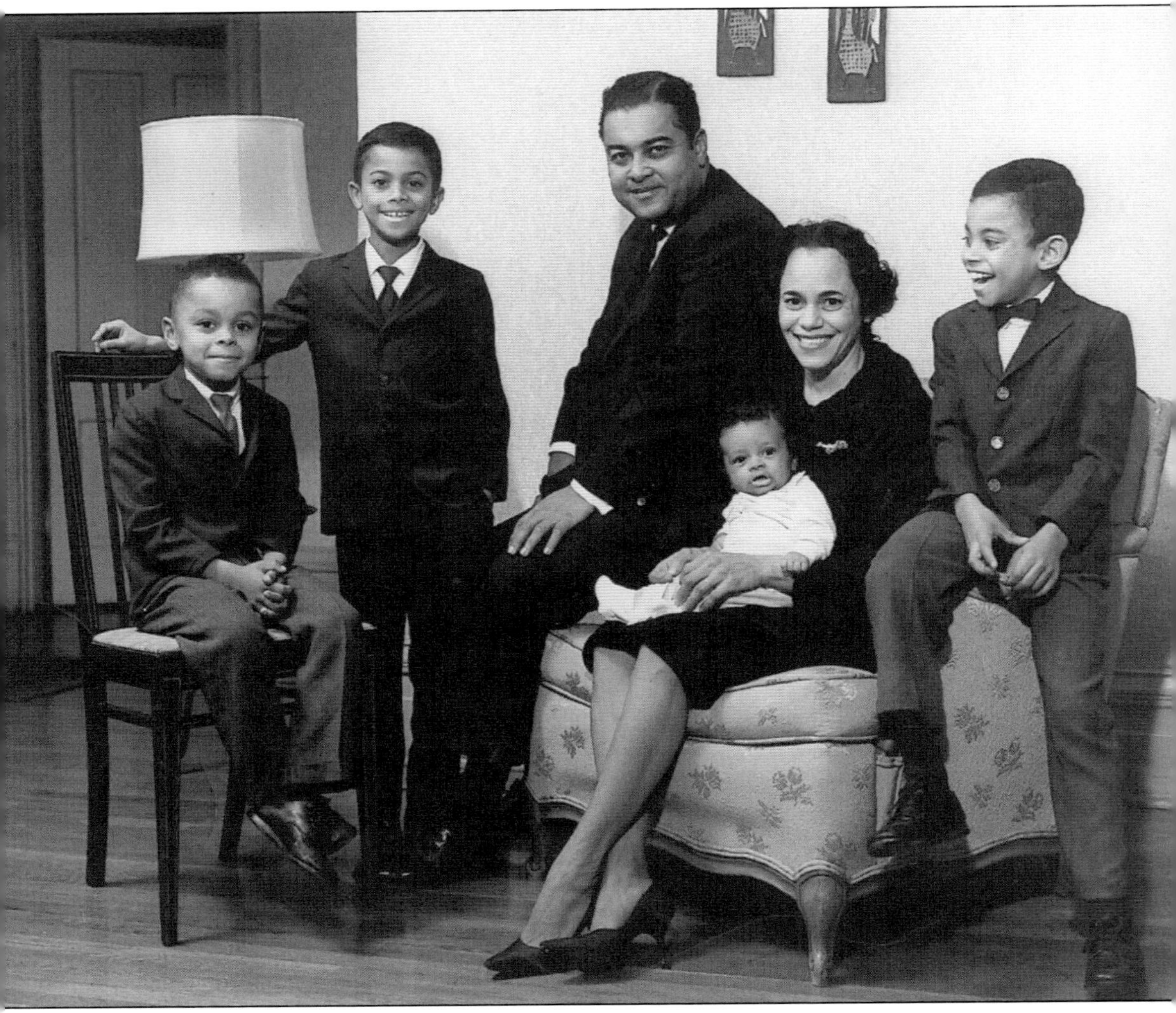

O.M. Travis and Family. Realtor and independent insurance agent, Travis served three terms as a council representative for the first district. Described as a "down-to-earth" politician, he ran unsuccessfully for the 53rd District House seat in 1964 and 1966. Travis was a member of St. Paul's A.ME. Church, and he died in 1979. (Courtesy of Miley Travis.)

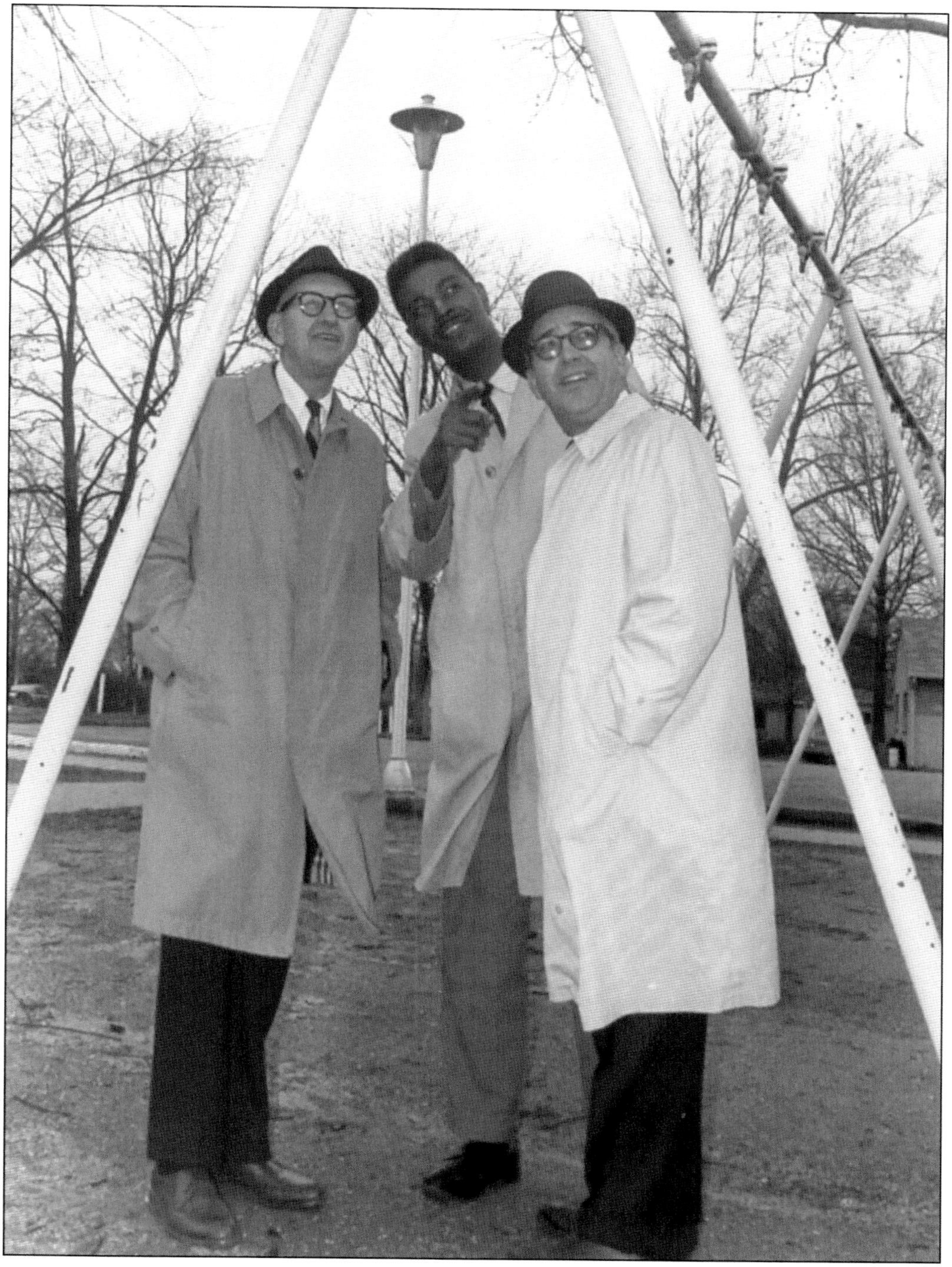

Harry Sykes. In 1963, Sykes became the first African American elected as a city commissioner. A former member of the Harlem Globetrotters, school teacher, and realtor, Sykes was active in community affairs and city and state government. In 1971, he was defeated in his bid for mayor by Foster Pettit. A highly respected administrator, he served as Acting City Manager and vice-chairman of the Committee to Insure Good Government in the early 1970s. (Courtesy of *Lexington Herald Leader*.)

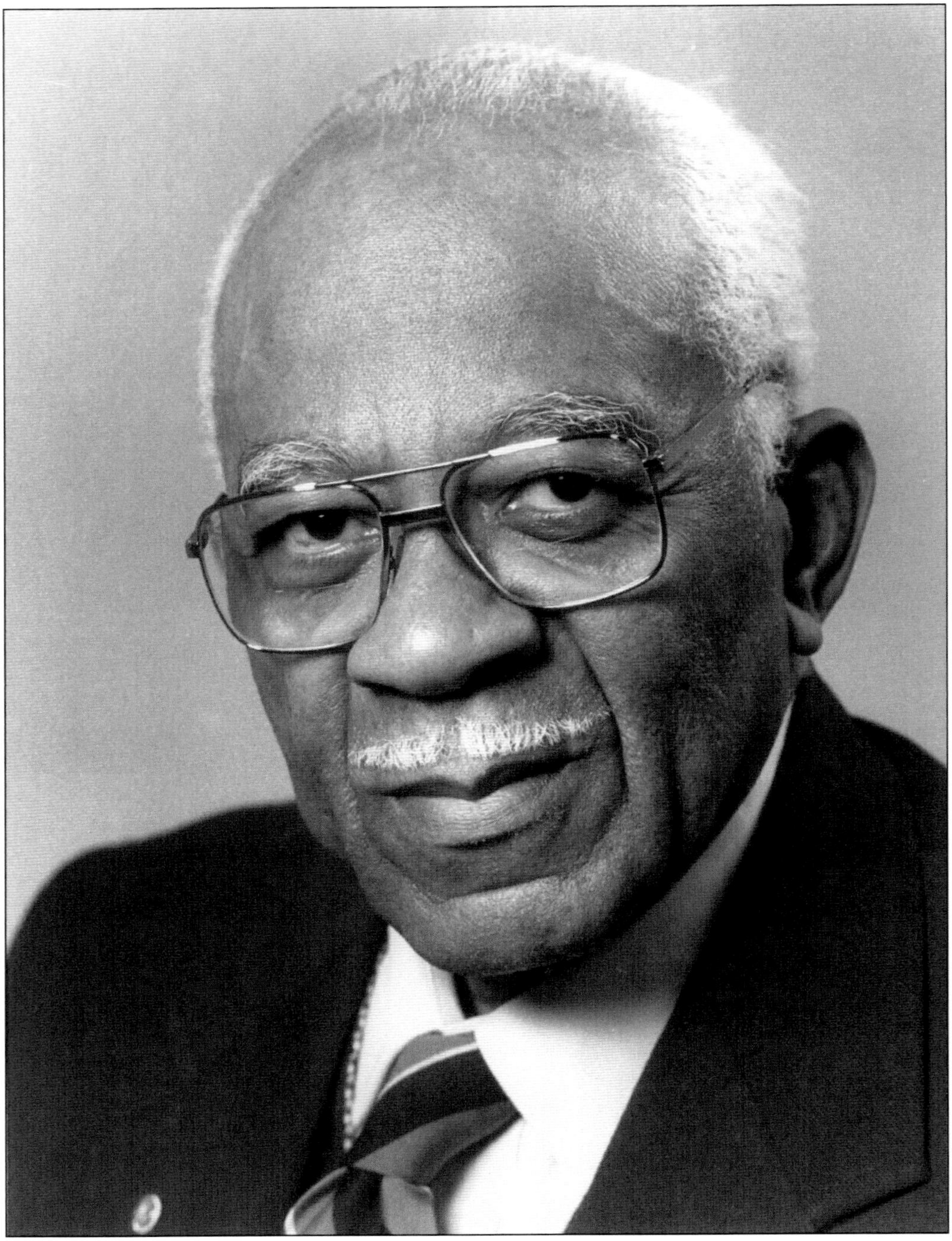

MAURICE STRIDER. Born in Lexington in 1913, Strider was a teacher, artist, historian, musician, and photographer. He taught at Dunbar High School for many years before accepting a position as an assistant professor in the art department at Morehead State University. Strider was a correspondent and photographer for the *Louisville Defender* and the *Pittsburgh Courier*. He died in 1989. (Courtesy of *Lexington Herald Leader*.)

Six

Fun and Games

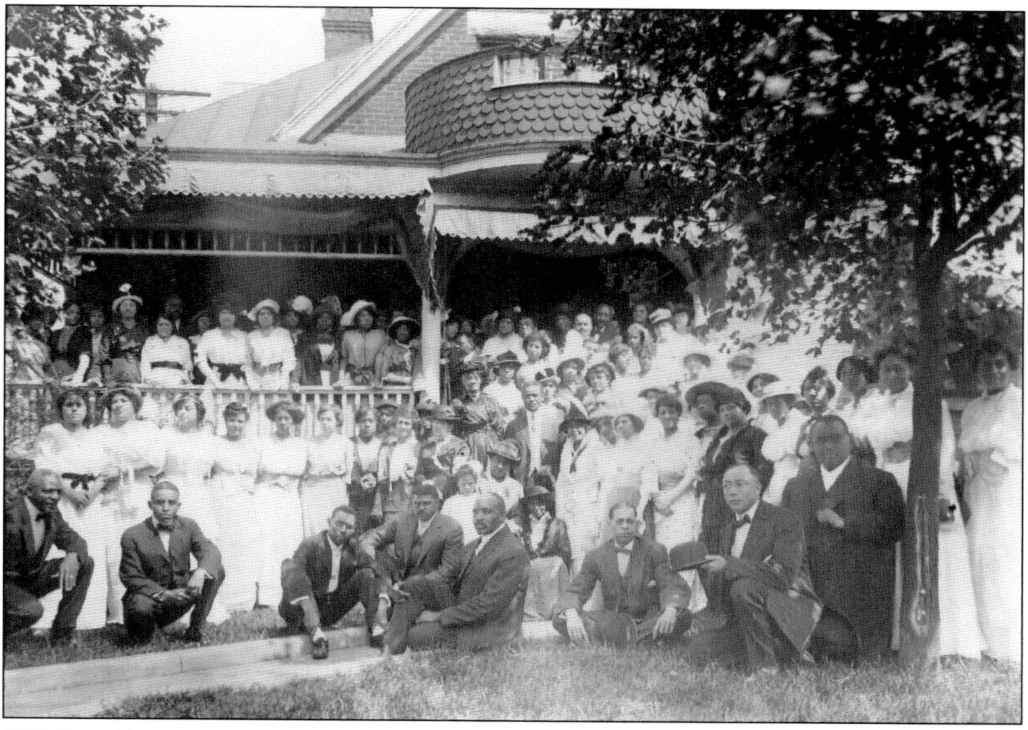

335 East Third Street. African Americans enjoyed a vibrant social life during segregation. Pictured is a large group of distinguished guests in the front lawn of Dr. T.T. Wendell's residence on September 12, 1914. (Courtesy of Dr. T.T. Wendell Collection, Kentucky Historical Society, Special Collections and Archives.)

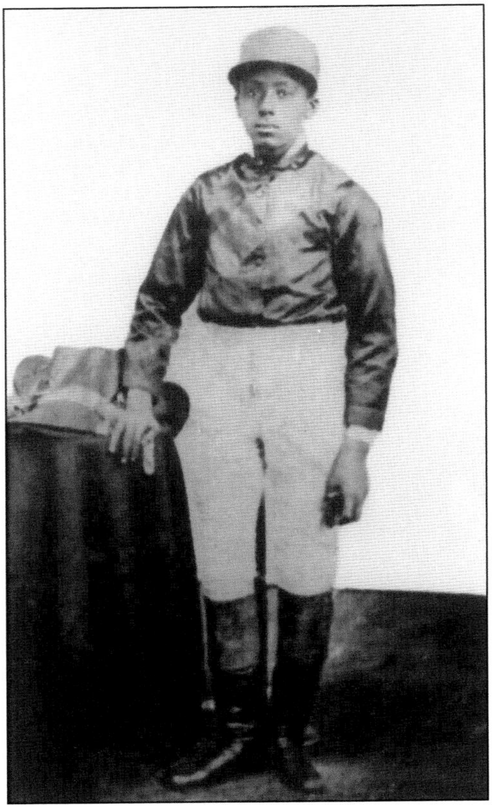

Isaac Murphy. Born in 1861, Murphy was an honest and outstanding jockey. He won the Kentucky Derby in 1884, 1890, and 1891. He died in 1896 and was buried in the African Cemetery on East Seventh Street. It was not until 1955 that Murphy was inducted into the Jockey's Hall of Fame at Saratoga. His body was reinterred at the Kentucky Horse Park in 1977. (Courtesy of P.W.L Jones Collection, Kentucky State University.)

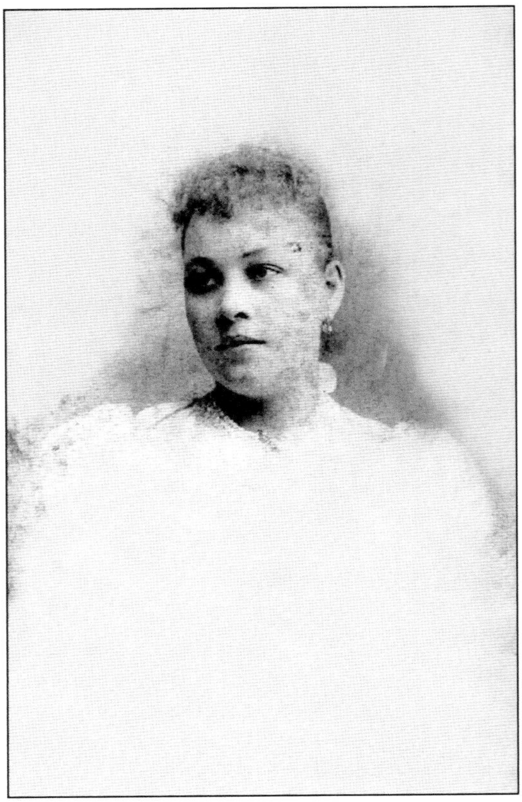

Lucy Murphy. Married to Isaac Murphy in 1882, Mrs. Murphy shared with her husband his success as a jockey. When Isaac died, she supposedly, in her grief, hired a carriage driver for several days to transport her to the cemetery on East Seventh Street so she could place flowers on his grave. She died in 1910 at the age of 40 at her residence on North Limestone Street. (Courtesy of Dr. T.T. Wendell Collection, Kentucky Historical Society, Special Collections and Archives.)

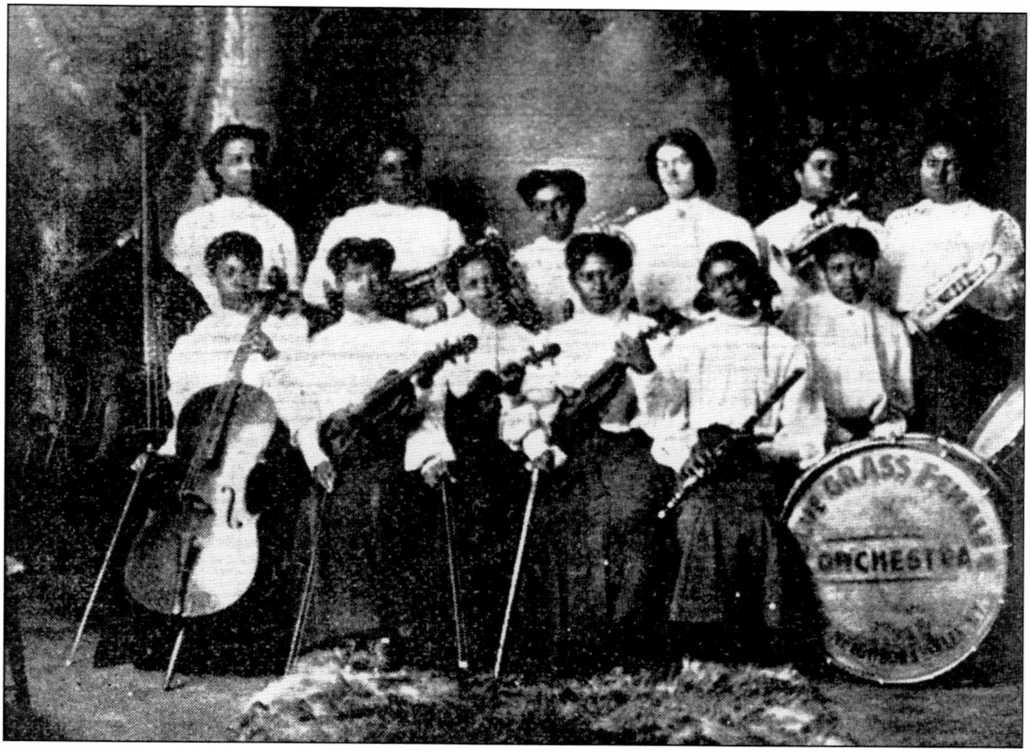

Blue Grass Orchestra, 1907. Historically, African Americans in Lexington have organized various kinds of musical groups. The African-American women in the photograph above comprised a local orchestra. (Courtesy of Negro Population of Lexington, 1907.)

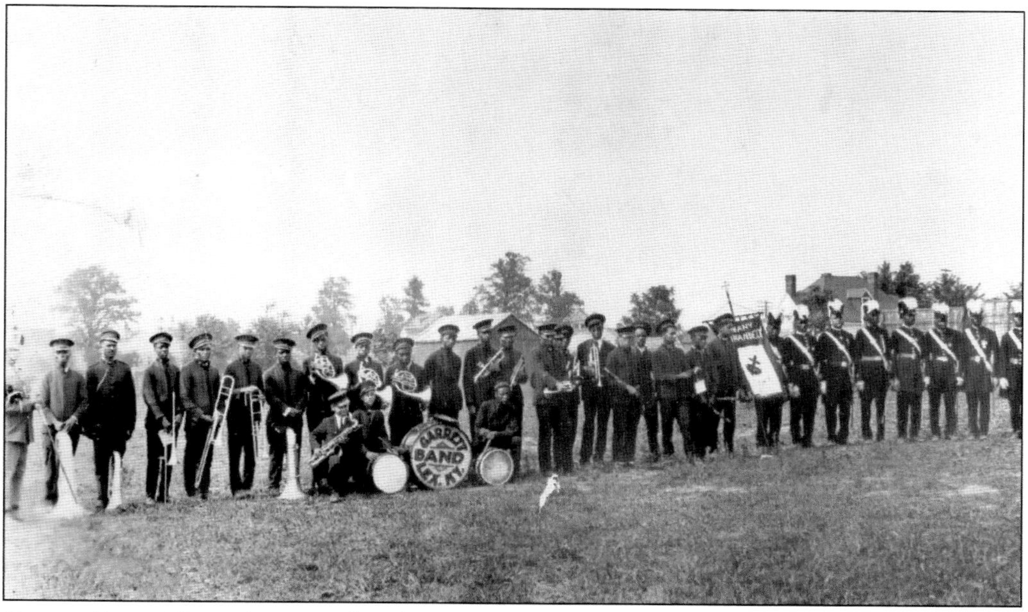

Garrett Band. African-American bands were performing in Lexington in the late 19th century. The Garrett Band of Lexington was known to have performed at the Colored Fair. (Courtesy of Dr. T.T. Wendell Collection, Kentucky Historical Society, Special Collections and Archives.)

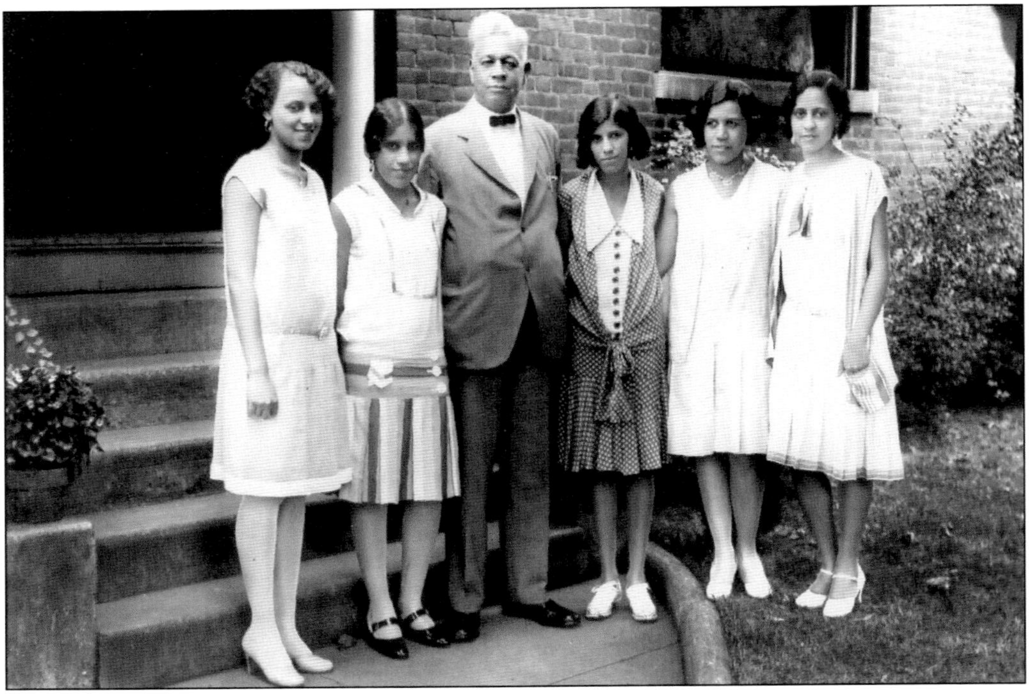

A Distinguished Visitor. Pictured here, in the front yard of Dr. T.T. Wendell's home at 335 East Third Street, is Oscar DePriest, the first African American elected to the United States Congress in the 20th century. DePriest represented Illinois in the House of Representatives from 1929 to 1935. Here, DePriest poses with Wendell's three daughters and two other young ladies. Pictured from left to right are an unidentified woman, Jennie V. Wendell, Laura Wendell, and Clara Wendell. (Courtesy of Dr. T.T. Wendell Collection, Kentucky Historical Society, Special Collections and Archives.)

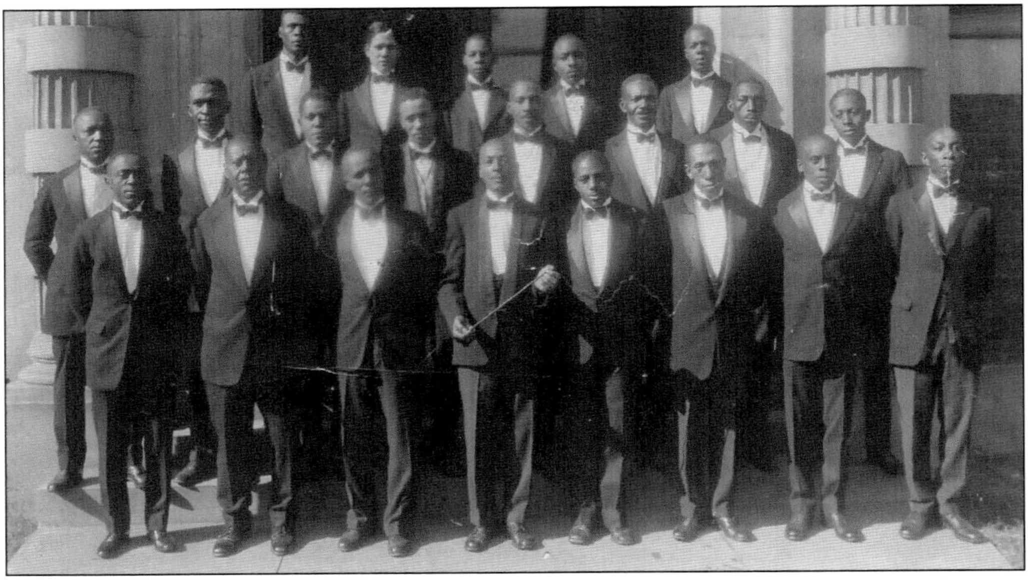

Lexington Jubilee Singers. Frank Brown occupies the top row far right space in this 1930 image. (Courtesy of Sharon Engles.)

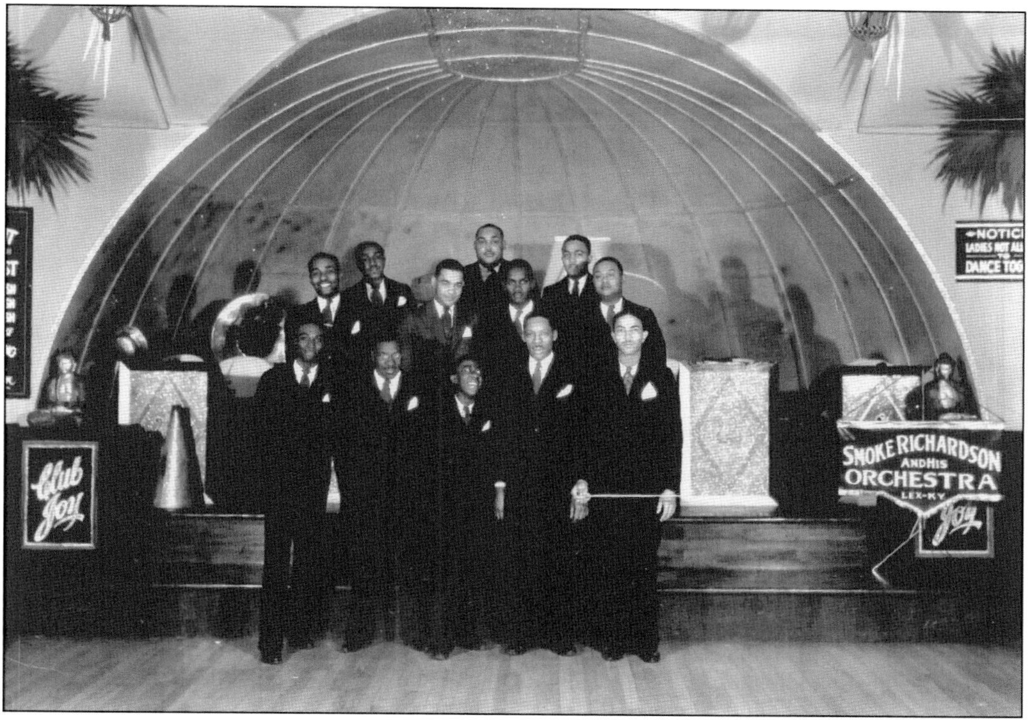

"Smoke" Richardson's Orchestra. Richardson was known throughout Kentucky. He played at schools and clubs throughout the city. One of his most popular selections was the poem "Trees." Richardson stands on the top row center at Club Joy in April 1934. (Courtesy of Lafayette Collection, UK Special Collections.)

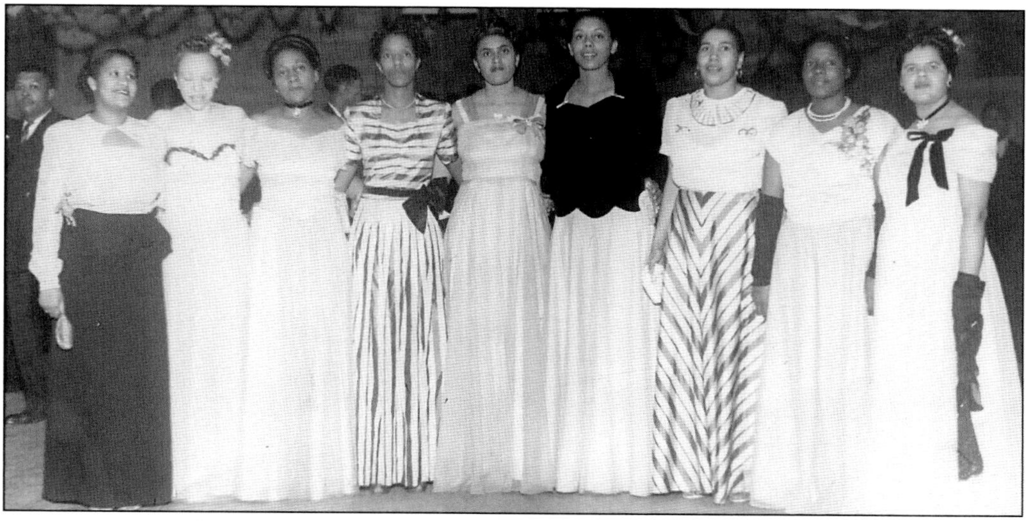

Economics Club. African-American men and women organized a number of different social clubs in the city. In doing so, they established lasting friendships and organized events and programs to benefit the African American community at large. The Economics Club met bi-weekly. Members ate food, played games, and talked. They also raised money for the needy. The picture includes indentifier Lilla Bentley, standing fifth from the left, and others at the club's charity ball in the late 1930s. (Courtesy of Lilla Bentley.)

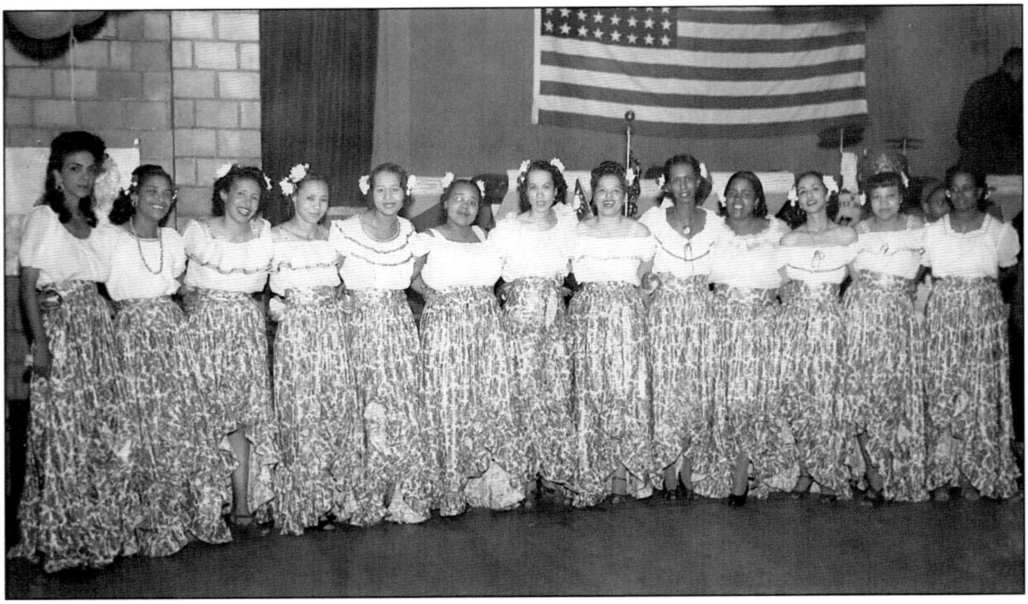

Tops Club. African-American women established lasting friendships in the social clubs they formed. The outings these clubs sponsored offered expanding opportunities for social and cultural activities. Pictured are members of one of the city's well-known clubs during segregation. (Courtesy of Amanda Elliott.)

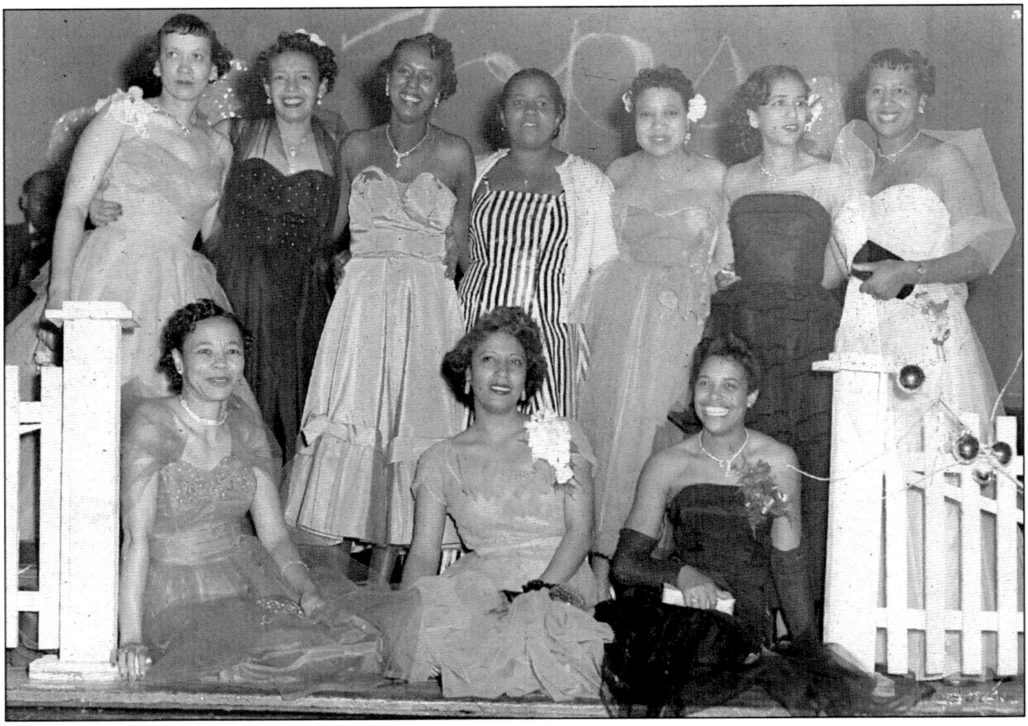

Tops Club. Club members, from left to right, are (front row) Mary Roach, an unidentified member, and Evelyn Livisay; (second row) two unidentified members, Dorothy Cooper, Myrtle Boss, Mariah Dunn Williams, Thelma Halliday, and Arnetta O'Neal. (Courtesy of Amanda Elliott.)

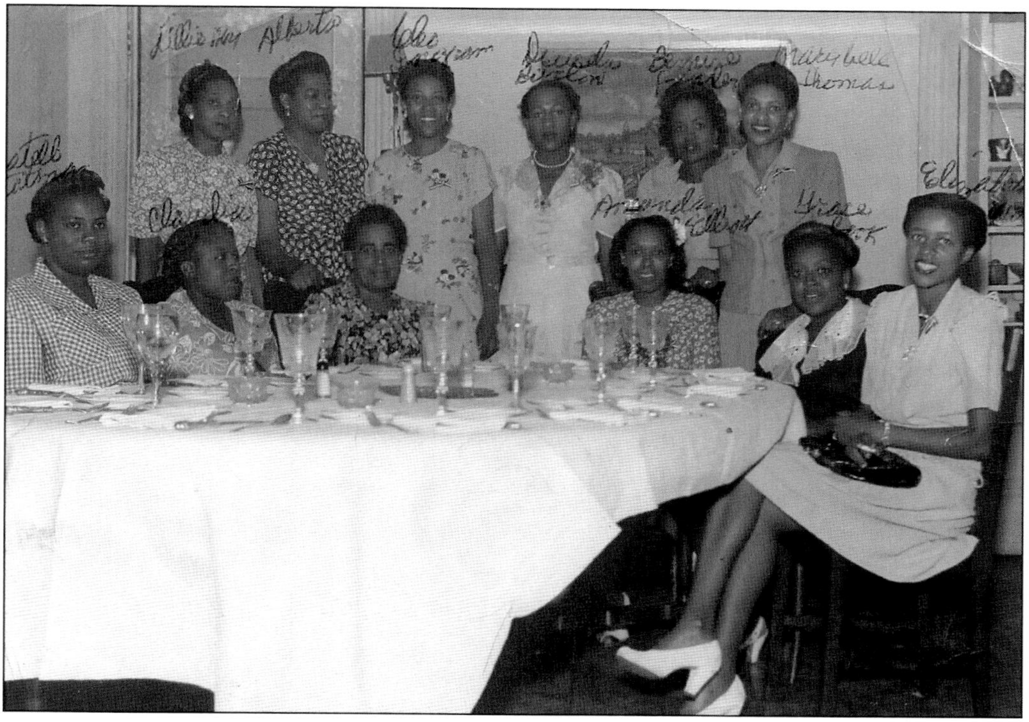

War Wives Club Having Dinner at Abbie's Food Shop, *c.* 1944. Seated, from left to right, are Estella Tatman, Claudia Matchen, Mrs. Abbie, Amanda Elliot, Grace Cook, and Elizabeth Woods. Standing, from left to right, Lillie Barber, Alberta Aurthor, Cleo Ingram, Drucella Barlow, Bernice Fender, and Maybell Thomas. (Courtesy of Cleo Ingram.)

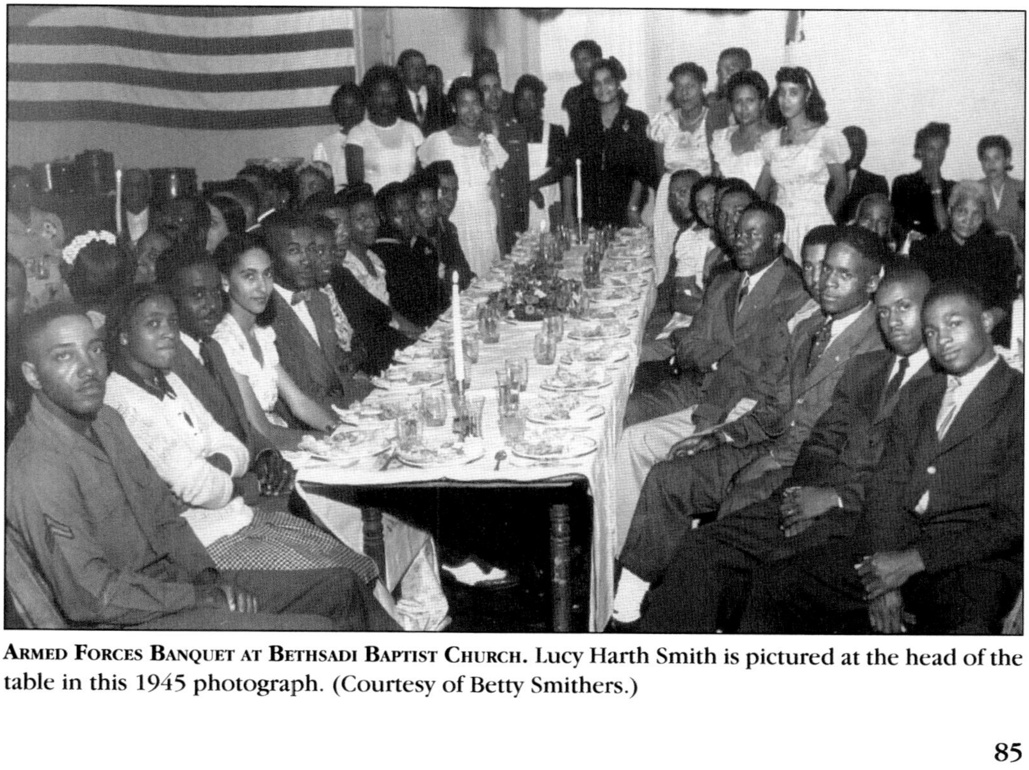

Armed Forces Banquet at Bethsadi Baptist Church. Lucy Harth Smith is pictured at the head of the table in this 1945 photograph. (Courtesy of Betty Smithers.)

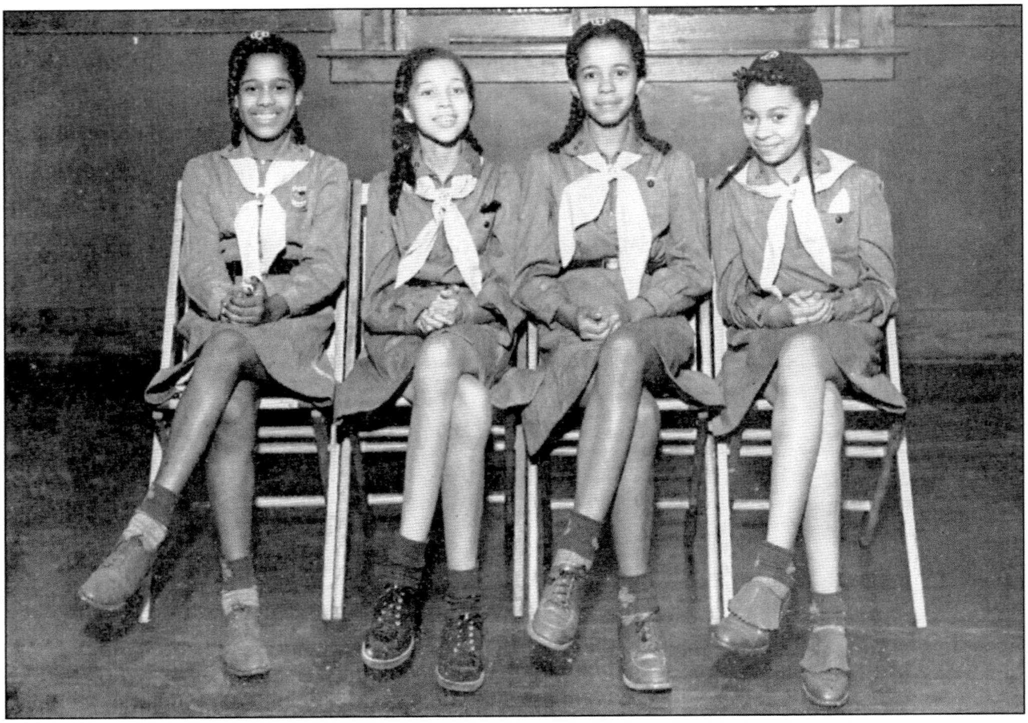

Girl Scouts at First Baptist Church, 1940. Pictured in the photograph above, from left to right, are Virginia Washington, Anne Bruce Hinnant, Anna E. Mack, and Dorothy Berry. (Courtesy of Sallie Price Collection, First Baptist Church Souvenir Booklet, 1940, UK Special Collections.)

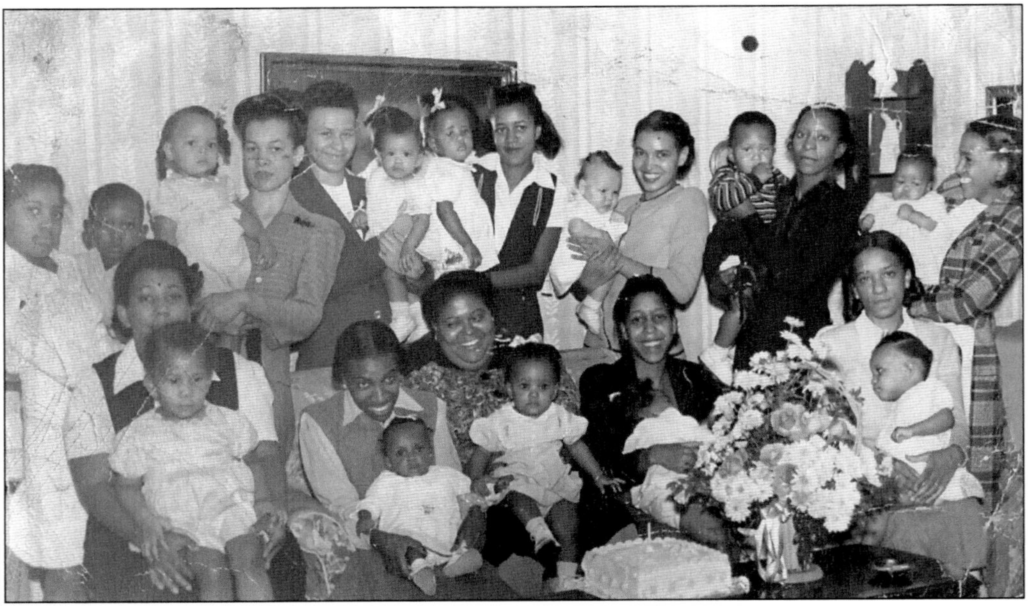

Birthday Party on Ohio Street. Henrietta Fisher Fender celebrates her first birthday. She and several of the other children pictured here had fathers who were serving in World War II at the time of this photo. Fender is pictured wearing a ribbon and is seated, center, in the lap of her mother, Mary Fisher Calloway. (Courtesy of Henrietta Fender.)

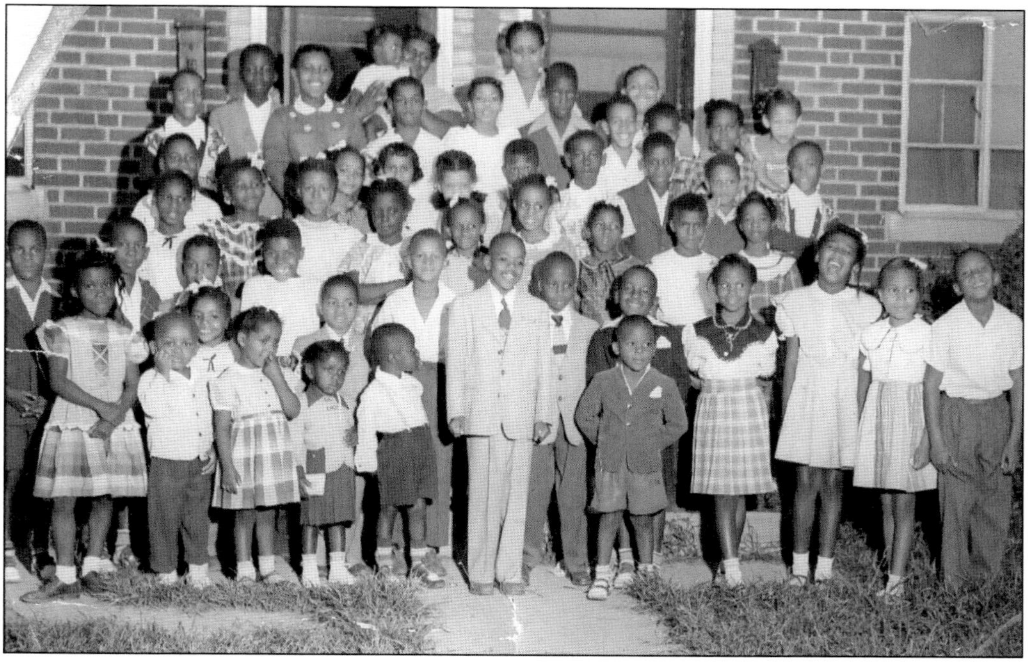

Birthday Party in Charlotte Court. Located between Georgetown Street and Newton Pike, Charlotte Court was one of two public housing projects established for African Americans during segregation. William Cook, center and wearing a suit, is pictured with his friends in the early 1950s. Charlotte Court has since been torn down for new housing construction. (Courtesy of Yolanda Douglass.)

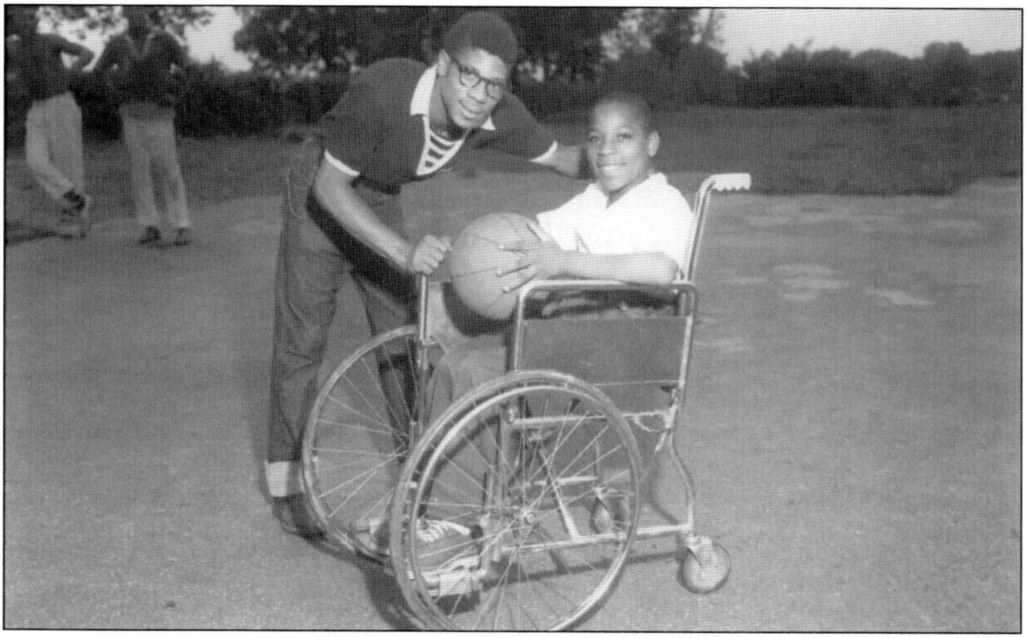

Having Fun at the Park. A new playground was built at the site of the old Douglass School on Chiles Avenue. Taylor Seals, director of the playground, and Carl Cummins, in the wheelchair, are pictured here in 1953. (Courtesy of *Lexington Herald Leader*.)

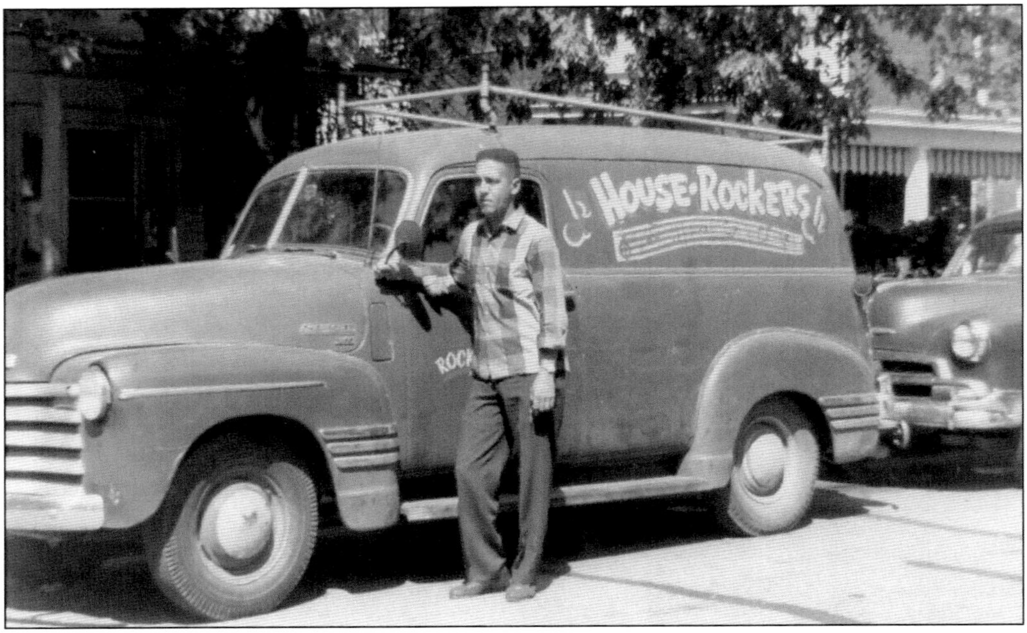

The House Rockers. In 1950, students from the old Ed Davis High School in Georgetown formed a band called the House Rockers. This popular band played at school dances, house parties, and several clubs in Lexington until the 1970s. Leslie Todd Bailey, the group's organist and alto saxophone player, stands beside the group's bus in 1957. (Courtesy of Alice Bailey.)

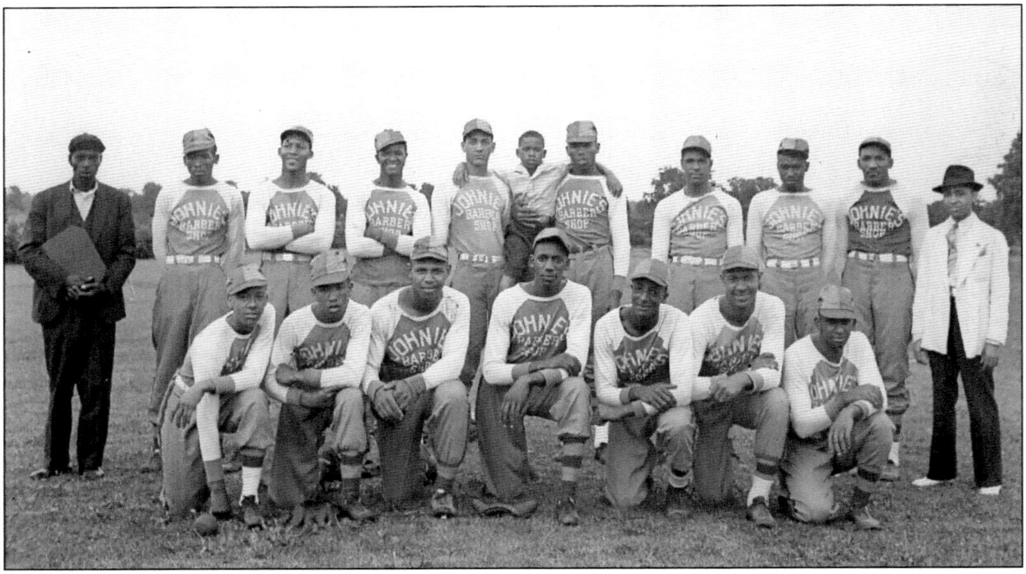

Johnnie's Barbershop Fast Pitch Softball Team. Organized by Johnnie Jackson, a local barber, this team won the city championship six straight years at Douglass Park during the 1930s. Team members, from left to right, are (front row) Robert Burbage, J.W. Simpson, Bill Dennis, James Young, John Will "The Mighty Scoop" Brown, R.B. Mitchell, and "Stonewall" Jackson; (back row) an unidentified person, M.T. Simpson, Robert Carson, Chum Davis, three unidentified people, Bernie Cooper, James Fields, Raymond Young, and Johnnie Jackson. (Courtesy of Winston Powell.)

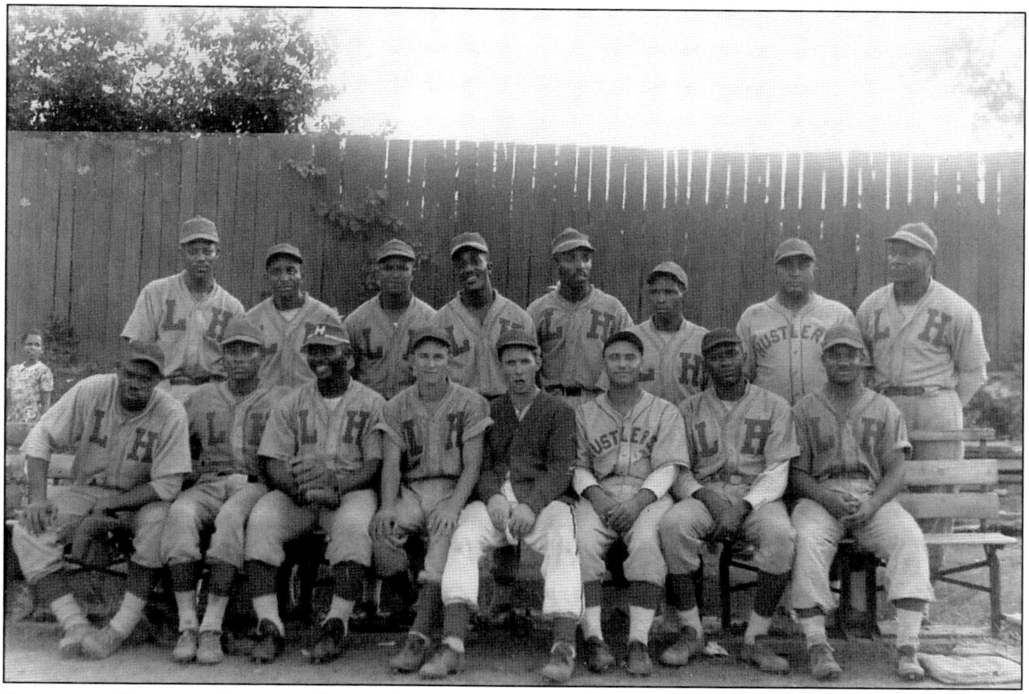

Lexington Hustlers. Organized in 1945, the Lexington Hustlers were a semi-professional baseball team owned and operated by African Americans. The team included white and black players. Local games were played at the Bluegrass Athletic Club field on Newtown Pike. The Hustlers played against several African-American baseball legends such as Hank Aaron and Josh Gibson. Pictured is an early team photo. (Courtesy of Winston Powell.)

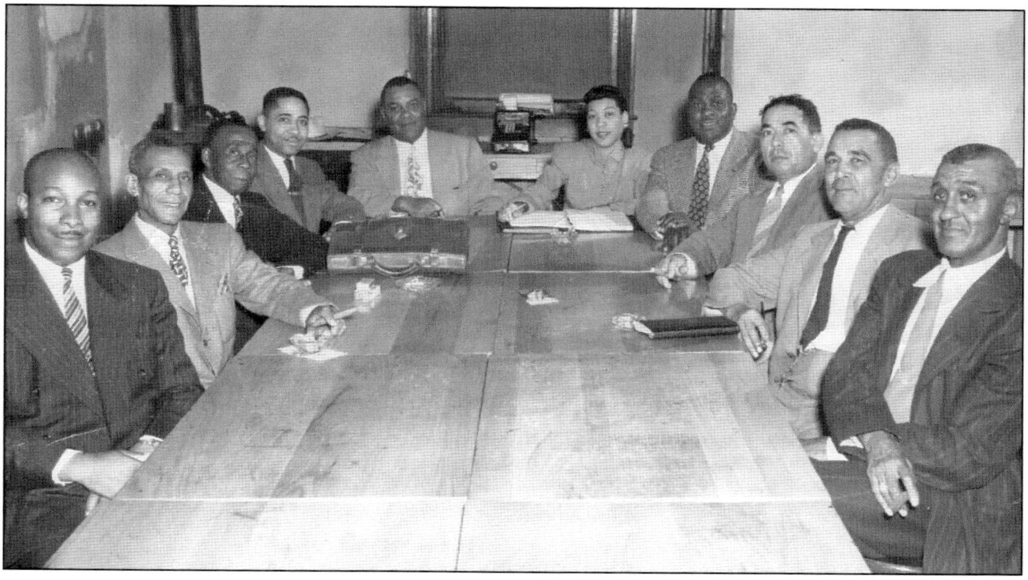

Board of Directors Meeting of the Lexington Hustlers. Board members, from left to right, are Earl Van Meter, Ernest Marshall, William Hughes, Johnnie Jackson, Ovan Haskins, Georgia Riffe, Theophilus Hogue, Dr. J.R. Dalton, Robert McClaskey, and John Taylor. (Courtesy of Winston Powell.)

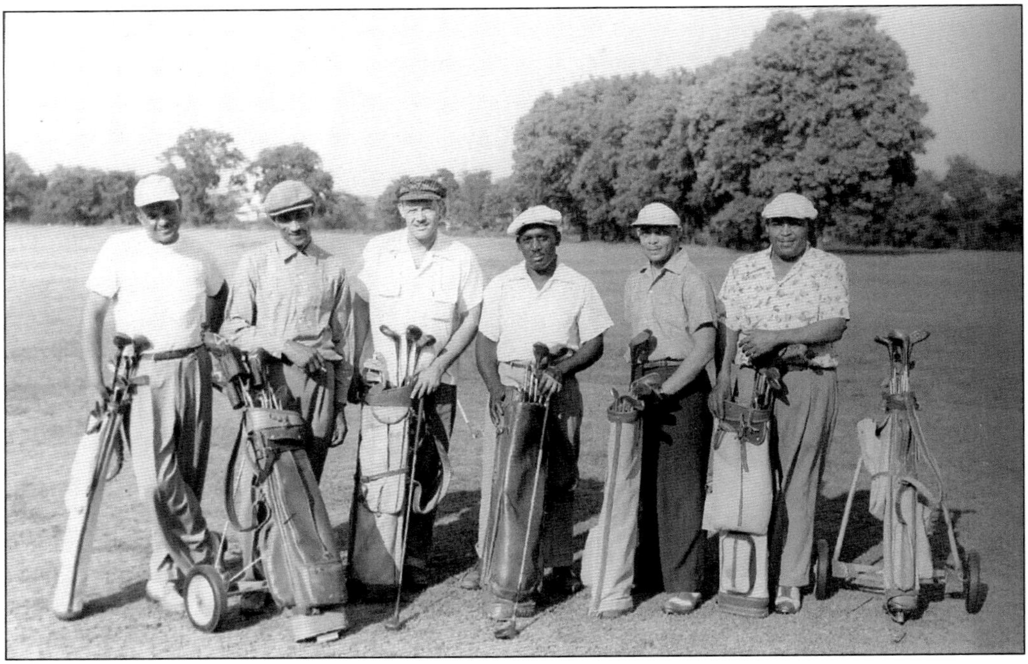

African-American Golfers at Douglass Park, *c.* 1945. Prohibited from playing in certain places because of their race, African Americans developed their own golf course at Douglass Park on Georgetown Street. George Livingston mowed the grass so that he and his friends could play on the weekends. From left to right are Bill Wilson, George Livingston, Gunoa Botts, "Trigger" Dunson, James "Red" Jones, and "Smoke" Richardson. (Courtesy of Gerri Botts.)

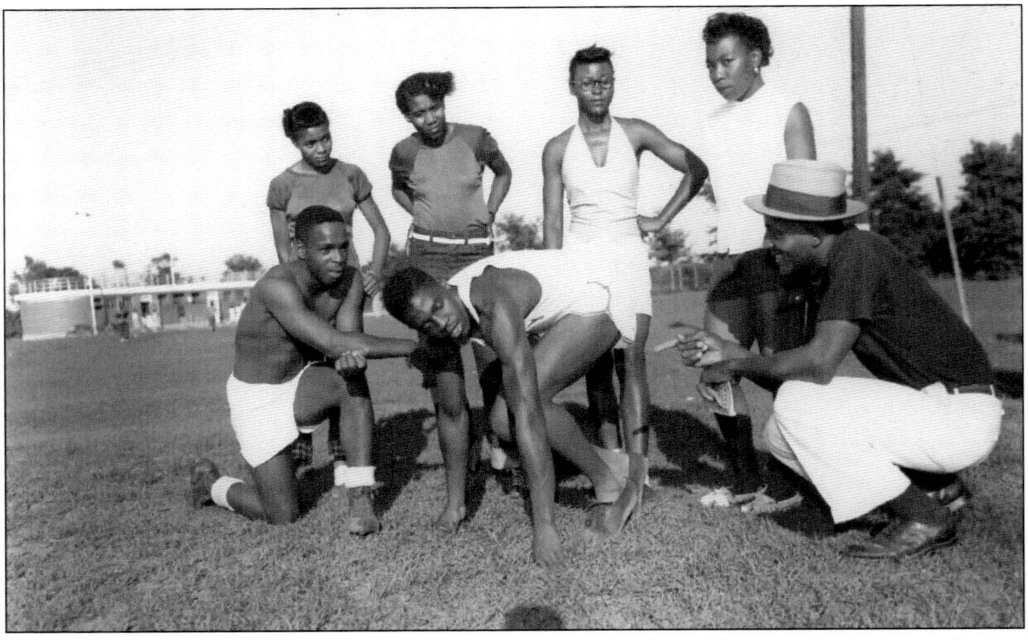

Track at Douglass Park. Pictured in this 1953 photo is John Will "Scoop" Brown, right and wearing a hat, assisting girls as they prepare for a girl's track meet at the park. (Courtesy of *Lexington Herald Leader*.)

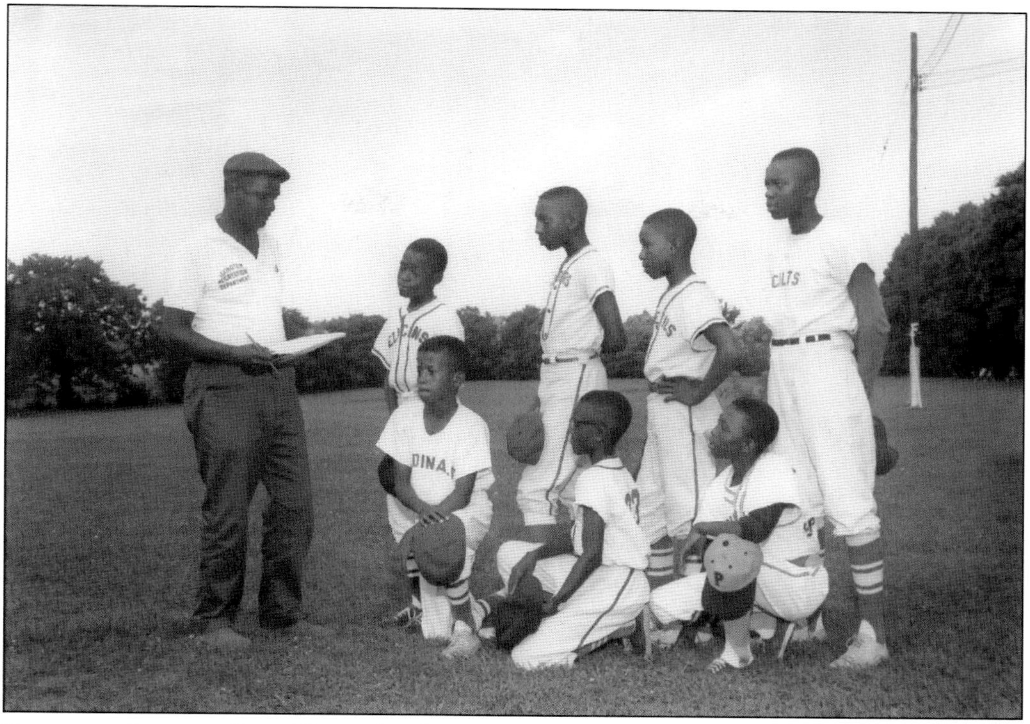

Baseball at Douglass Park. Pictured is director Willie Williams with players of different baseball teams in July 1961. (Courtesy of *Lexington Herald Leader*.)

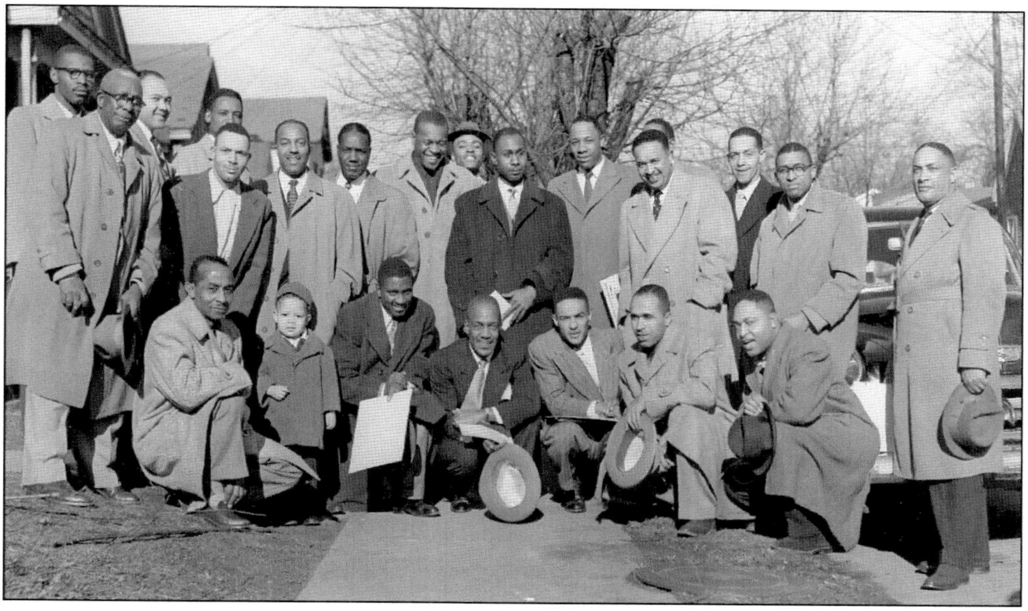

A Meeting of Coaches and Athletic Directors. Throughout much of segregation, it was against the law for black and white schools to play against one another. African-American coaches formed their own league, the Kentucky High School Athletic League. In 1957, this group merged with the Kentucky High School Athletic Association. Pictured is a gathering of members of the Kentucky High School Athletic League. (Courtesy of Annetta Bibbs.)

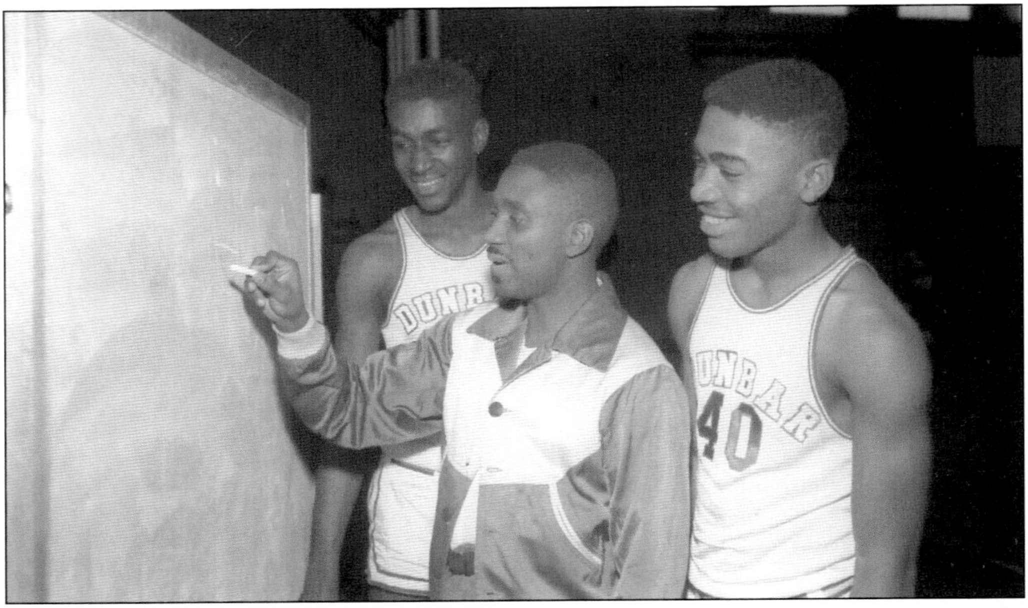

NORMAN PASSMORE. Beloved teacher, minister, administrator, and coach, Passmore gained the respect of his students, players, and the community at large. He coached football and basketball at old Dunbar and later served as associate principal at Henry Clay High School. (Courtesy of *Lexington Herald Leader*.)

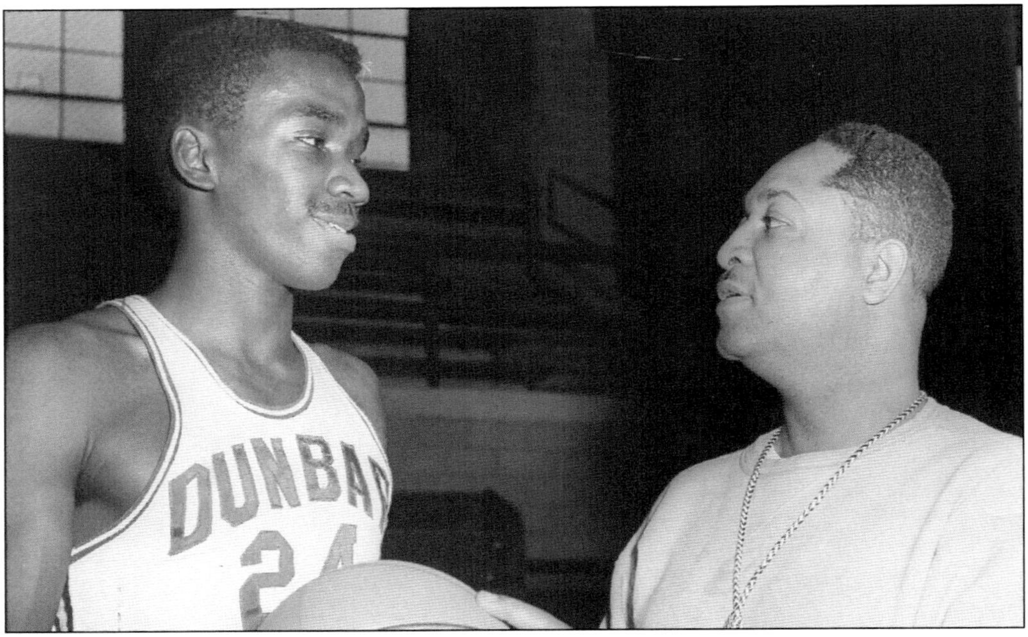

SANFORD T. ROACH. Teacher, administrator, civic leader, and basketball coach, Roach has had a positive influence on young people throughout the Lexington community. He was a successful basketball coach at Dunbar High School from 1943 to 1965. The recipient of numerous well-deserved honors, Roach was awarded an honorary doctorate from the University of Kentucky in 2002. Roach is pictured here with one of his players, George Wilson. (*Lexington Herald Leader* photo, Courtesy of S.T. Roach.)

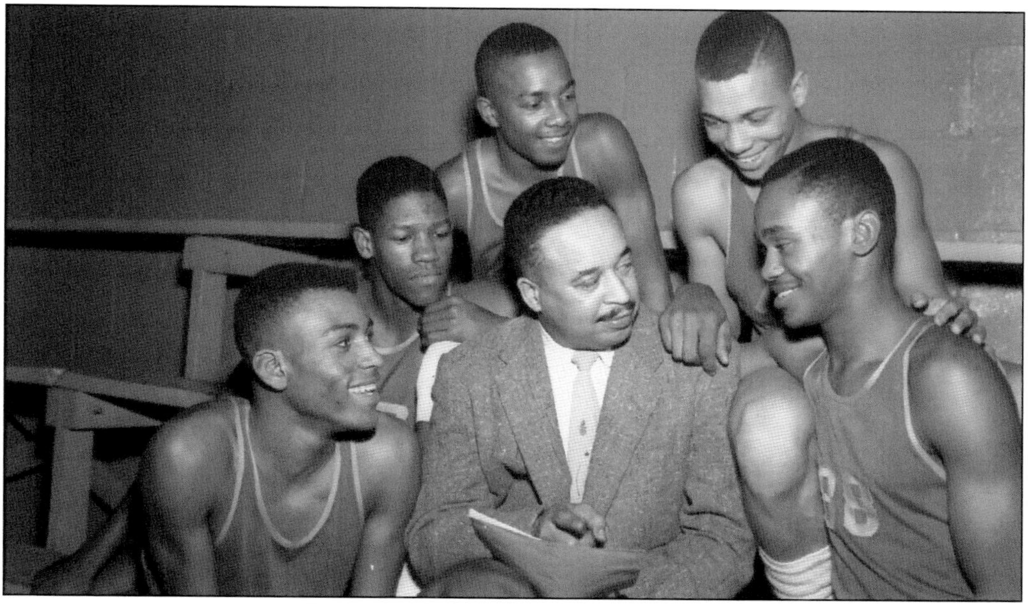

Charles H. Livisay. Respected teacher, coach, civic leader, and politician, Livisay taught and coached at Douglass High School for 18 years and did the same at Bryan Station High School from 1966 to 1974. He served as a councilman for the First District in 1979 and was a member of the YMCA and YWCA boards. Livisay died at the age of 77 in 1989. (*Lexington Herald Leader* photo, Courtesy of S.T. Roach.)

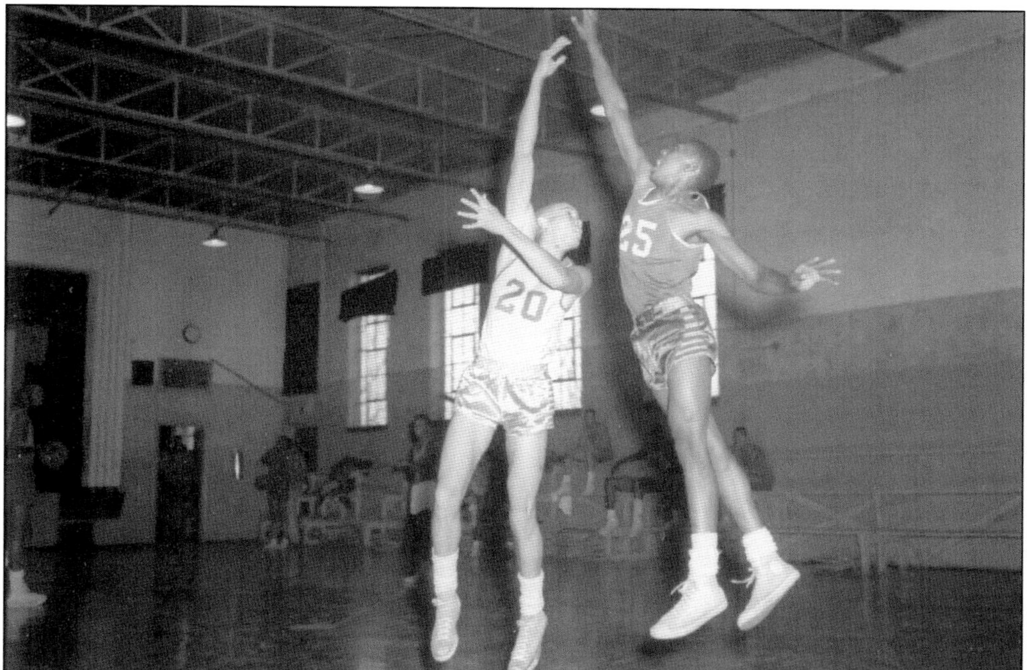

Henry Bell. A standout player at Douglass High School, Bell scored 54 points in a win over Lincoln Institute. Here, Bell shoots over teammate James Bention in 1957. (Courtesy of *Lexington Herald Leader*.)

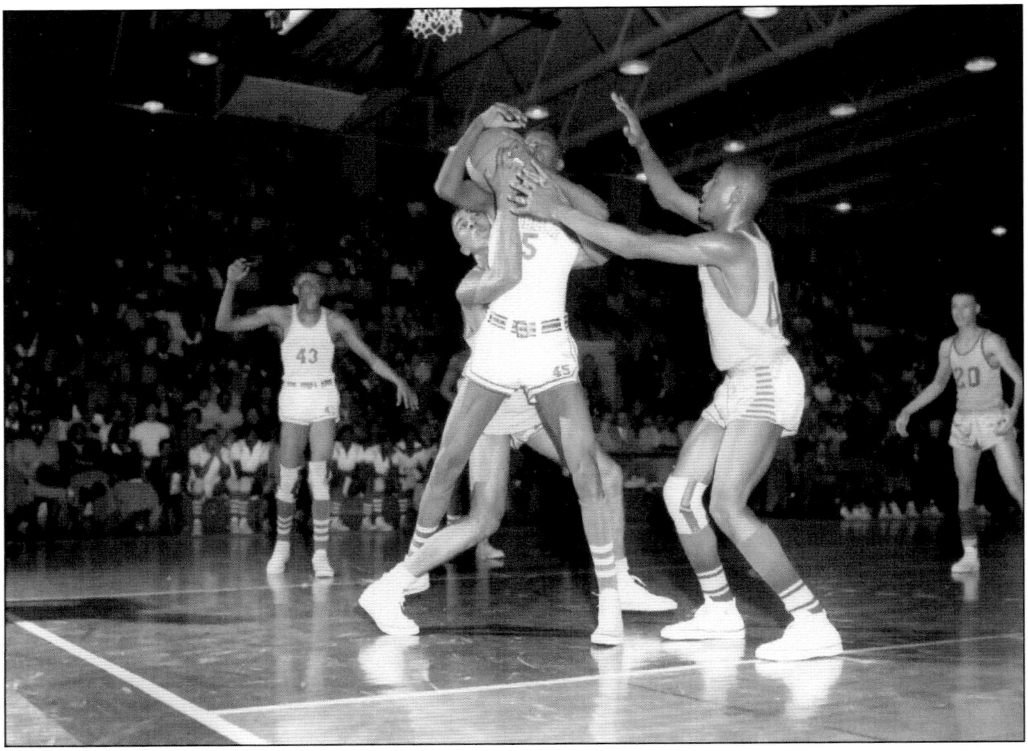

Dunbar vs. Douglass Basketball Game. In the 1950s and 1960s, basketball games between the two schools were major events in the community. Fans arrived early in order to get a seat for the game. Pictured is a game at Dunbar's gym in January 1958. Dunbar won the contest 63-61. (Courtesy of *Lexington Herald Leader*.)

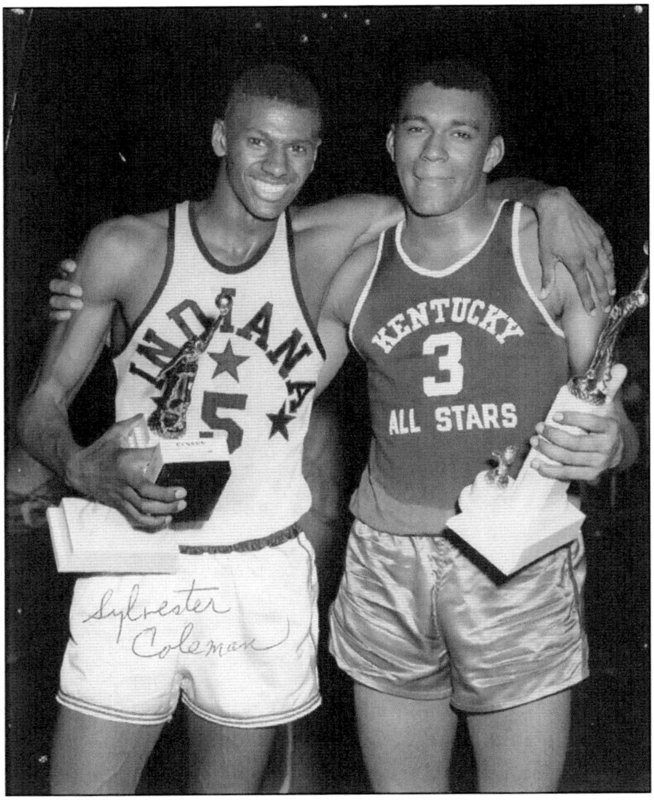

Basketball Stars. Pictured is Syl Coleman, left, and Julius Berry, right. Berry was selected as Kentucky's "star of stars" in a game against Indiana's best high school players in 1959. Berry, an outstanding player at Dunbar High School, scored 20 points and pulled down 17 rebounds in the game. (*Lexington Herald Leader* photo, Courtesy of S.T. Roach.)

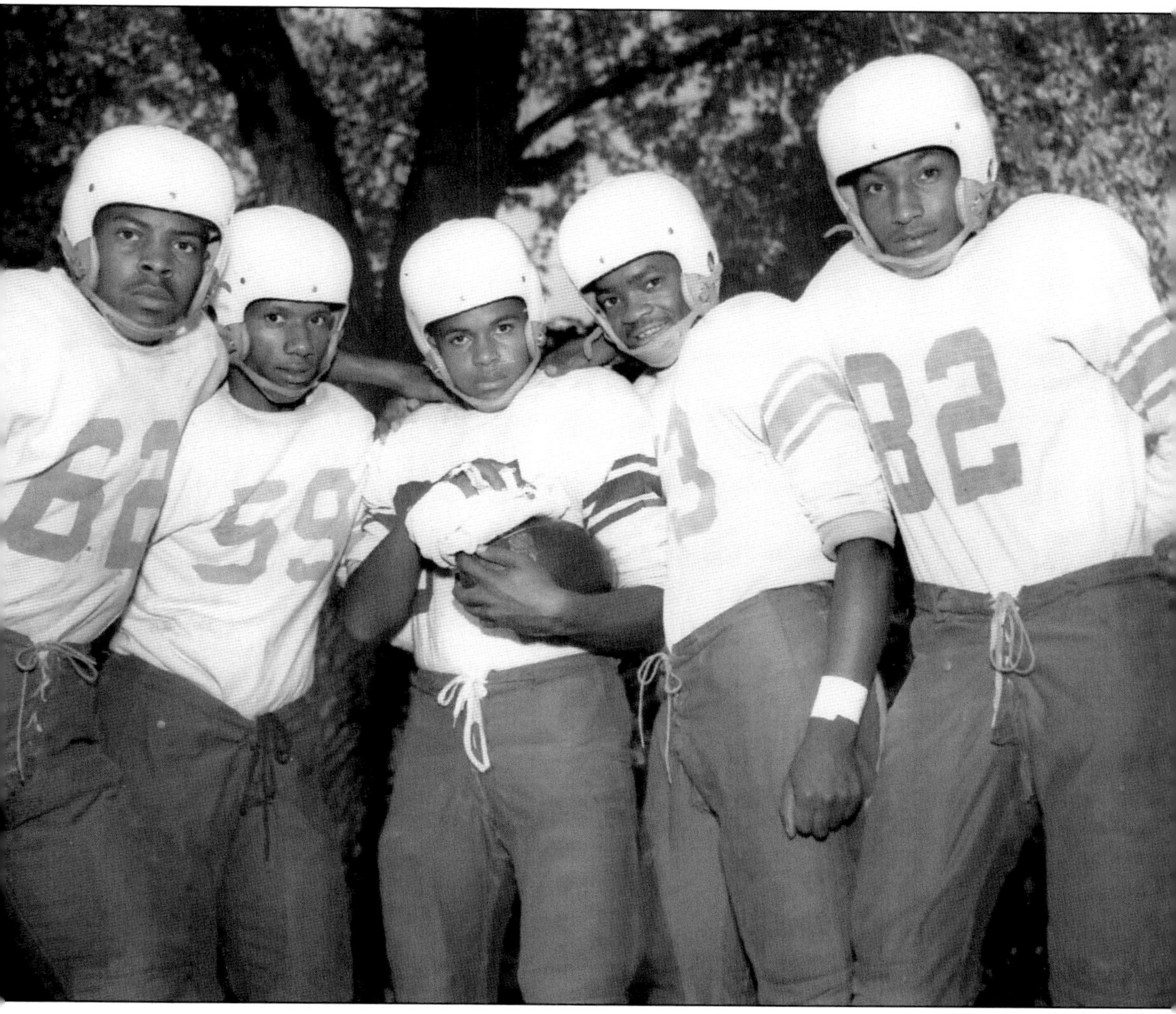

Football Players. Players from Dunbar High School are pictured in this 1954 photo. (Courtesy of *Lexington Herald Leader*.)

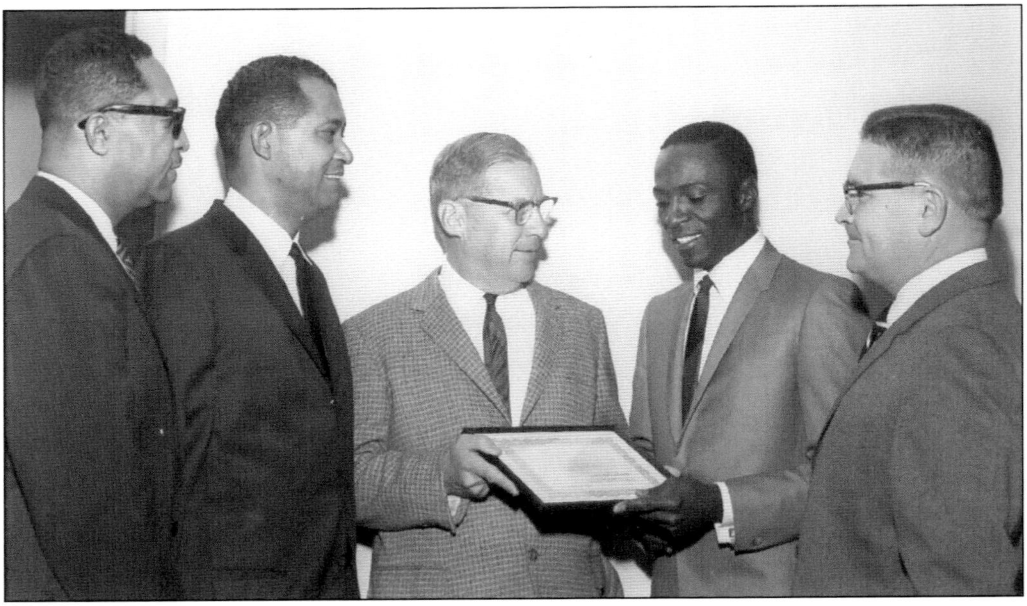

Lou Johnson. A 1951 graduate of Dunbar High School, Johnson was a star baseball player for the champion Los Angeles Dodgers in the 1965 World Series. In this photo, representatives of the city school system present him the distinguished alumnus award. S.T. Roach, far left, and Carl Lynem, next to Roach, witness the presentation. (Courtesy of *Lexington Herald Leader*.)

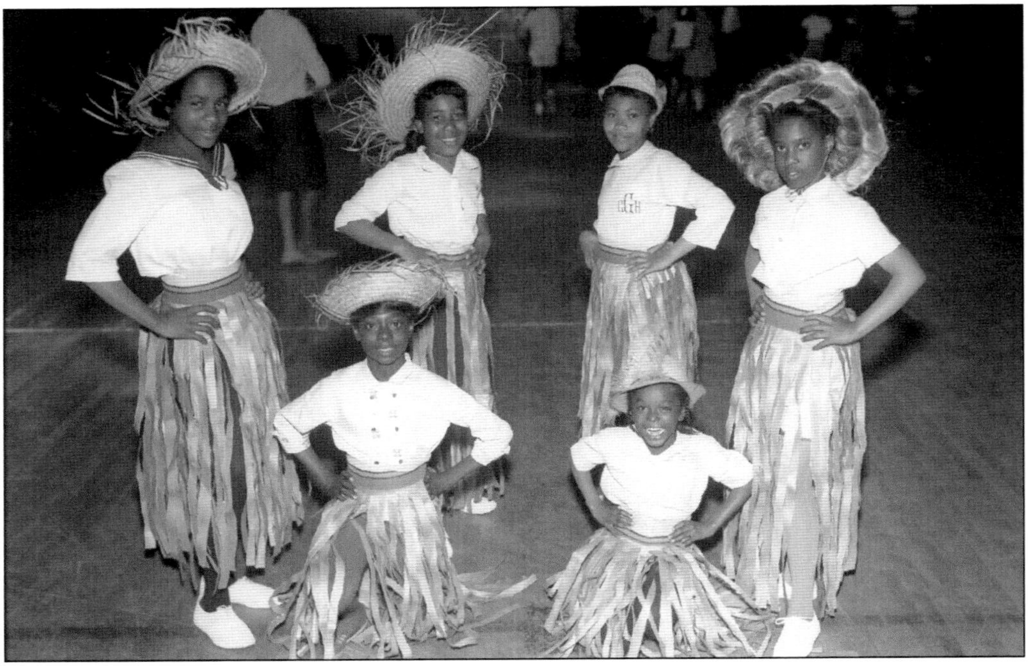

Dancers at Charles Young Community Center. Named for a distinguished African-American military officer born in Mayslick, Kentucky, the center was constructed in the early 1930s on East Third Street. It has served as an important center for social and cultural activities. Pictured are students from Russell School dressed as Cha Cha dancers in the annual Kiddie Revue in April 1962. (Courtesy of *Lexington Herald Leader*.)

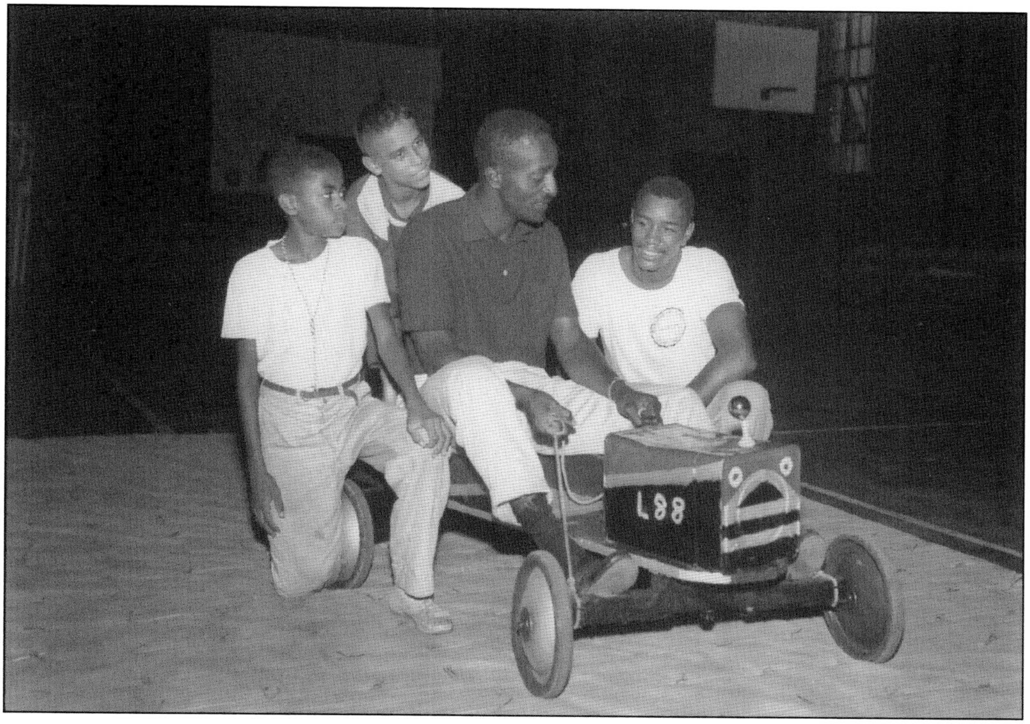

Pushmobile Derby. John Will "Scoop" Brown, supervisor of the Lexington Recreation Department, is pictured sitting in a pushmobile with participants looking on in this July 1957 photo. (Courtesy of *Lexington Herald Leader*.)

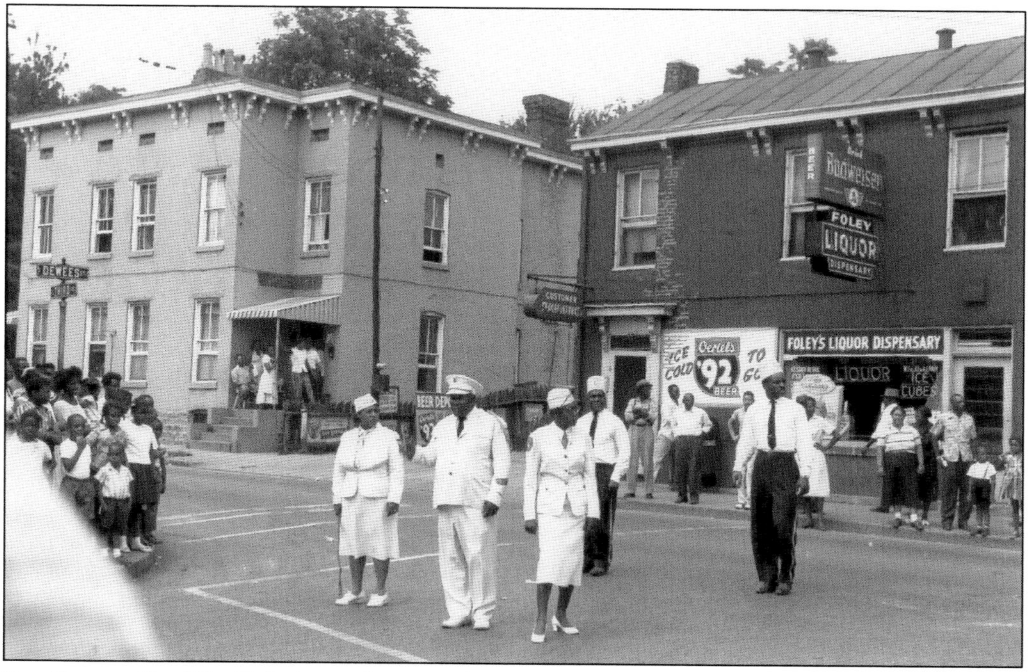

Elks Parade. The Elks Club, located on Northeastern Street, sponsored a parade in the late 1950s. Pictured are marchers at the corner of Third and Deweese Street. (Courtesy of Calvert McCann.)

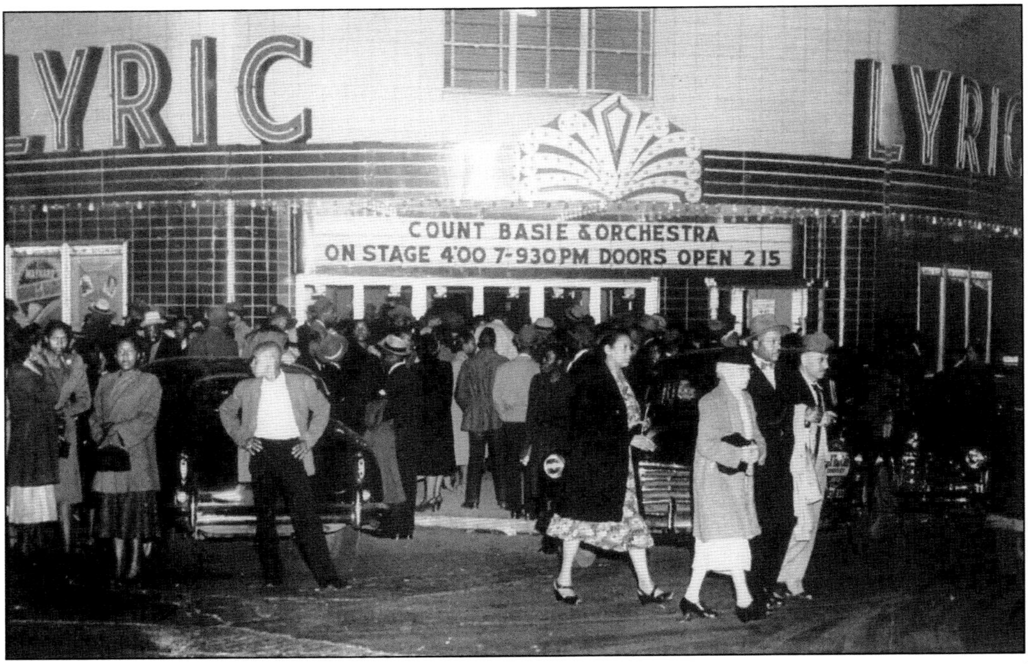

Lyric Theater. Opened in 1948 on the corner of Third and Elm Tree Lane (then a section of Deweese Street), the Lyric housed a restaurant and seated 924 people. It was the showplace for first-run movies as well as cartoons on Saturdays for children. Several headline entertainers performed at the theater including Duke Ellington and Jackie "Moms" Mabley. It closed in 1963. This is a photo of patrons outside the theater. (Courtesy of *Lexington Herald Leader*.)

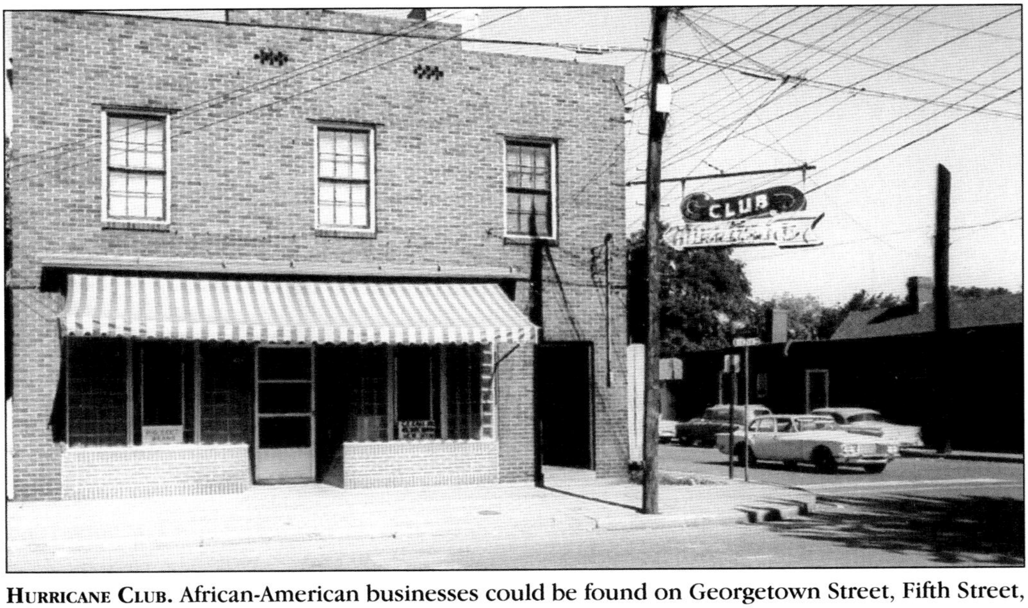

Hurricane Club. African-American businesses could be found on Georgetown Street, Fifth Street, East Second and Third Streets, and South Broadway. Deweese Street was the central black business district in Lexington. Barbershops, restaurants, clubs, and other establishments lined the street, which was always crowded on Friday and Saturday nights. The popular Hurricane Club is shown here on Deweese Street. (Courtesy of LFUCG Archives.)

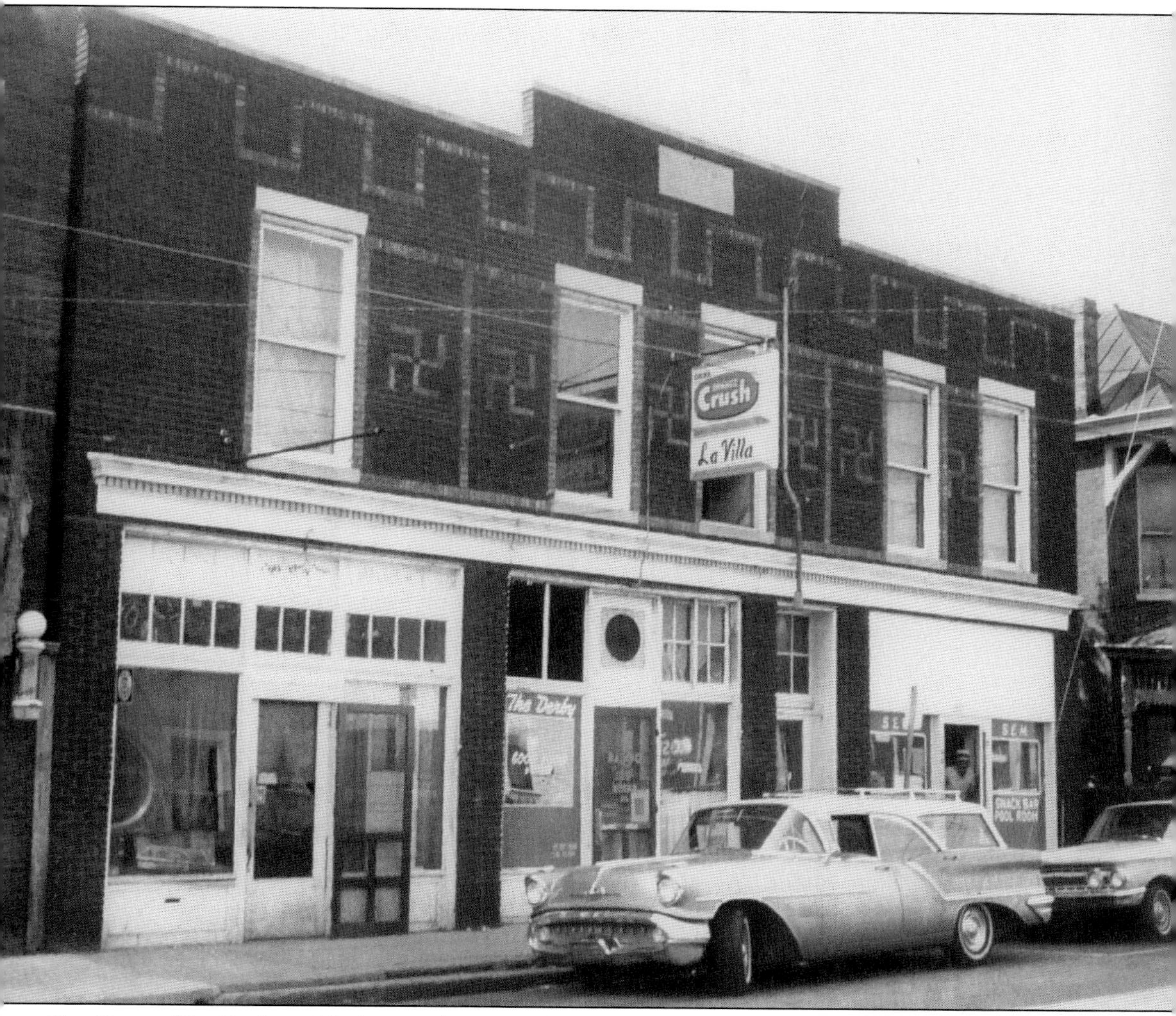

The Derby. The Derby, with the sign hanging above the door, was an establishment on Deweese Street. (Courtesy of LFUCG Archives.)

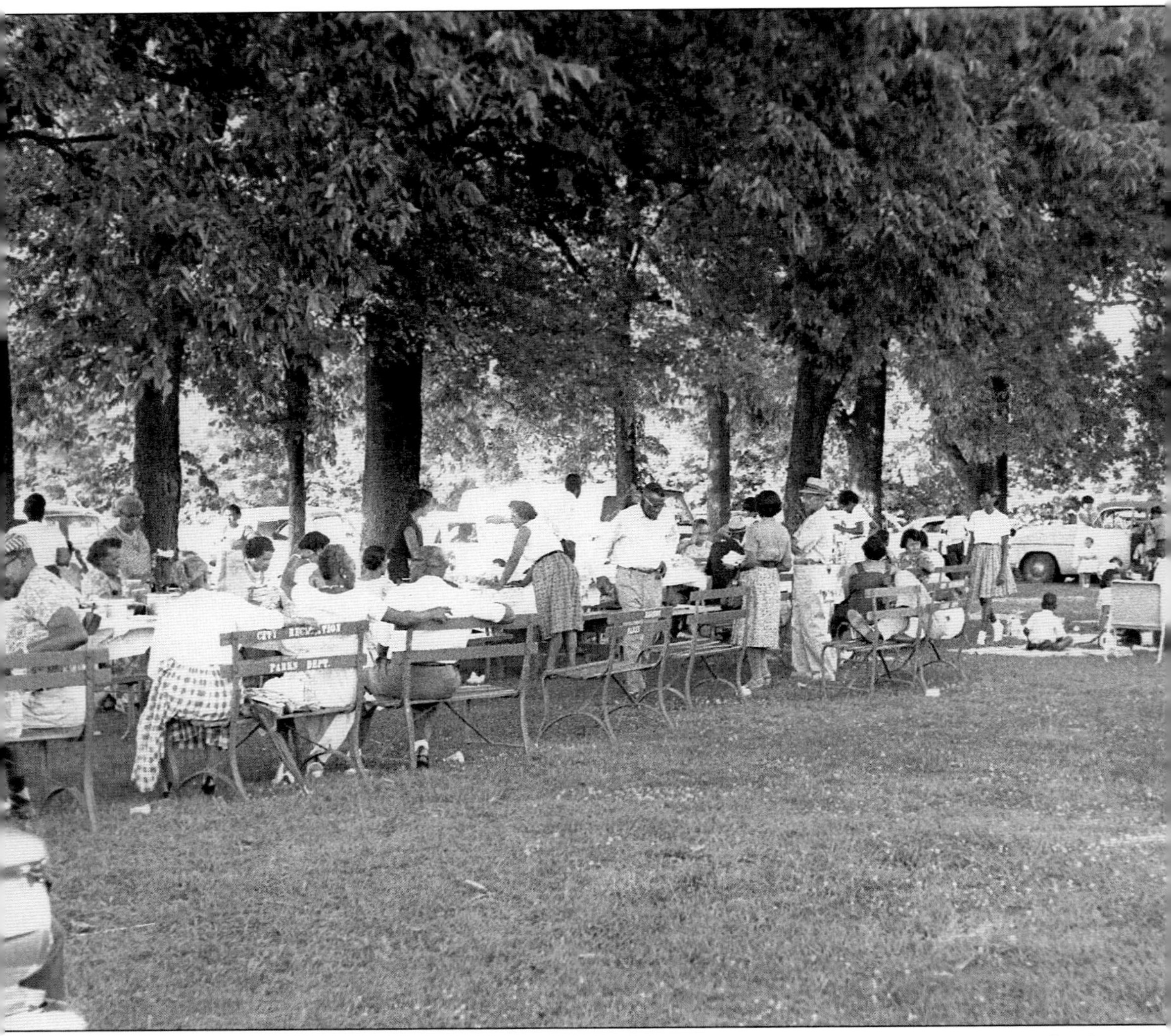

Douglass Park. Located on Georgetown Street, the park was dedicated on July 4, 1916. The July 5 edition of the *Lexington Herald* referred to the park as Lexington's "first colored public amusement place." Through the years, the park has been a popular site for family reunions, picnics, athletic events, and other special programs. Pictured is a family gathering, *c.* 1960. (Courtesy of Calvert McCann.)

Seven

Barriers Worth Breaking

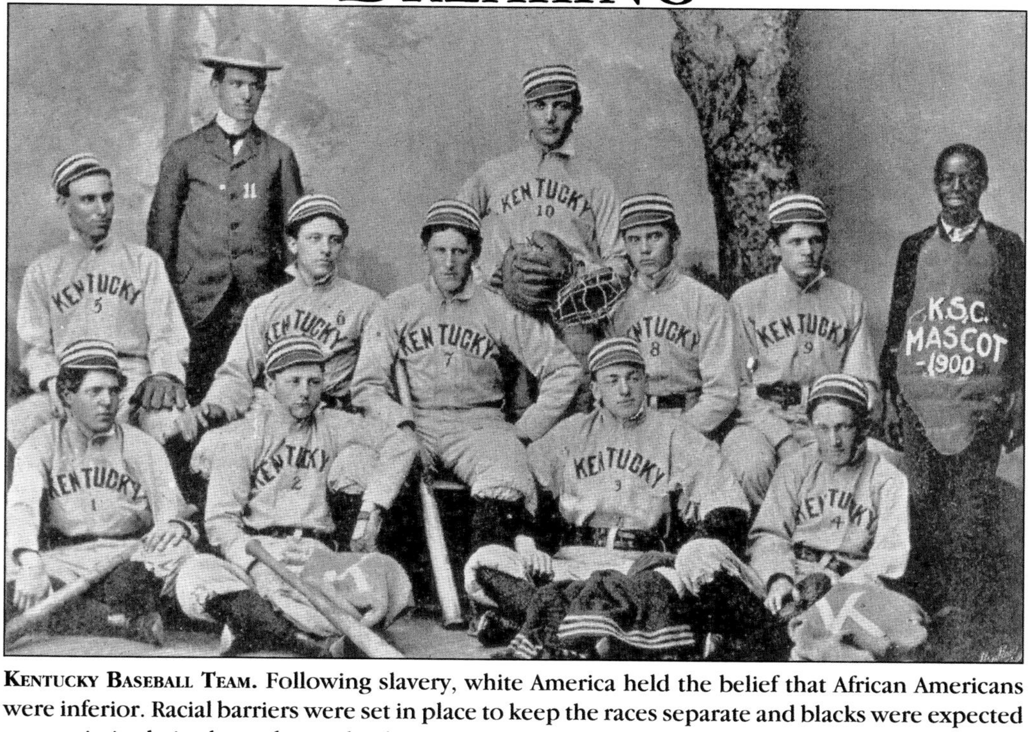

Kentucky Baseball Team. Following slavery, white America held the belief that African Americans were inferior. Racial barriers were set in place to keep the races separate and blacks were expected to remain in their place—beneath whites. Employment opportunities for African Americans were limited, housing was poor and substandard, and education was separate and unequal. This early 1900 photo depicts an image of a young African-American male who was not allowed to try out for the baseball team because of his race, but who qualified to be the school's mascot. (Courtesy of UK Special Collections.)

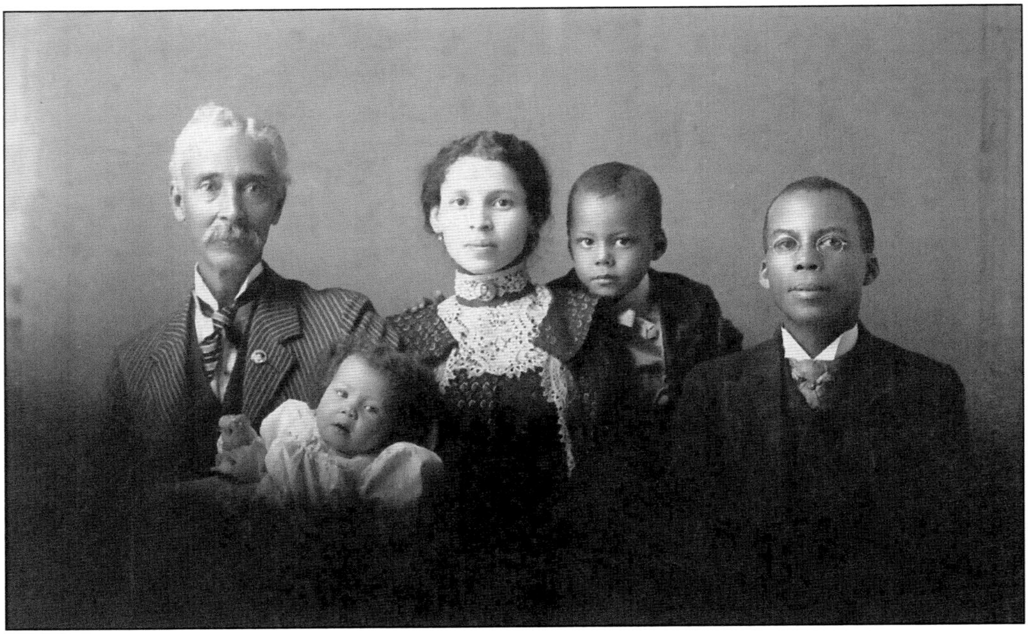

A Tragic Death on October 2, 1900. R.C.O. Benjamin, far right, was shot in the back and killed on the corner of Spring and Water Streets, following an argument with a white man who was challenging African-American voters. Authorities found a gun in Benjamin's pocket with one empty chamber. Although it could not be determined when the gun was last fired, the case against Benjamin's assailant was dismissed on the grounds of self-defense. Benjamin is pictured with his wife, two children, and father-in-law. (Courtesy of UK Special Collections.)

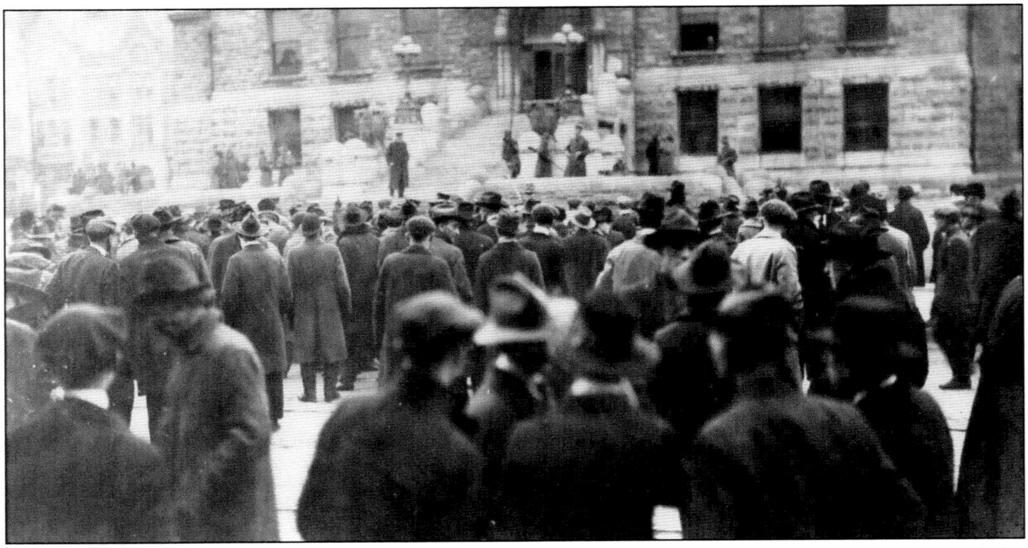

Will Lockett Trial. On February 9, 1920, several thousand people gathered in front of the courthouse on Main Street to witness this historic trial. Lockett, a black man, was tried for the rape and murder of a 10-year-old white girl. Local papers predicted a brief trial. Lockett pleaded guilty and, despite his request for a life sentence, was ordered to die in the electric chair in a trial that lasted 30 minutes. Pictured is the crowd outside the courthouse. (Courtesy of Coleman Collection, Transylvania University.)

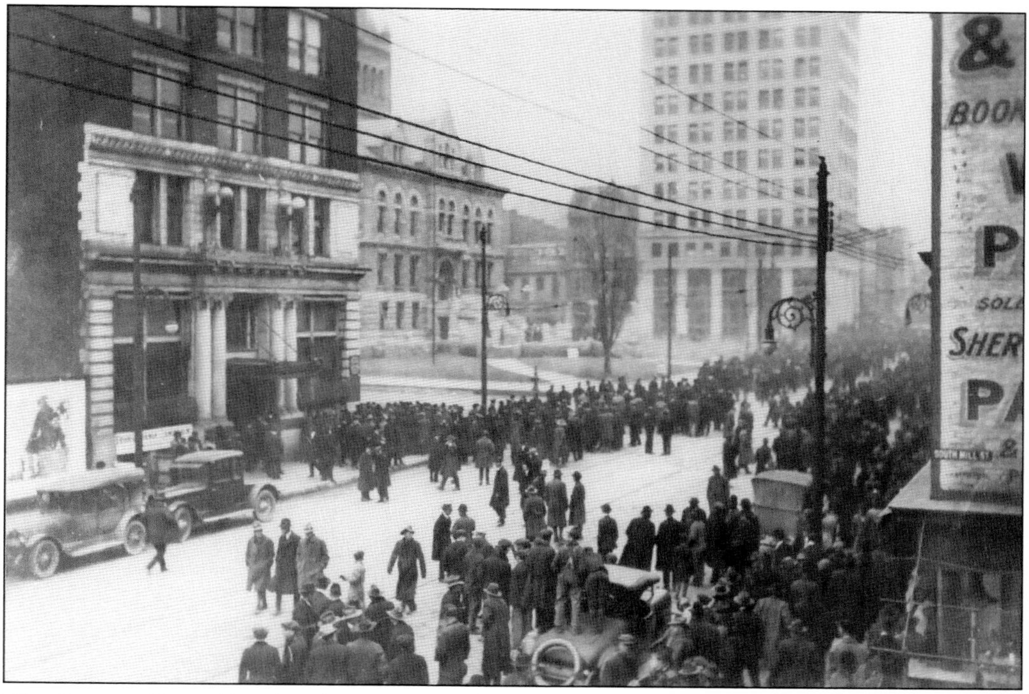

Will Lockett Trial. Despite the presence of state troopers, the local police force, and a steel cable around the courthouse, a riot broke out. Six people were killed and many were wounded. The governor declared the city under martial law. Pictured is another view of the downtown courthouse scene. (Courtesy of Coleman Collection, Transylvania University.)

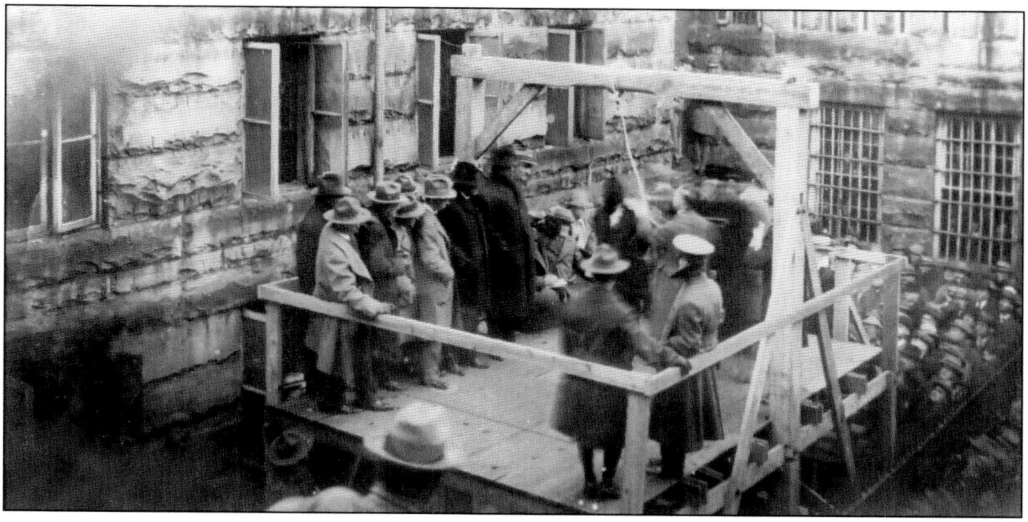

Ed Harris Hanging. Harris was arrested for murdering a white family. He was charged with killing Clarence Bryant and his two children on January 19, 1926. His wife, who was also attacked, identified Harris as the murderer. Harris, a former employee of the family, eventually confessed to the murder. The local papers predicted a "speedy trial." It lasted 16 minutes. Pictured is Harris with a black hood on his head standing on the scaffold with authorities in the county jail courtyard on East Short Street. The hanging took place on March 5, 1926. (Courtesy of Coleman Collection, Transylvania University.)

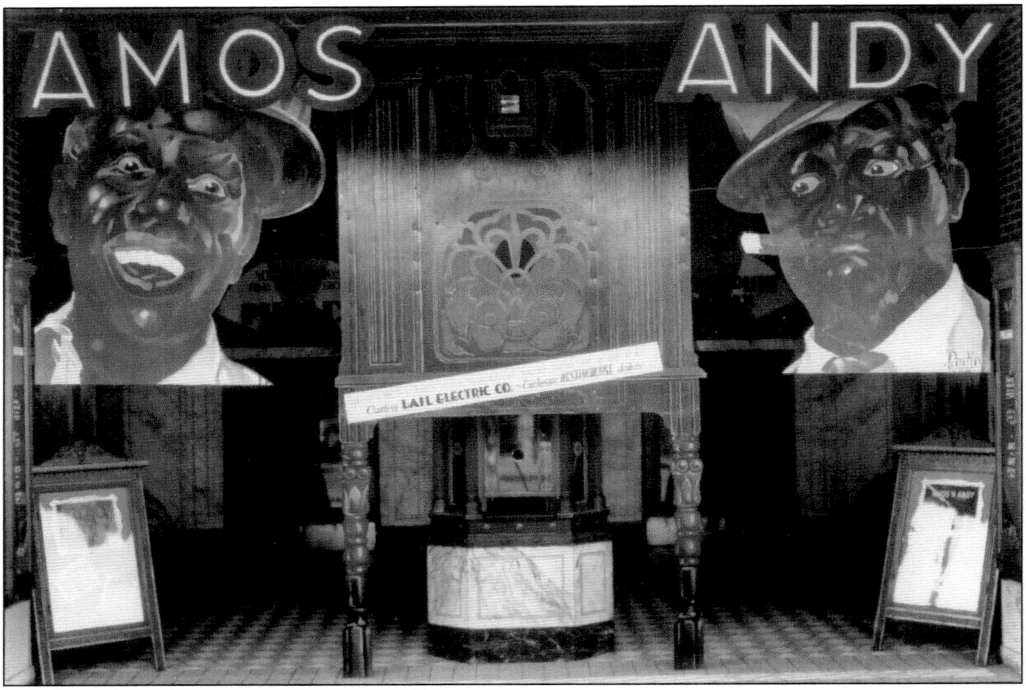

Amos n' Andy. In 1930, millions of Americans were listening to this popular radio program, which featured two white actors, Freeman Gosden and Charles Correll, who portrayed two southern African Americans adjusting to life in the urban north. Many African Americans found the program demeaning because of the negative stereotypes it promoted. Pictured is a sign in the window at the Kentucky Theater on October 25, 1931. (Courtesy of Lafayette Collection, UK Special Collections.)

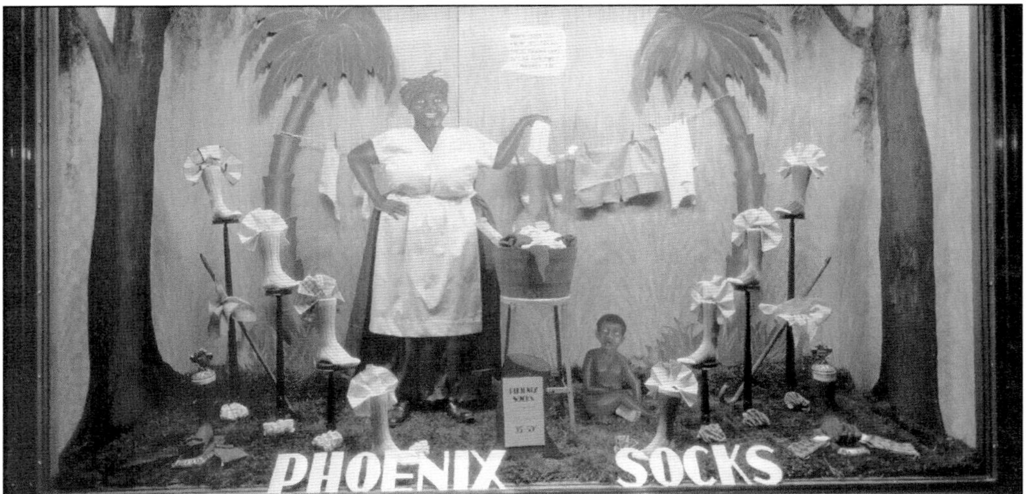

A Display in the Window of Kaufman's Clothing Store on Main Street, May 6, 1935. This kind of image served to reinforce negative stereotypes of African Americans that permeated the South. That this display was prominently shown on Main Street clearly demonstrates the racial attitudes that prevailed in a city in which African Americans lived. (Courtesy of *Lafayette Collections, UK Special Collections.*)

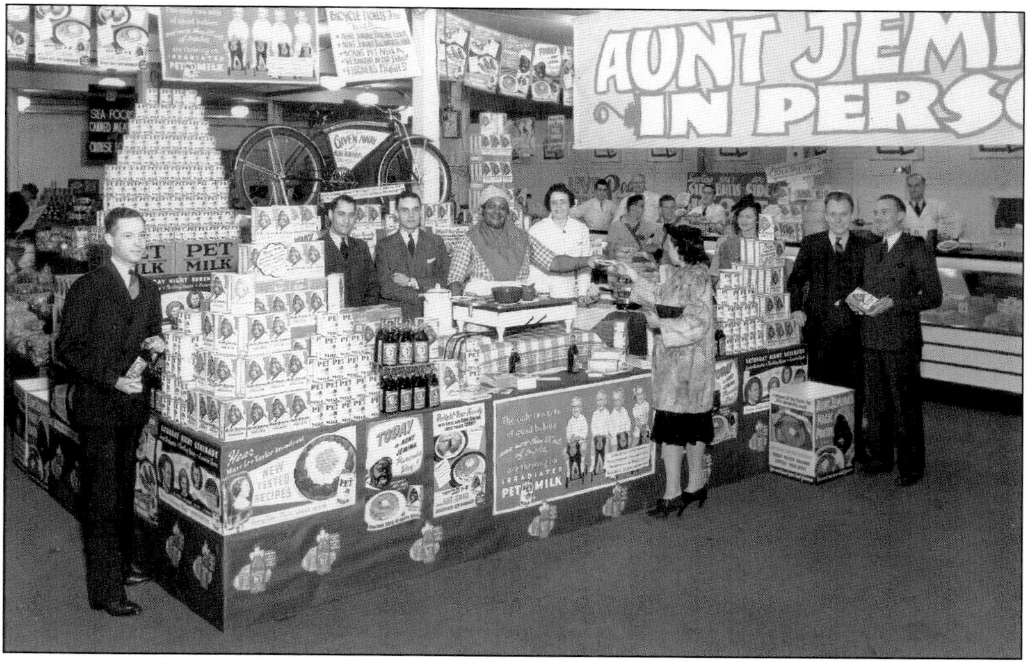

Aunt Jemima. The promotion of a self-rising pancake mix named Aunt Jemima began in the late 19th century. In 1893, an African-American woman named Nancy Green, originally from Kentucky, was hired to make pancakes and greet people at the World's Columbian Exposition in Chicago. Anna Robinson was "Aunt Jemima in person" in the 1930s. This kind of advertising campaign was popular among whites. Pictured is Aunt Jemima at Bahers Market on West Main Street in December 1939. (Courtesy of Lafayette Collections, UK Special Collections.)

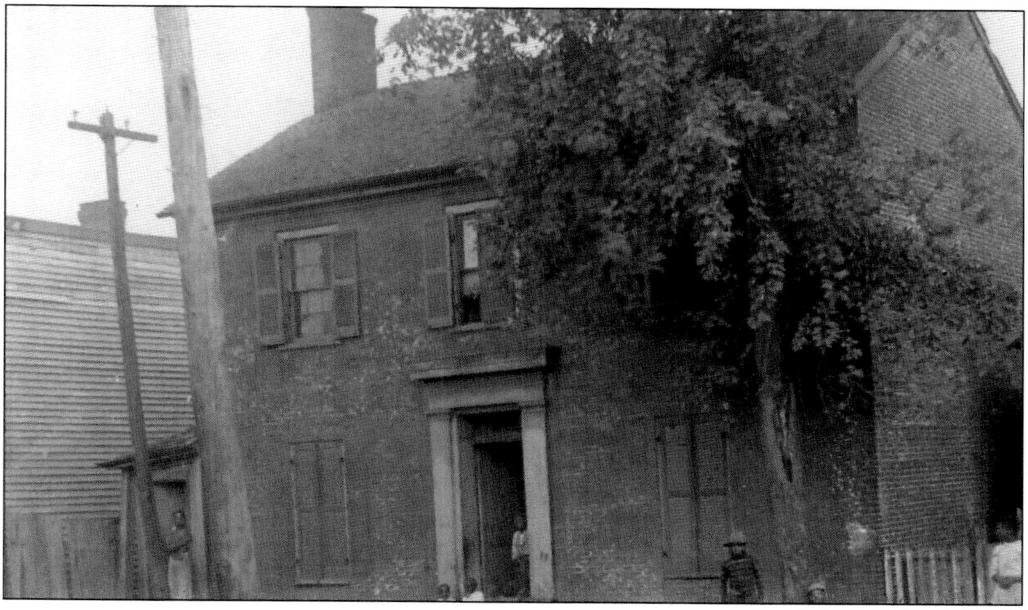

A House on Winslow between Limestone and Upper. Sub-standard housing was one of the most pressing problems facing African Americans in Lexington during segregation. (Courtesy of Bullock Collection, Transylvania.)

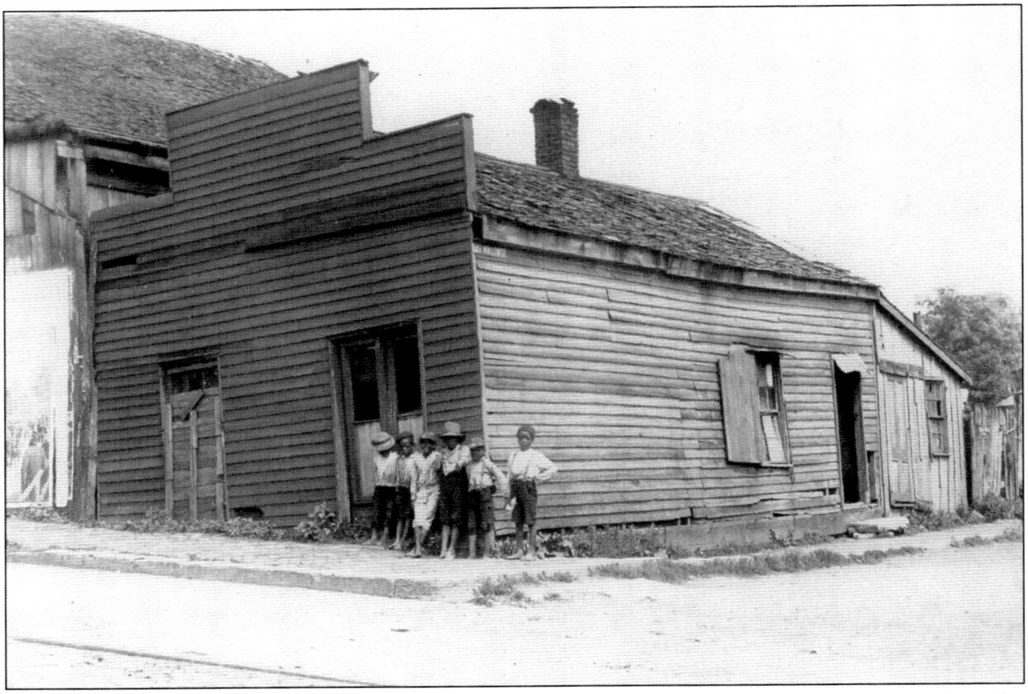

Children outside a House on the East Corner of Limestone and Winslow Streets. Within the shadows of the University of Kentucky were several poorly constructed houses occupied by African Americans. This photo was probably taken in the late 19th or early 20th century. (Courtesy of *Bullock Collection, Transylvania.*)

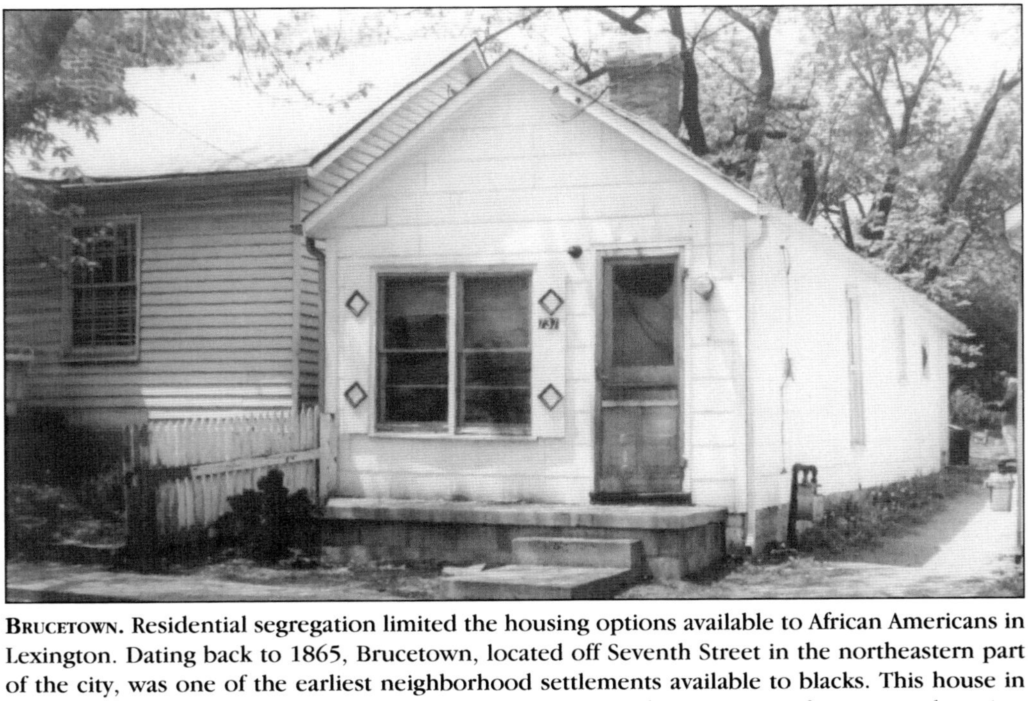

Brucetown. Residential segregation limited the housing options available to African Americans in Lexington. Dating back to 1865, Brucetown, located off Seventh Street in the northeastern part of the city, was one of the earliest neighborhood settlements available to blacks. This house in Brucetown on Florida Street rented for $12.50 a week in 1962. (Courtesy of LFUCG Archives.)

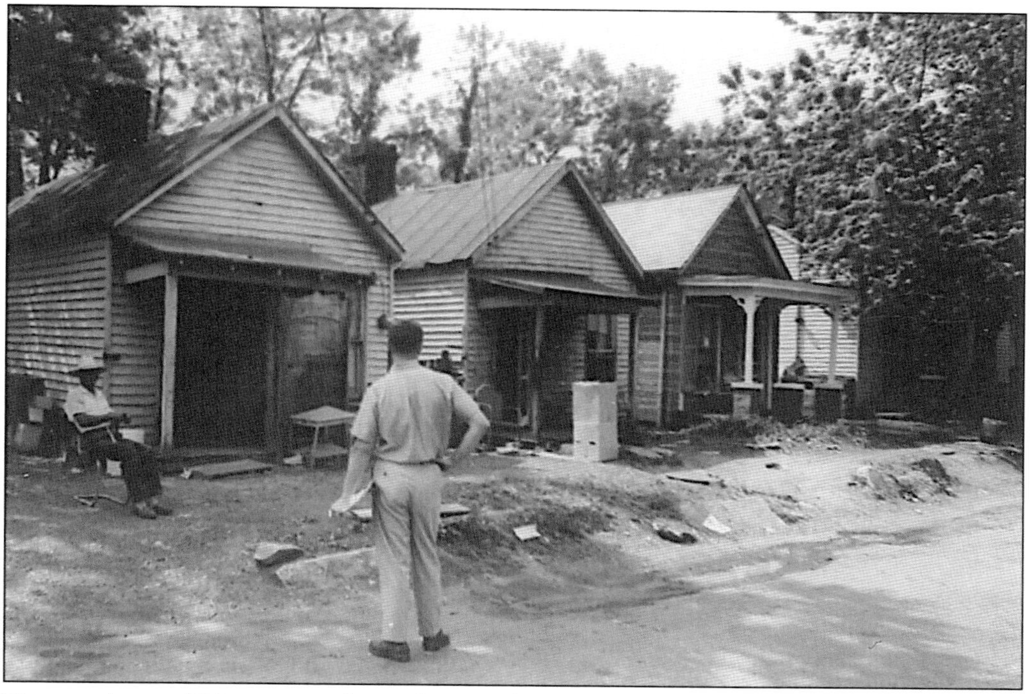

WARNOCK AVENUE. This property, located in Goodloetown, near Midland Avenue and Race Street, did not have sewage and rented for $30 a month in 1962. (Courtesy of LFUCG Archives.)

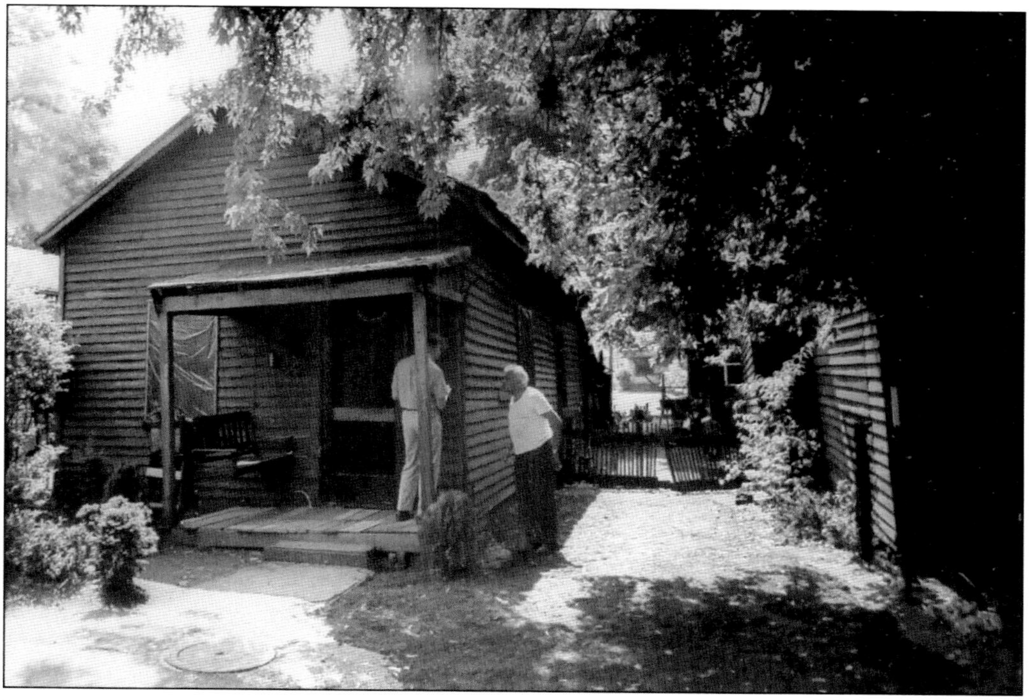

KINKEADTOWN. This house pictured in a black neighborhood settlement named Kinkead, east off Fourth Street, offers an example of the shotgun style homes in which African Americans have lived. This house still did not have sewage in the early 1960s. (Courtesy of LFUCG Archives.)

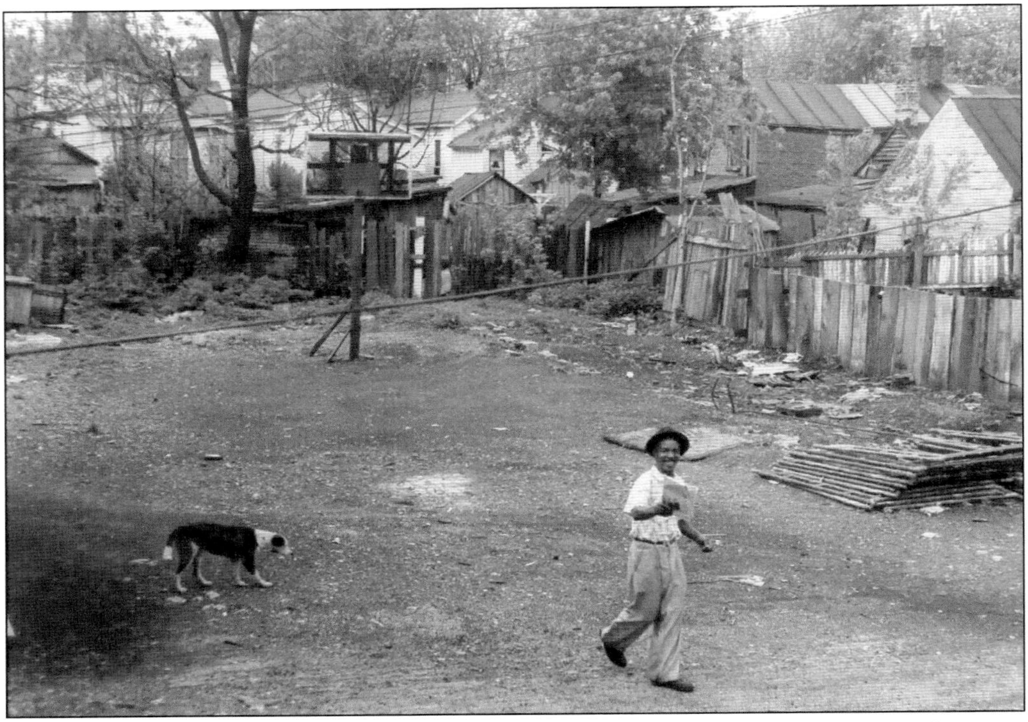

Vacant Lot. The city's unwillingness to invest in the upkeep of African-American neighborhoods is depicted in this early 1960s photograph, which shows Conley Street in the vicinity of Race and Fourth Streets. (Courtesy of LFUCG Archives.)

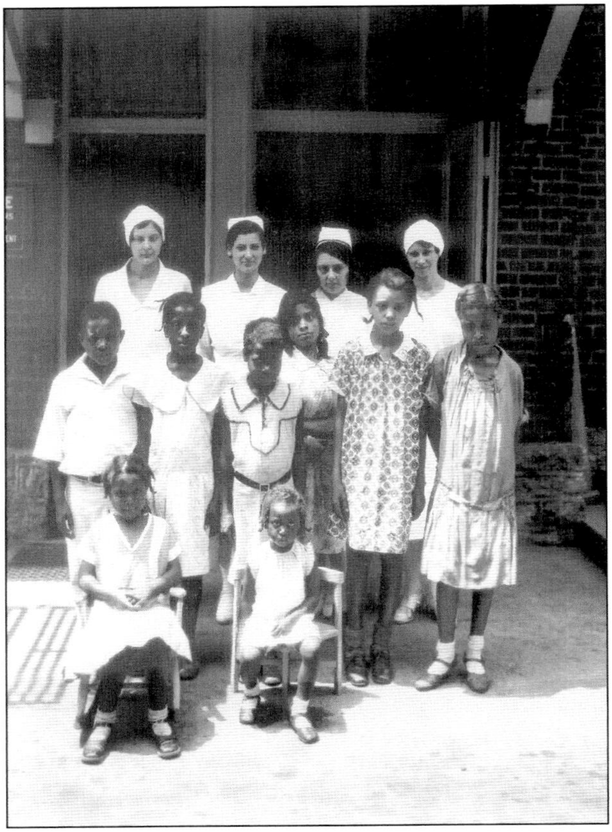

Children in the St. Joseph Hospital "Colored Ward." Barriers were in place to keep the races separate in a variety of ways. This photo was taken on December 12, 1930. (Courtesy of Lafayette Collections, UK Special Collections.)

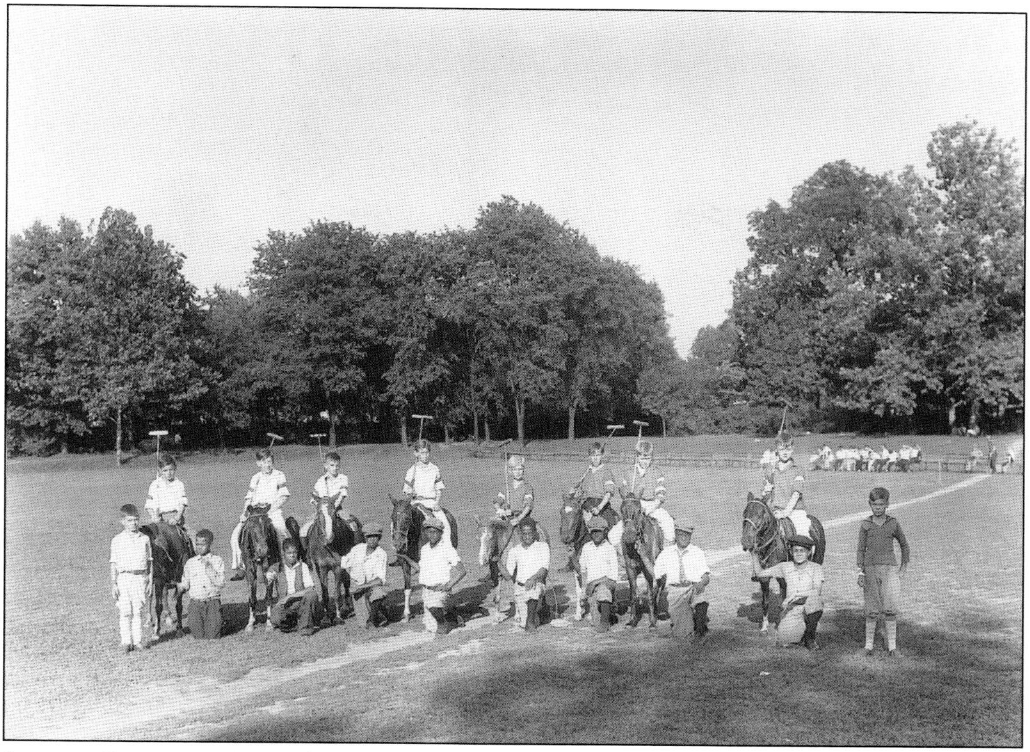

Shetland Pony Polo Teams. This photo captures African-American boys kneeling beside the horses of the red and white polo teams of the Iroquois Hunt and Polo Club. In August 1931, the teams played against one another at Woodland Park for the junior championship of Kentucky. (Courtesy of Lafayette Collections, UK Special Collections.)

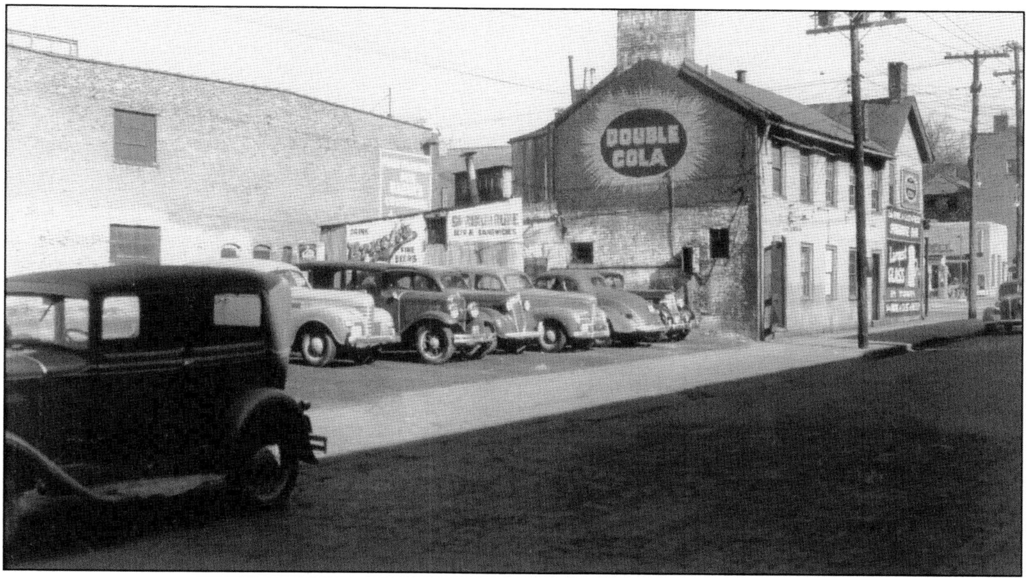

A "Colored" Entrance on the Side of an Old Building on Main and Spring Streets, 1941. African Americans were expected to abide by the customs of racial segregation or risk facing the consequences. (Courtesy of Lafayette Collections, UK Special Collections.)

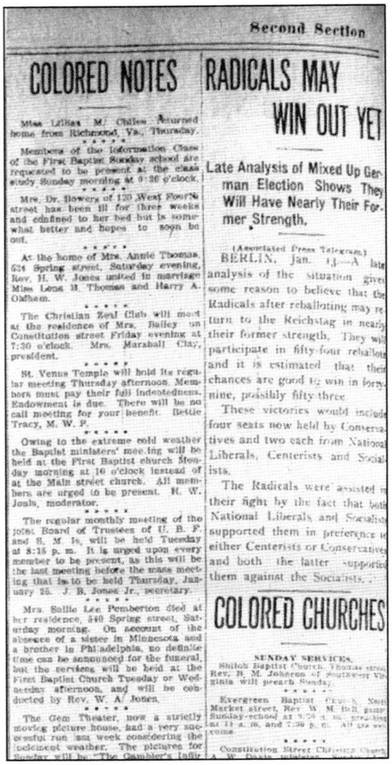

Second Section

COLORED NOTES

Miss Lillian M. Chiles returned home from Richmond, Va., Thursday.

* * * * *

Members of the Information Class of the First Baptist Sunday school are requested to be present at the class study Sunday morning at 9:30 o'clock.

* * * * *

Mrs. Dr. Bowers of 130 West Fourth street has been ill for three weeks and confined to her bed but is somewhat better and hopes to soon be out.

* * * * *

At the home of Mrs. Annie Thomas, 624 Spring street, Saturday evening, Rev. H. W. Jones united in marriage Miss Lena B. Thomas and Harry A. Oldham.

* * * * *

The Christian Zeal Club will meet at the residence of Mrs. Bailey on Constitution street Friday evening at 7:30 o'clock. Mrs. Marshall Clay, president.

* * * * *

St. Venus Temple will hold its regular meeting Thursday afternoon. Members must pay their full indebtedness. Endowment is due. There will be no call meeting for your benefit. Bettie Tracy, M. W. P.

* * * * *

Owing to the extreme cold weather the Baptist ministers' meeting will be held at the First Baptist church Monday morning at 10 o'clock instead of at the Main street church. All members are urged to be present. H. W. Jones, moderator.

* * * * *

The regular monthly meeting of the joint Board of Trustees of U. B. F. and S. M. Ts, will be held Tuesday at 8:15 p. m. It is urged upon every member to be present, as this will be the last meeting before the mass meeting that is to be held Thursday, January 25. J. B. Jones Jr., secretary.

* * * * *

Mrs. Sallie Lee Pemberton died at her residence, 540 Spring street, Saturday morning. On account of the absence of a sister in Minnesota and a brother in Philadelphia, no definite time can be announced for the funeral, but the services will be held at the First Baptist Church Tuesday or Wednesday afternoon, and will be conducted by Rev. W. A. Jones.

* * * * *

The Gem Theater, now a strictly moving picture house, had a very successful run last week considering the inclement weather. The pictures for Sunday will be "The Gambler's [illegible]

RADICALS MAY WIN OUT YET

Late Analysis of Mixed Up German Election Shows They Will Have Nearly Their Former Strength.

(Associated Press Telegram.)

BERLIN, Jan. 13—A late analysis of the situation gives some reason to believe that the Radicals after reballoting may return to the Reichstag in nearly their former strength. They will participate in fifty-four reballots and it is estimated that their chances are good to win in forty-nine, possibly fifty-three.

These victories would include four seats now held by Conservatives and two each from National Liberals, Centerists and Socialists.

The Radicals were assisted in their fight by the fact that both National Liberals and Socialists supported them in preference to either Centerists or Conservatives and both the latter supported them against the Socialists.

COLORED CHURCHES

SUNDAY SERVICES.

Shiloh Baptist Church, Thomas street, Rev. R. M. Johnson of Southwest Virginia will preach Sunday.

* * * * *

“COLORED NOTES.” In the early 1900s, the *Lexington Leader* published a column titled “Colored Circles.” The paper later changed the title to “Colored Notes.” Funeral notices, programs, and organizational meetings were the main news items mentioned in this column. In the 1960s, African Americans protested the publication of this section, which was reserved for black announcements. By the end of 1964, the paper had stopped titling the section “Colored Notes,” but the reserved section for African Americans remained. It was maintained by an African-American woman whose face appeared before the column. This practice did not end until the later 1960s. This facsimile is from the January 14, 1912 edition of the *Leader*.

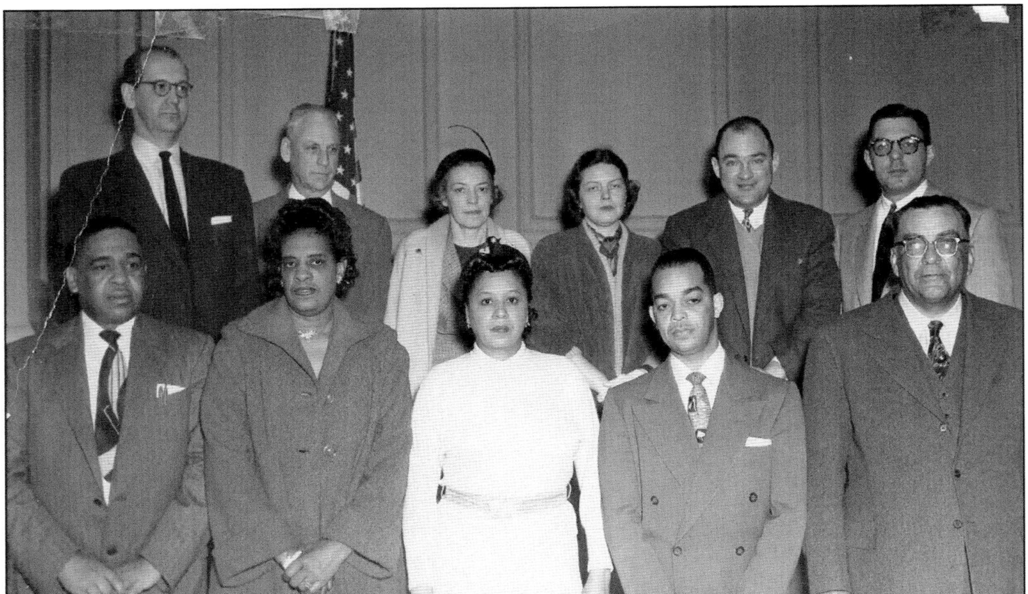

PARK COMMISSIONERS. In the early 1950s, Lexington still had white and “colored” boards of park commissioners. In the front row, from left to right, are members of the colored board. Included are William H. Goodwin, Sadie Brown, Lucy Estill, James O. Jones, and J.C. Smith. The Kentucky Court of Appeals outlawed segregation in all public recreational facilities in the state in 1955. (Courtesy of Annetta Bibbs.)

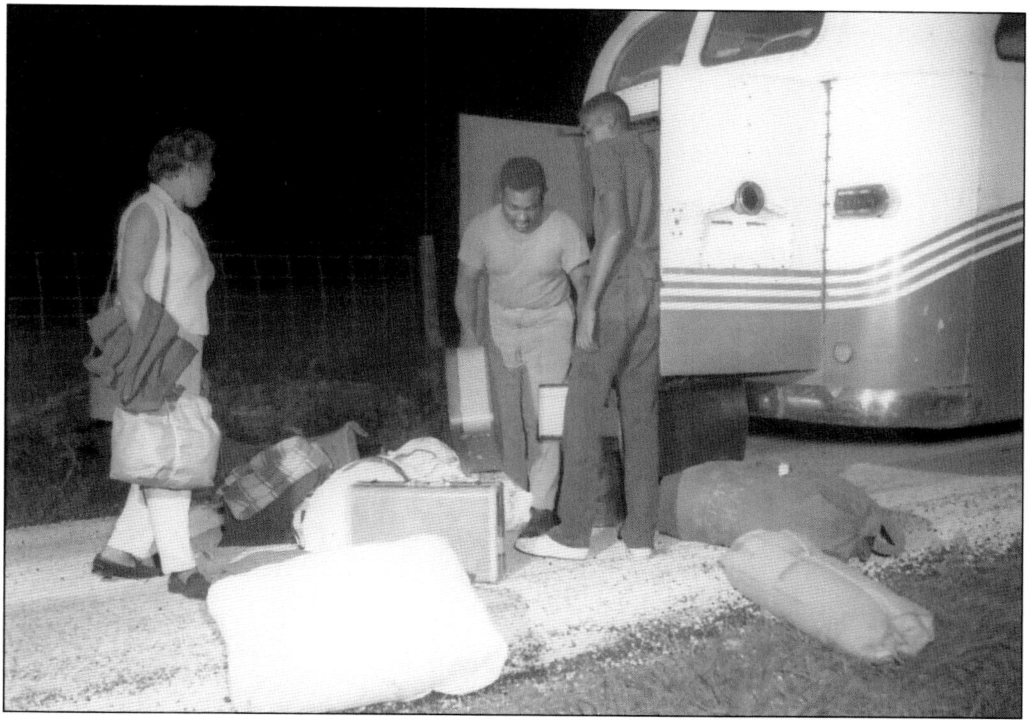

African Americans Leaving Camp Otonka After Threats. On August 13, 1959, 27 African-American girls from the Lexington area were nearing the end of a two-week camping trip at Camp Otonka. The camp was located 11 miles from Versailles on the Kentucky River. However, a group of white men fired shots near the camp and tried to burn down a cabin. None of the girls were injured and the culprits were not identified. In this picture, the girls and camp workers load a bus to leave and return to Lexington. (Courtesy of *Lexington Herald Leader*.)

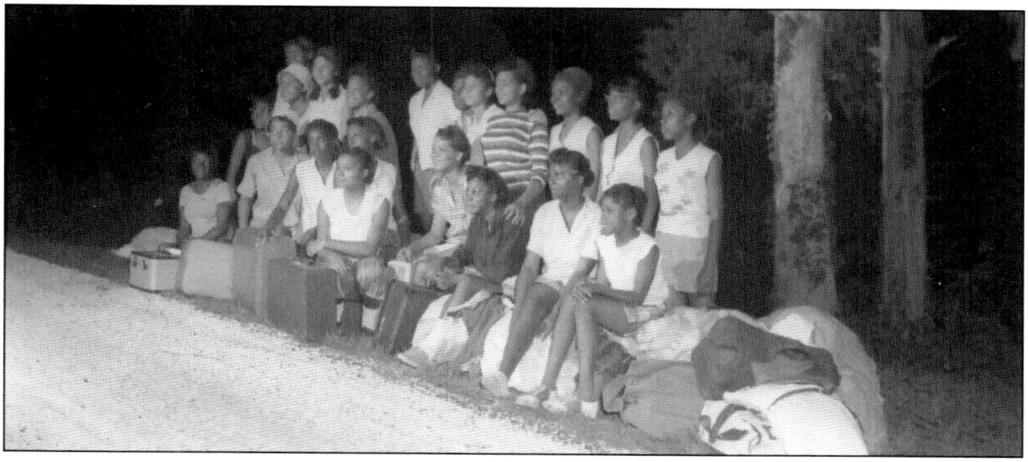

Camp Otonka. The camp was open to African Americans two weeks out of the year. Upon investigation of the incidents that took place on this trip, a young boy who lived across the street from the camp informed a state detective that he had received an anonymous phone call from someone who said that "they were going to run the Negroes out, burn everything in the camp and kill whoever tries to stop them." In this picture, campers wait to board their bus back to Lexington. (Courtesy of *Lexington Herald Leader*.)

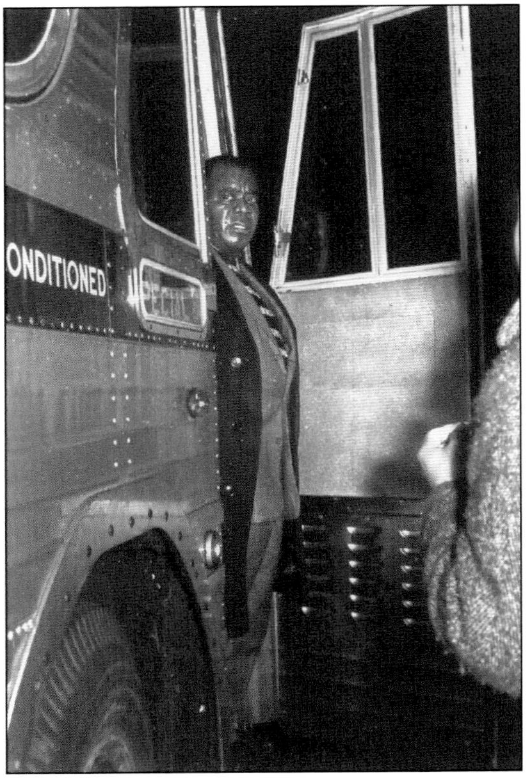

Louis Armstrong. In December 1961, Armstrong came to Lexington to perform at a private party at the Phoenix Hotel. When he saw demonstrators protesting the hotel's discriminatory policies, he refused to cross the picket line. Not wanting Armstrong to be sued for breaking a contract, demonstrators disbanded their line for him to cross. Armstrong said if he had known the Phoenix discriminated against blacks, he would not have accepted the engagement. (Courtesy of Calvert McCann.)

Friends Determined to Eat Together. Because of segregation, co-workers Barbara Olson (white) and Harrietta Jackson (black) were not able to eat lunch together at downtown restaurants. Pictured is Olson seated in the foreground on the left and Jackson across from her seated second, joined by friends, in the garden of Olsen's father at 417 Clifton Avenue in the late 1940s. (Courtesy of Ellen Allen.)

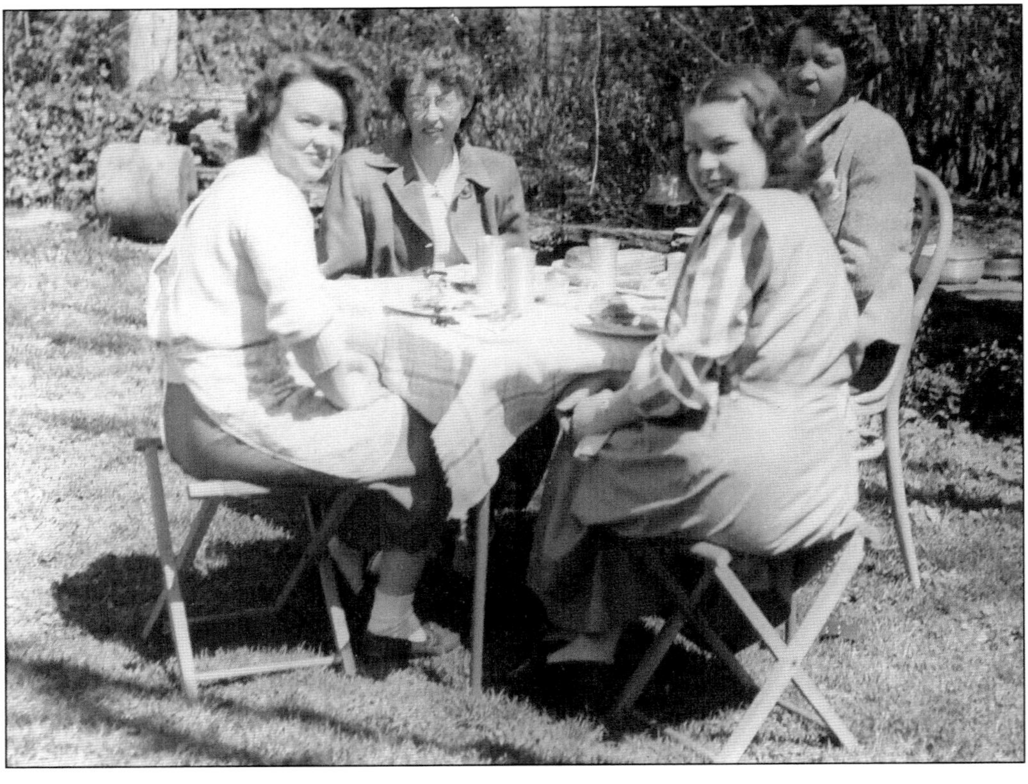

Eight

Civil Demonstrations

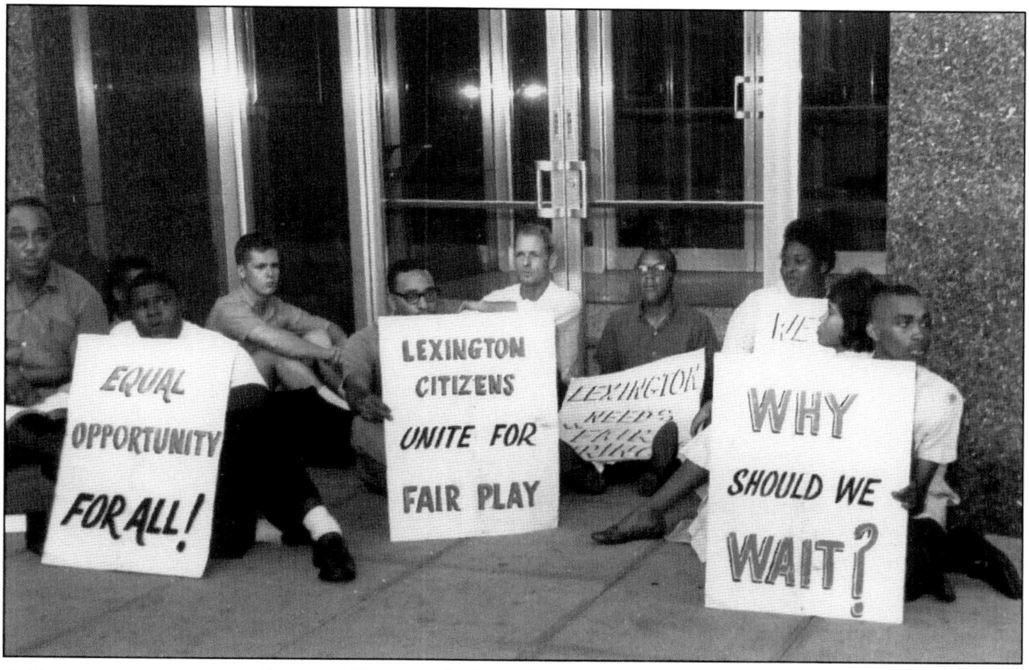

A Protest for Equality. In the 1950s and '60s whites joined African Americans in the struggle for racial equality in Lexington. The Congress of Racial Equality (CORE) and members of the local chapter of the NAACP were persistent in their efforts to break down racial barriers that had been firmly planted in the community. Sit-ins, stand-ins, and economic boycotts all took place, as well as marches in protest of racial segregation in front of Main Street stores. Calvert McCann participated in the movement and documented it with his camera. Pictured is a demonstration in front of city hall demanding employment opportunities for African Americans. The people above include Reverend Wade Washington, Jerry Williams, Calvert McCann, Julia Lewis, and Ronald Berry. (Courtesy of Calvert McCann.)

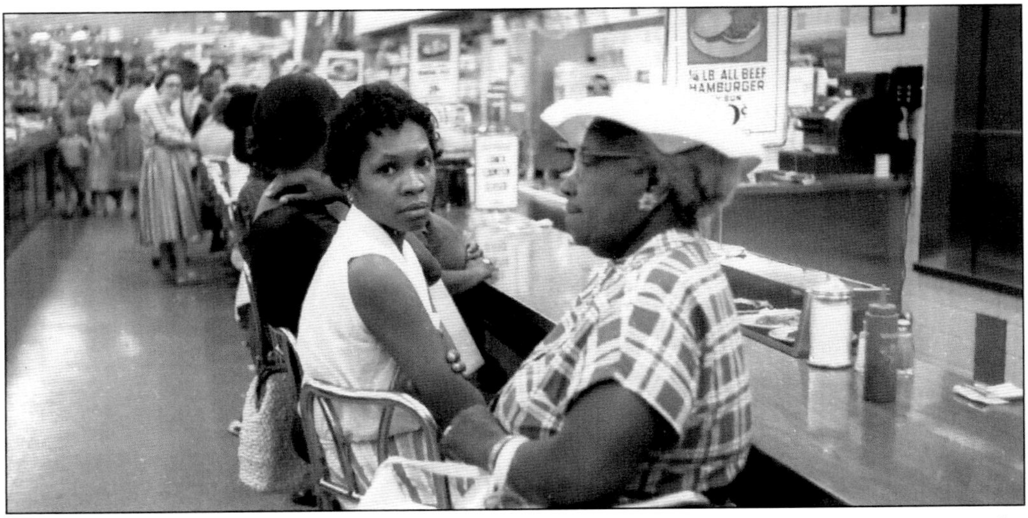

Sit-in Demonstrations. African Americans were not allowed to eat at the lunch counters in the dime stores in downtown Lexington. Rather, they were expected to purchase food and leave or stand at the snack bar. In protest of this policy, blacks and whites in the late '50s and early '60s organized sit-in demonstrations at lunch counters. They would occupy lunch counter seats so that no whites could sit there. Pictured are African-American women participating in one of the sit-in demonstrations in downtown Lexington.

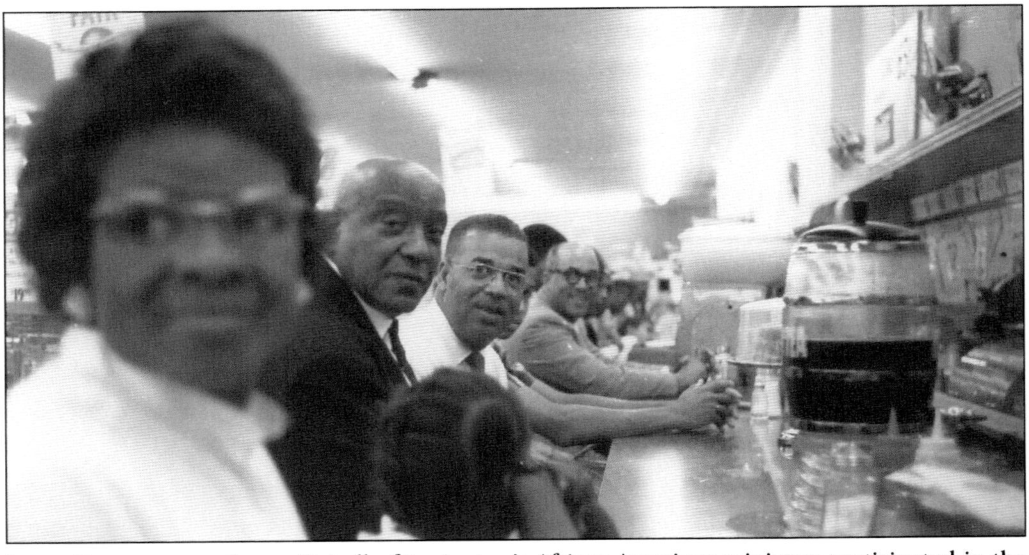

Local Ministers at a Sit-in. Not all of Lexington's African-American ministers participated in the demonstrations. Only a few were actively engaged in the struggle on a regular basis. Some were advanced in age and could not physically participate; others believed the demonstrations were outside the mission of the church; and then some did not want to disrupt the relationships they had developed with whites. Rev. W. A. Jones Sr. (pastor of Historic Pleasant Green Baptist Church), Rev. Walter Taylor; and Rev. A.B. Lee of Liberty Baptist Church were early supporters of the local Civil Rights Movement. Pictured are three other ministers who joined the sit-in movement. From left to right are an unidentified woman, Rev. W.H. Howard (pastor of Consolidated Baptist Church), Rev. J.S. Beverly (pastor of Bethel Baptist Church), and Rev. A.B. Lee. (Courtesy of Calvert McCann.)

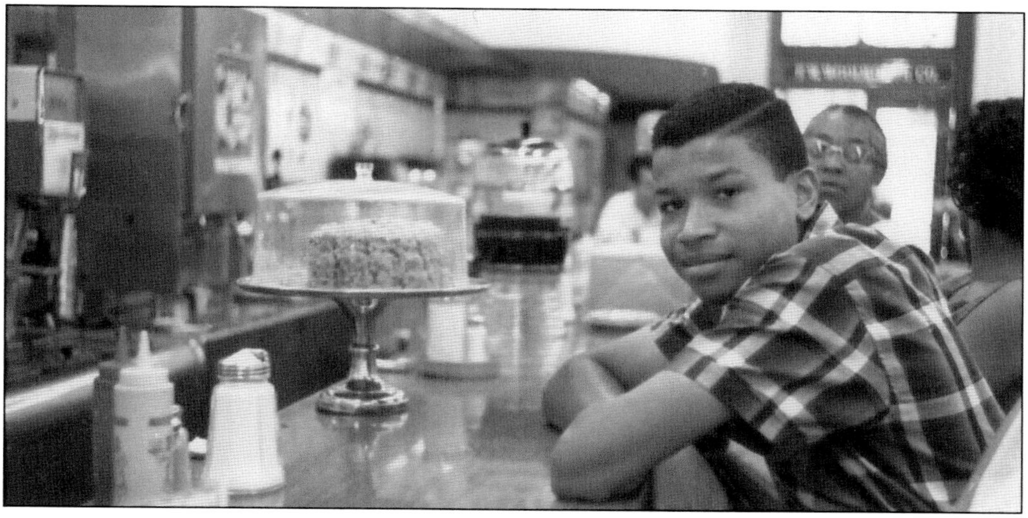

THE SIT-IN MOVEMENT. On February 1, 1960, four black college students led a sit-in movement at Woolworths in Greensboro, North Carolina. Following their arrest, high school and college students around the country launched sit-ins. CORE, a national civil rights organization, sought to abolish segregation at lunch counters through nonviolent direct action. The organization sponsored workshops to train persons how to be nonviolent. A local CORE chapter was established in Lexington in 1959. Lexington's first sit-in took place on July 11, 1959 at a restaurant near the University of Kentucky campus. The first publicized demonstration occurred February 27, 1960, at H. L. Green and Company. Pictured above is a high school student during a demonstration at F.W. Woolworth's lunch counter. (Courtesy of Calvert McCann.)

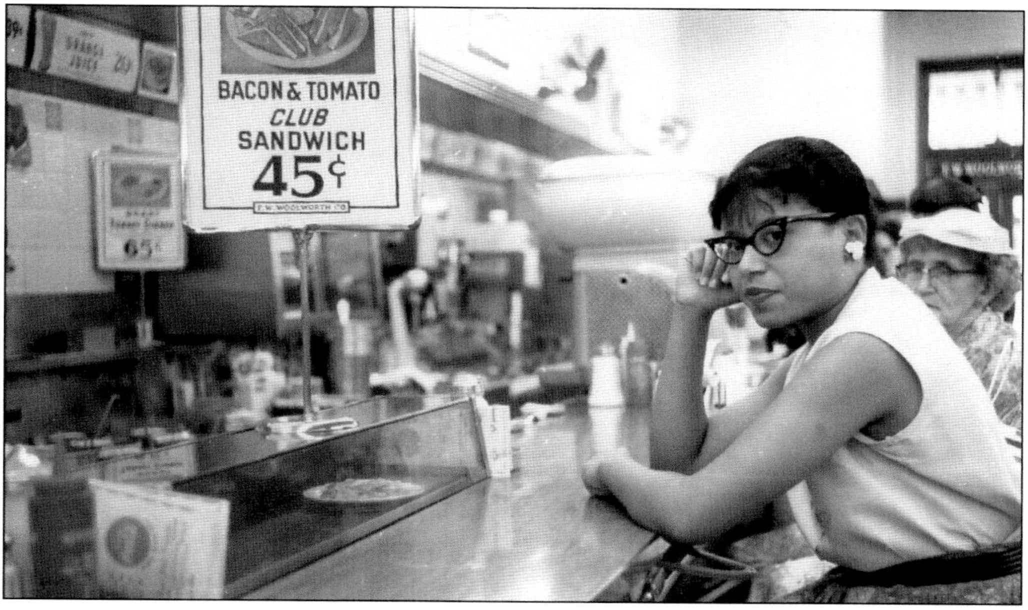

WAITING TO BE SERVED. White waitresses tried to ignore the demonstrators, but this was not always easy to do. At times blacks left alternating seats vacant at the lunch counters so that white customers would have to sit next to a black person. The objective was to show store managers that whites would sit next to blacks and eat if necessary. Pictured is another high school demonstrator at F.W. Woolworth's lunch counter. (Courtesy of Calvert McCann.)

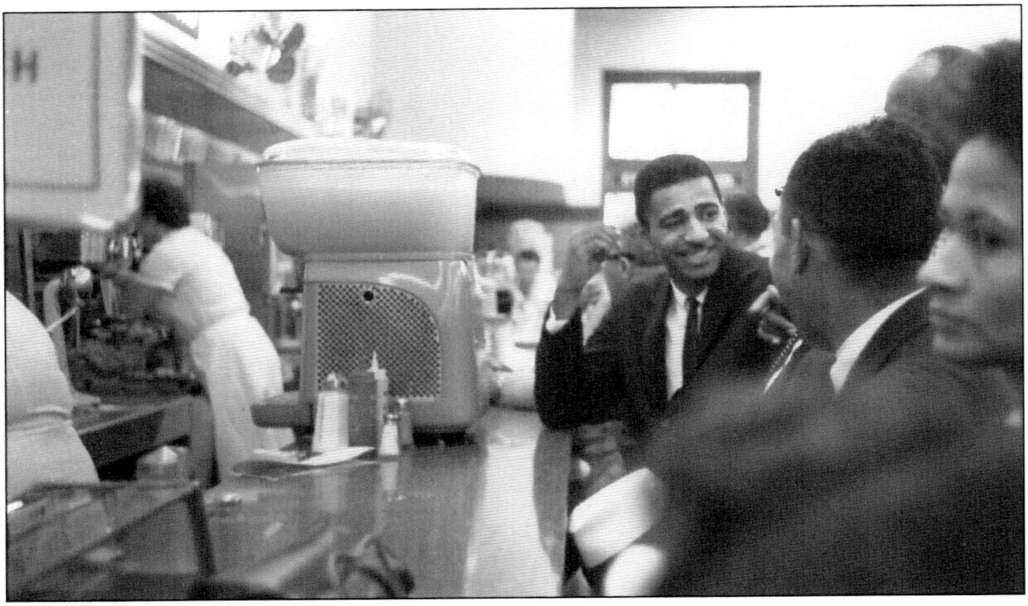

More Waiting. Lexington CORE also organized sit-ins at S.S. Kresge and McCrory's on Main Street. The demonstrations were effective. By August 1960 most downtown lunch counters were integrated. Pictured facing the camera is Reverend W.A. Jones Jr. during a sit-in at the lunch counter in F.W. Woolworth's. (Courtesy of Calvert McCann.)

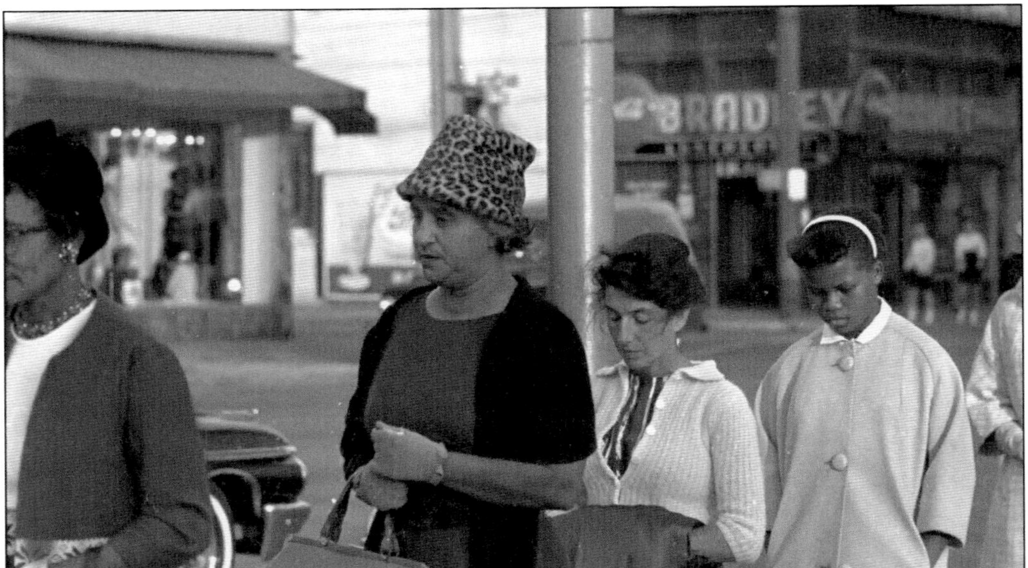

Women Activists. African-American women played leadership roles in the Civil Rights Movement throughout Kentucky. In Lexington, Julia Lewis led the local CORE Chapter and Audrey Grevious chaired the Lexington NAACP chapter. Both women were organizers and active participants in the struggle. Abby Marlatt, a white University of Kentucky professor, was a valuable contributor to the efforts of CORE. Throughout the 1960s several younger and older women protested segregation. Pictured here is Mary Jones, wife of Rev. W.A Jones, in a line of demonstrators on Main Street. (Courtesy of Calvert McCann.)

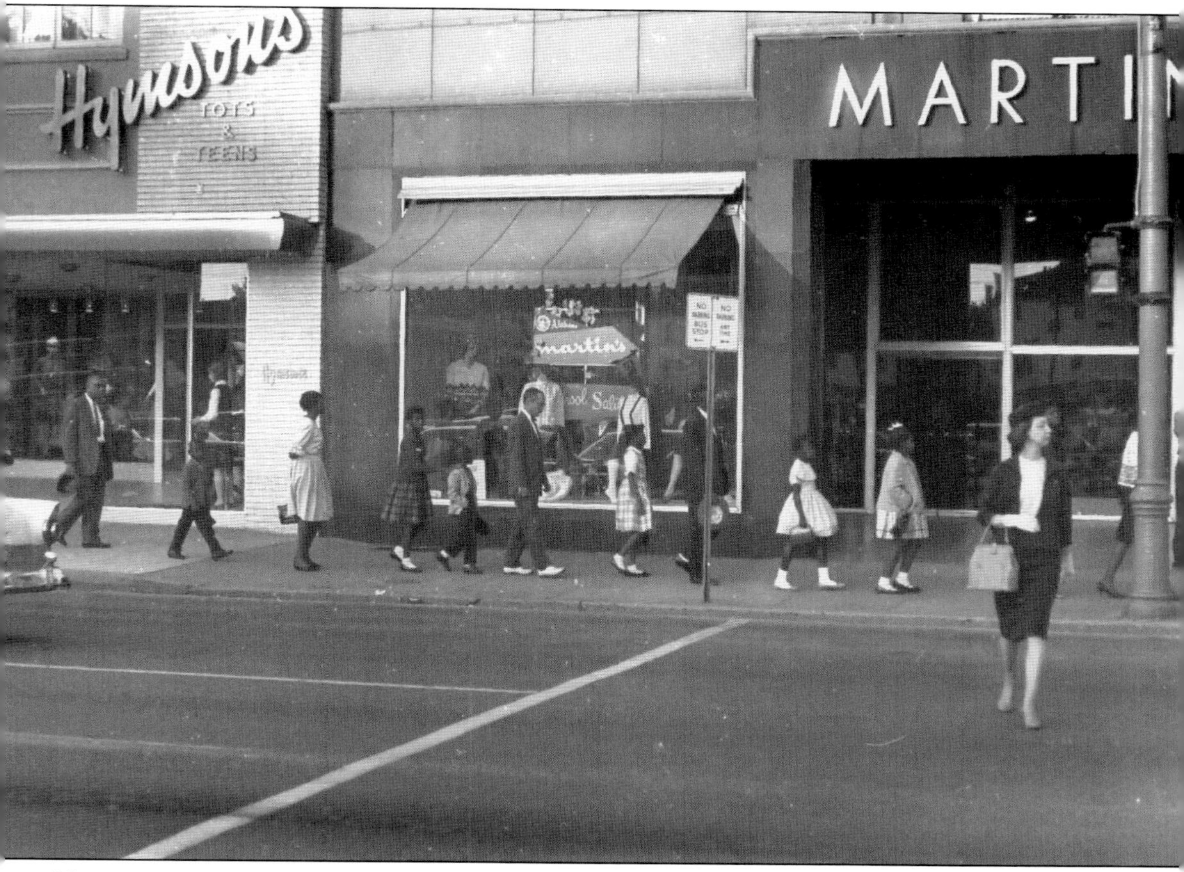

Marching for Freedom. Not all white establishments in Lexington were easily desegregated. Mass marches were organized to pressure the white community into desegregating all public accommodations and hire African Americans for white collar jobs that had been historically reserved for whites. On April 25, 1961, more than 200 demonstrators participated in a "Freedom Parade" through downtown Main Street. Pictured here is a diverse group of demonstrators who may have been a part of that "Freedom Parade." The group includes several young children all dressed up. (Courtesy of Calvert McCann.)

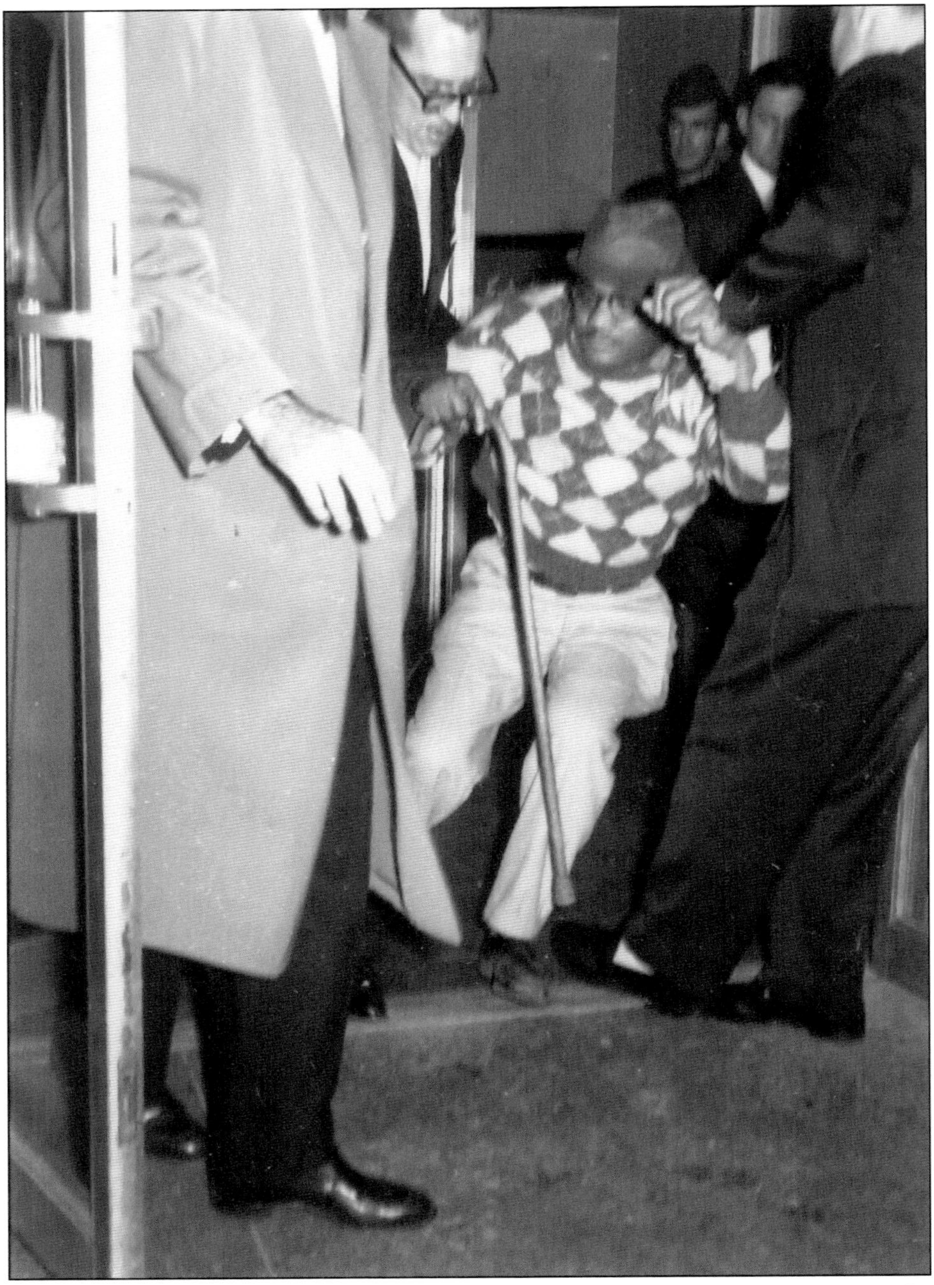

Phoenix Hotel. On Tuesday afternoon, October 17, 1961, several African-American members of the Boston Celtics basketball team were in Lexington to play an exhibition game against the St. Louis Hawks at Memorial Coliseum. When some of the players sought service in the Phoenix's coffee shop, they were asked whether they were guests at the hotel. Insulted, five players, including Hall of Famer Bill Russell, refused to play in the game and returned to Boston on a plane later that day. The incident sparked a series of protests against the hotel's policy of discriminating against blacks. Pictured is Simon Gentry, who was physically challenged, being thrown out of the Phoenix by hotel management. This photo was published in the *Louisville Defender* on December 14, 1961. (Courtesy of Calvert McCann.)

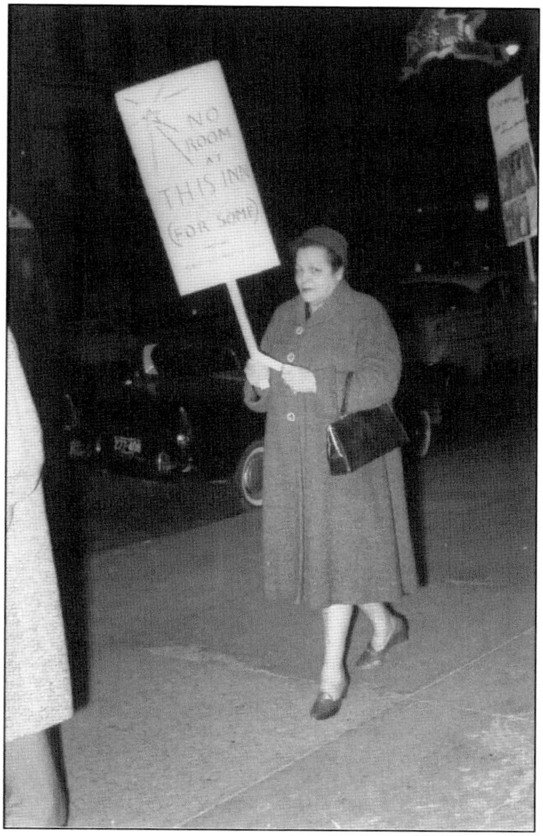

Protest at Night. The Phoenix Hotel did not allow blacks to register as guests unless they were "participating in a convention at the hotel." Bertha Wilkinson Simms carries a sign protesting the practices of the hotel.

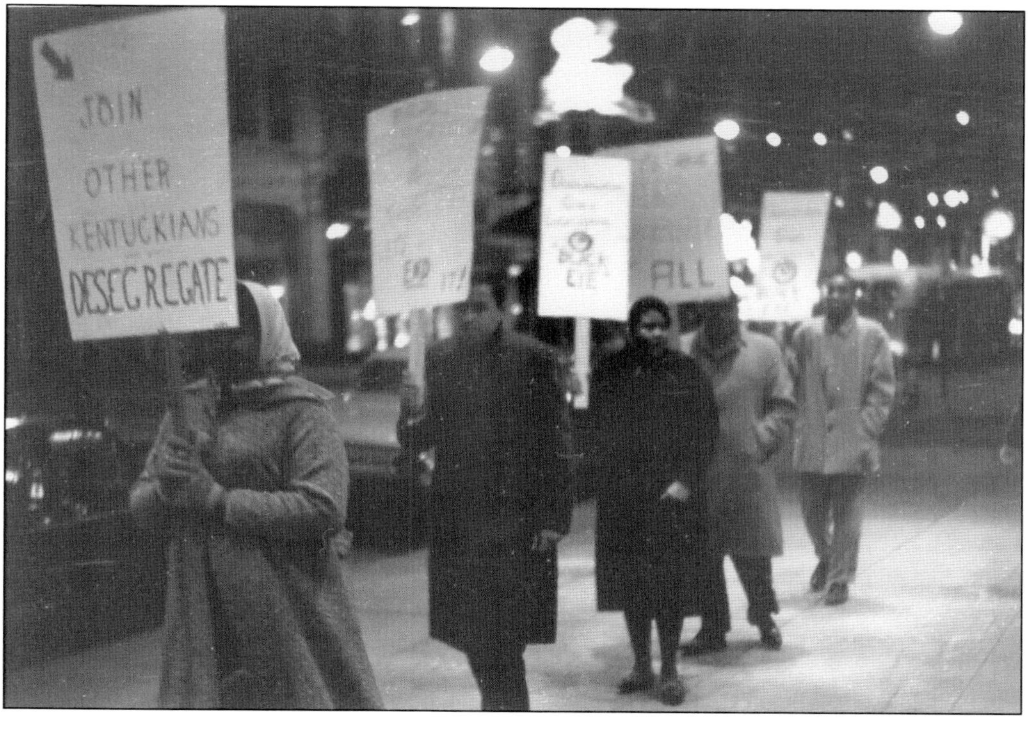

Picketing in the Winter Cold. African Americans were determined to end segregation in Lexington. Despite cold weather, they often demonstrated in small groups as a show of their persistence and determination to gain freedom and equality for local blacks.

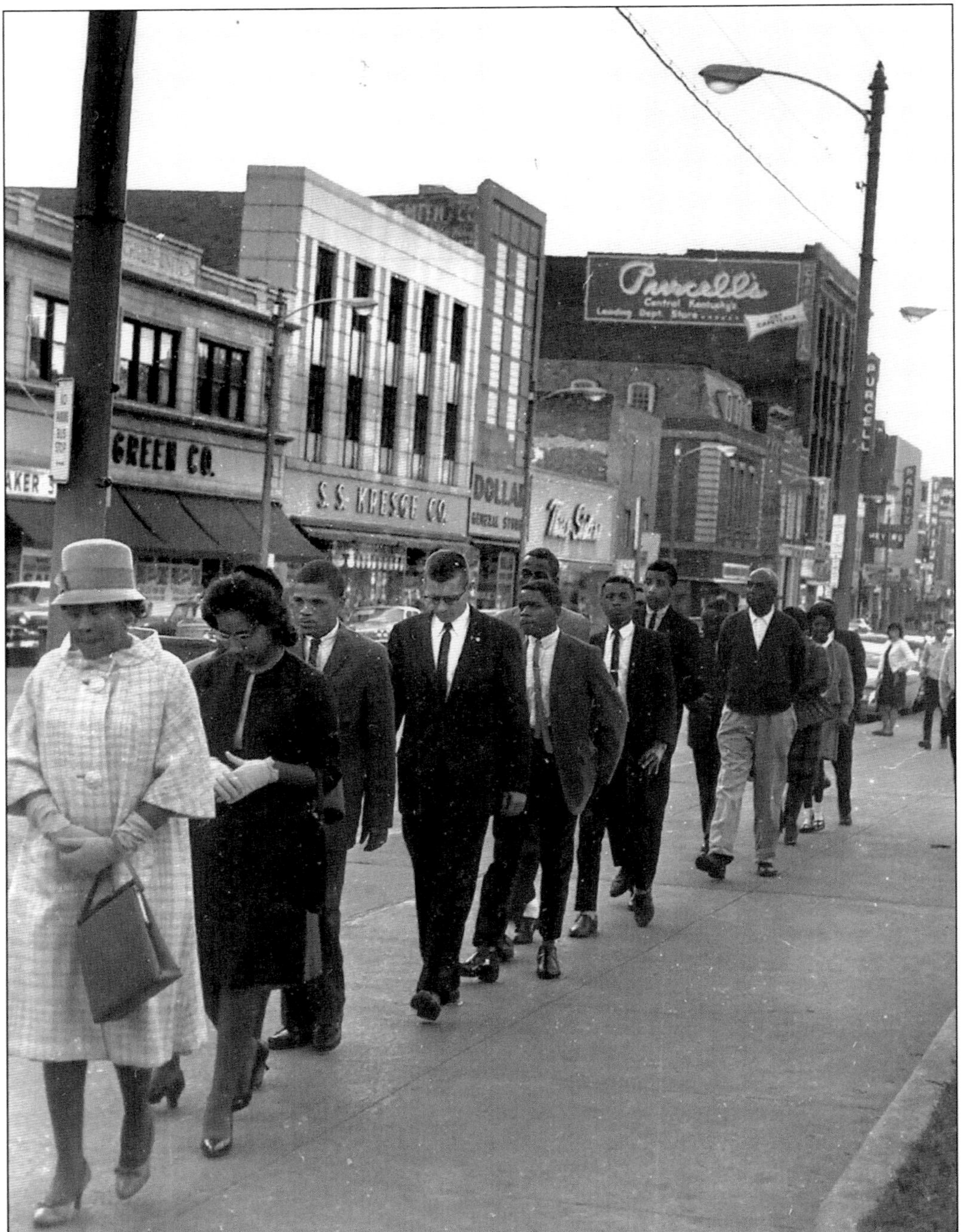

Dressed-up Demonstrators. African Americans were not always allowed to pay for their tickets to movies at the same window as whites. Many times, they had to go to a side entrance. After purchasing their tickets, they had to sit in the balcony of the theatre. Local African Americans began protesting this arrangement in the winter of 1961, organizing stand-ins in front of the Strand, Kentucky, and Ben Ali Theatres. By the summer of 1961 movie theaters in downtown Lexington had desegregated. Pictured is a group of demonstrators making their case for equality with class and dignity. (Courtesy of Calvert McCann.)

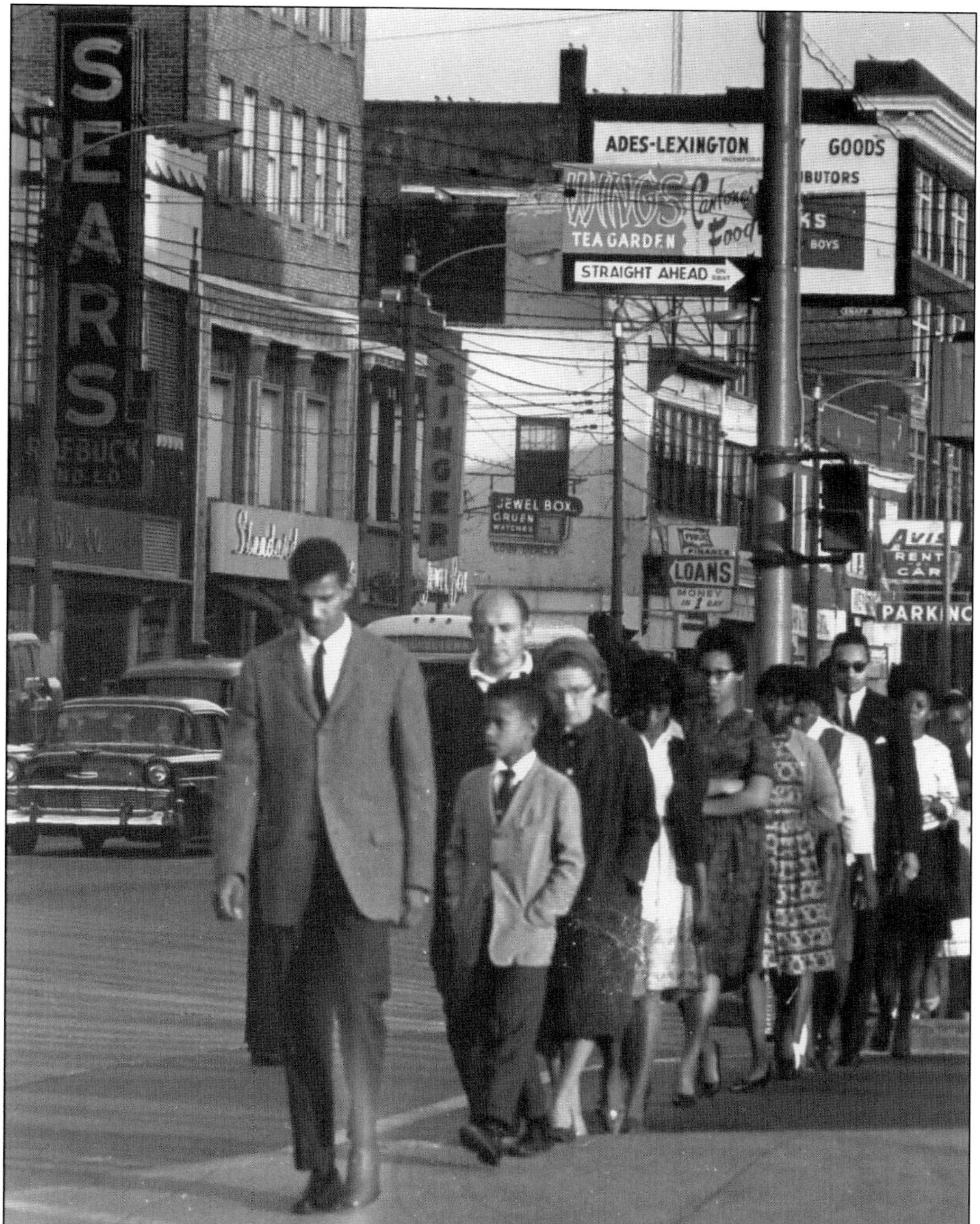

THE POWER OF NON-VIOLENCE. The Civil Rights Movement in Lexington did not receive much publicity. Pictures of demonstrations were not printed in the local newspaper, and articles about CORE activities were brief and offered few details. Unlike other places in the south, police brutality towards activists was not a significant issue in Lexington. Still, white resistance and harassment of demonstrators did occur during the 1960s. White pedestrians and those in cars were known to heckle protesters, but demonstrators—white and black—were undaunted by the comments. Pictured is Henry W. Jones being followed by his brother, Byron Timothy Jones. (Courtesy of Calvert McCann.)

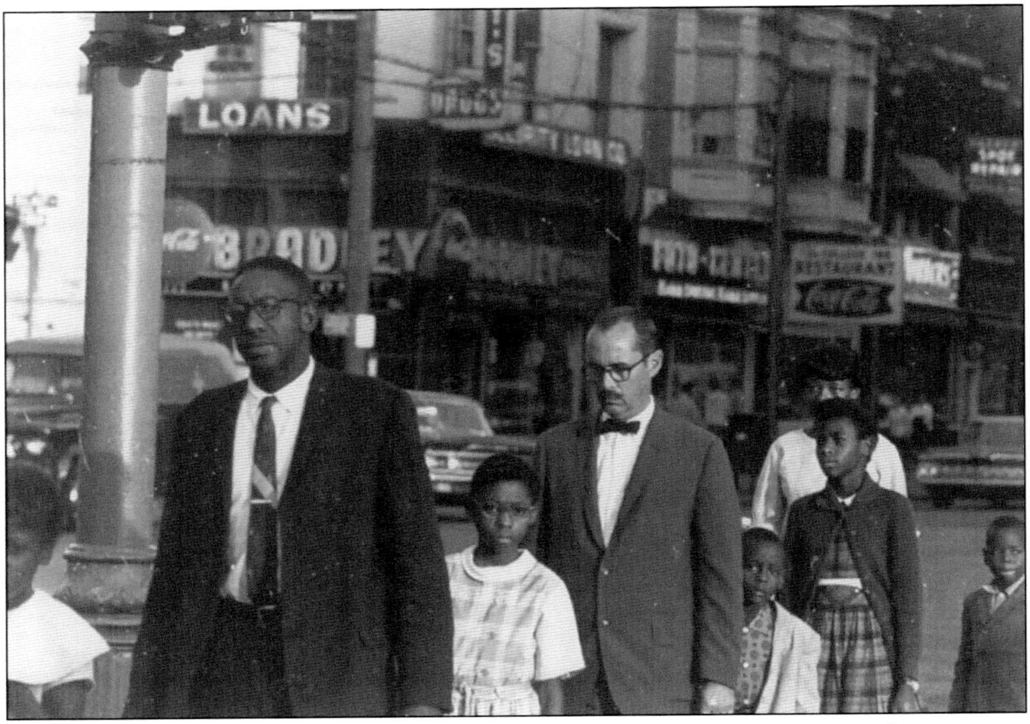

Child Demonstrators. Young African-American children joined their parents and other adult supervisors in challenging racial barriers designed to keep them in "their place." Pictured is Rev. Thomas Moore, an unidentified white man, and several children marching for freedom. (Courtesy of Calvert McCann.)

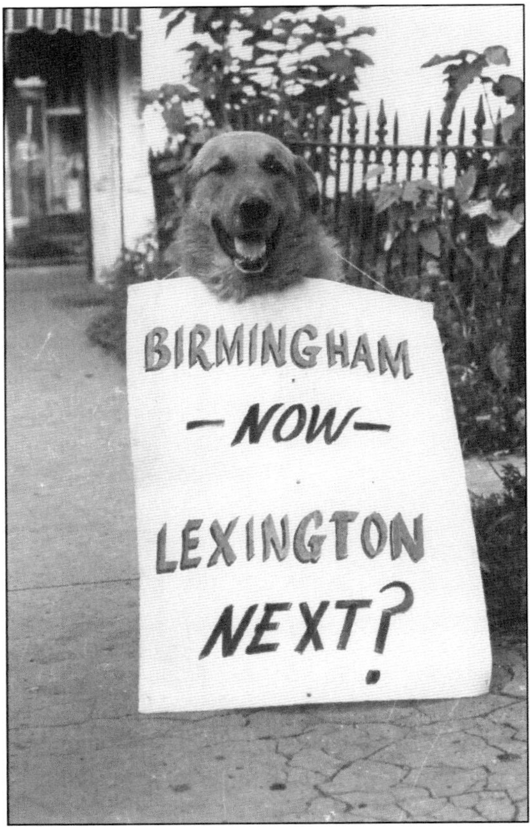

Bad Publicity. In May 1963, the nation watched Birmingham, Alabama Police Commissioner Eugene "Bull" Connor order his police force to spray fire hoses and unleash attack dogs on young demonstrators. The violence of the Birmingham demonstrations was embarrassing for the nation. White Lexingtonians did not want to see their city on the national news, and this photo was designed to send a message to the white community reminding them of Birmingham. (Courtesy of Calvert McCann.)

Equal Employment. Nine African Americans were arrested for lying in the aisles of Sears Roebuck department store on August 2, 1963, where they were protesting employment discrimination. Pictured in an evening demonstration, front to back, are Henry Jones, Jerry Williams (holding sign), and Ronald Berry as they march down Main Street in another demonstration. (Courtesy of Calvert McCann.)

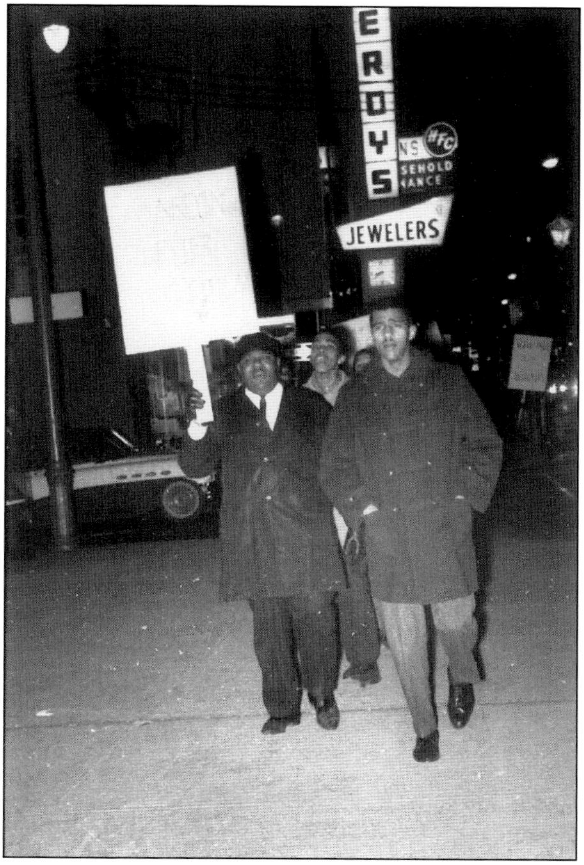

Historic Pleasant Green Missionary Baptist Church. Most of the meetings and rallies involving the local Civil Rights Movement were held in the sanctuary of Pleasant Green located on Maxwell Street. In the picture below Jerry Williams, left, and Ronald Berry, right, stand outside the church during a rally, (Courtesy of Calvert McCann.)

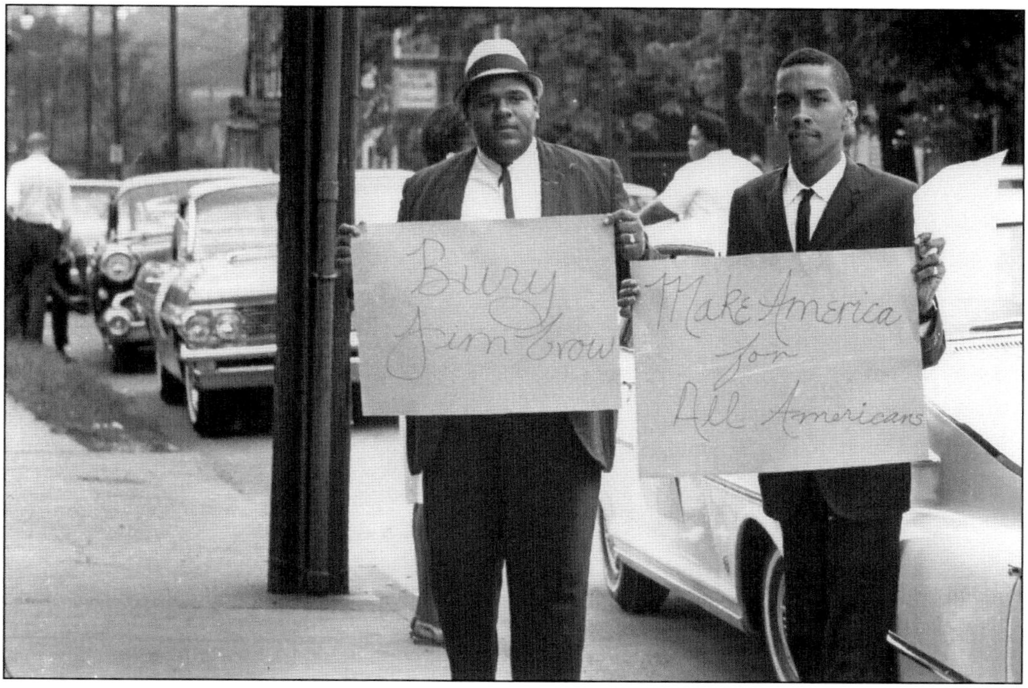

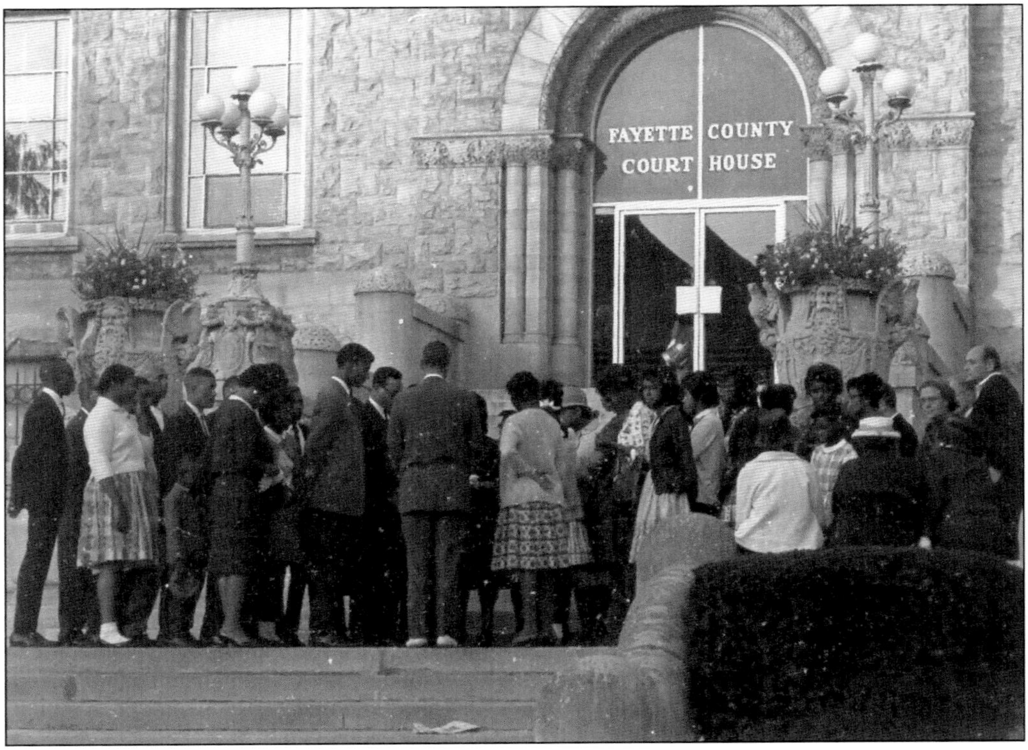

Prayer. On August 30, 1963, over 250 activists marched on downtown Lexington as well as the *Lexington Herald Leader*. The newspaper had continued to publish the "Colored Notes" despite black requests to retire the column. Following this march a small number of African Americans were hired in white collar jobs in downtown stores in Lexington. Pictured is a prayer vigil in front of the Fayette County Courthouse. (Courtesy of Calvert McCann.)

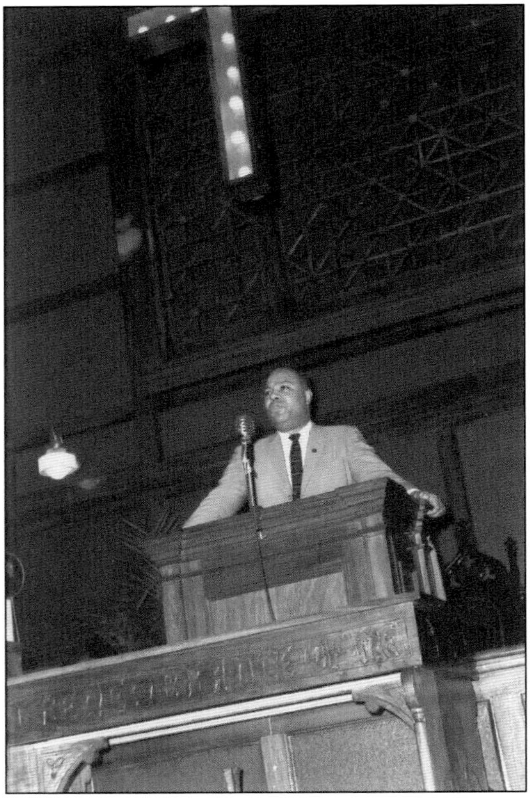

James Farmer. A major figure in the national Civil Rights Movement, Farmer led the freedom ride demonstrations through the south in 1961. He was the national director of CORE from 1961 to 1966. Farmer is pictured here speaking at a rally at Historic Pleasant Green Missionary Baptist Church. Courtesy of Calvert McCann)

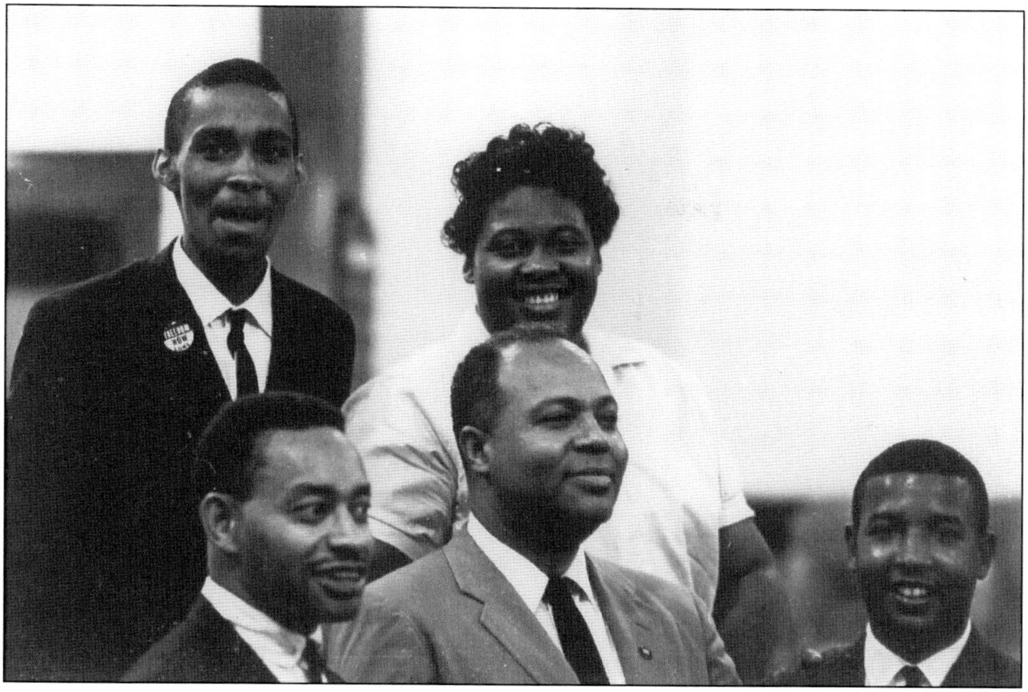

Freedom Fighters. Julia Lewis was a committed and forceful leader of the local movement. Pictured from left to right are (front row) Ernest Weaver, James Farmer, and Isaac Coleman; (back row) Ronald Berry and Julia Lewis. (Courtesy of Calvert McCann.)

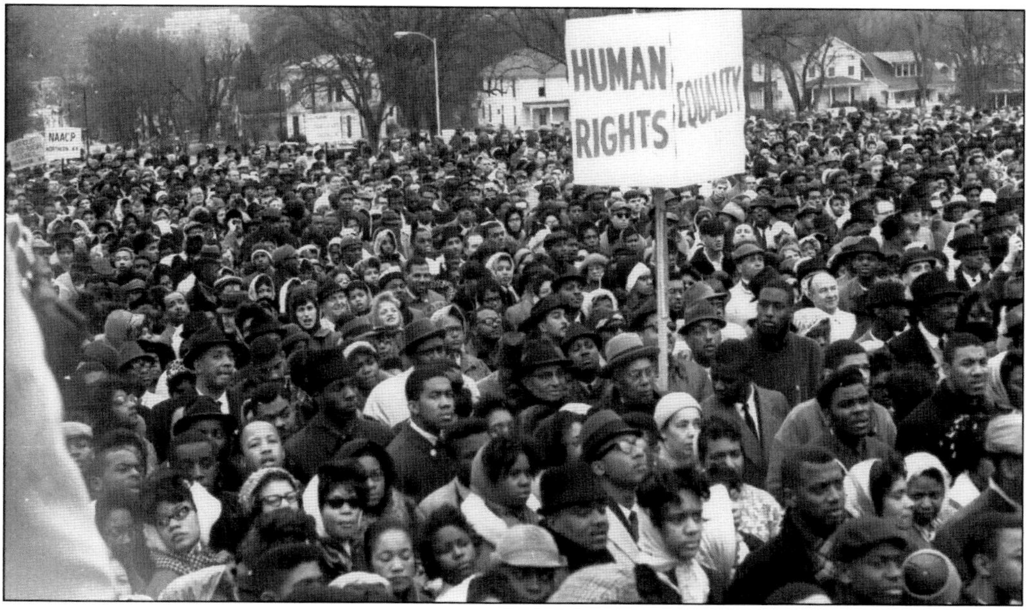

March on Frankfort. On March 5, 1964, Dr. Martin Luther King Jr. led more than 10,000 black and white Kentuckians in a march to the state capitol to lobby support for a state public accommodations bill. A contingent of Lexington civil rights activists attended that march. Pictured is some of the crowd that was present that day. The legislature refused to pass the bill. (Courtesy of Calvert McCann.)

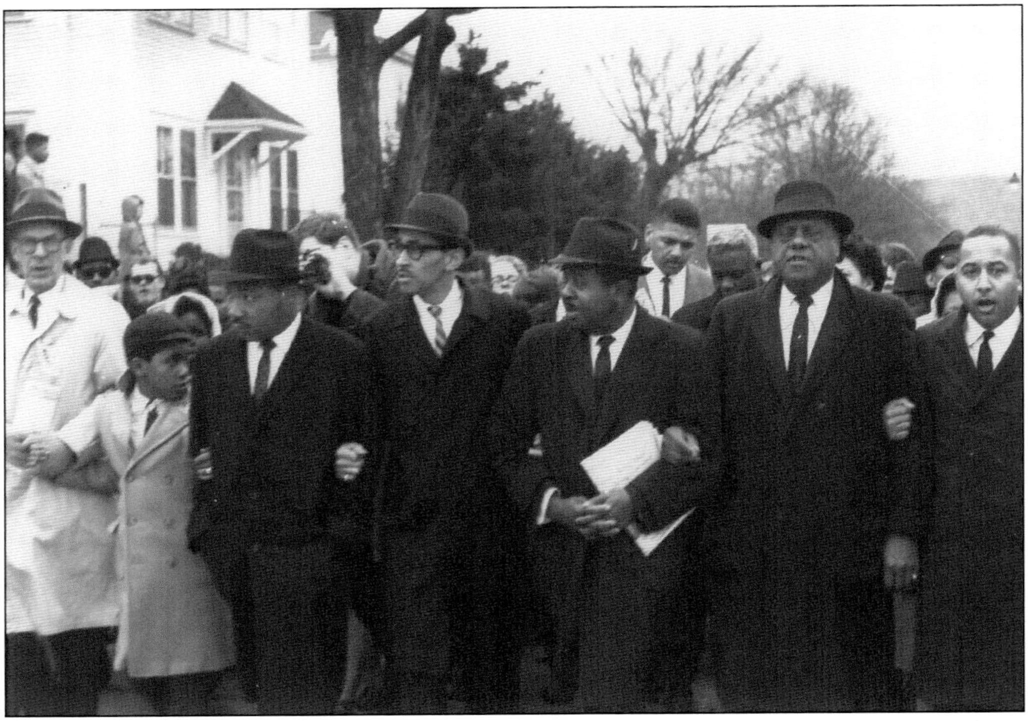

Martin Luther King Jr. Dr. King visited Kentucky often to spend time with his brother, A D., who pastored a church in Louisville. King led demonstrations against housing discrimination in Louisville in 1967 and is shown here, third from left. His close associate, Ralph Abernathy, is fifth from the left. (Courtesy of Calvert McCann.)

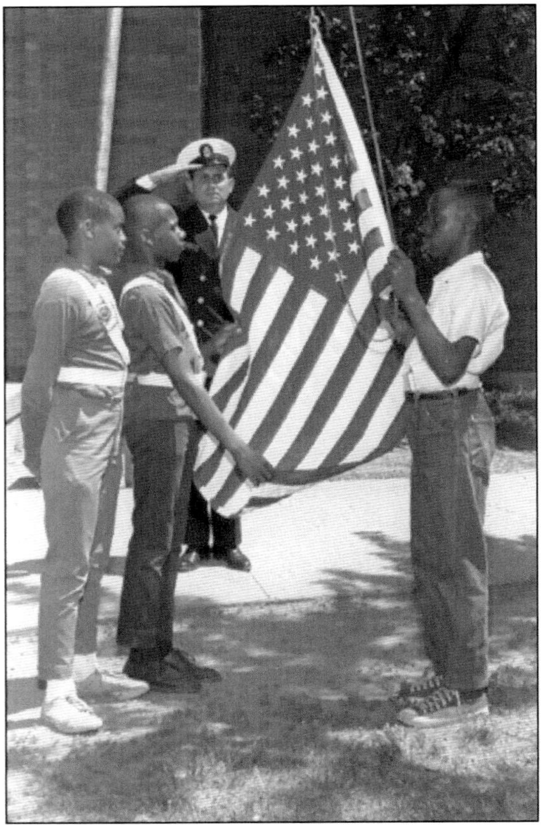

Raising the American Flag. On July 2, President Lyndon Johnson signed the historic Civil Rights Act of 1964, thereby making segregation in public accommodations unconstitutional. Two years later, the Kentucky General Assembly passed a state civil rights act that extended the coverage of the federal act. The bill was signed into law on January 27, 1966. The struggle to get this piece of legislation passed was not an ending. Instead, it was another milestone in the long march for freedom and equality. Pictured are students from Carver Elementary School raising the school's new flag in May 1964.

Selected Bibliography

Photographic Archives

Barton Battaile Collection, Lexington Public Library, Kentucky Room
Bullock Collection, Transylvania University Library
Dr. T.T. Wendell Collection, Kentucky Historical Society, Special Collections and Archives.
J. Winston Coleman Collection, Transylvania University Library
Lafayette Studio Collection, University of Kentucky, Department of Special Collections
Lexington Fayette Urban County Government Archives
Lucy Estill Papers, Lexington Fayette Urban County Government Archives
P.W.L. Jones Collection, Kentucky State University Archives and Special Collections
Whitney M. Young Sr. Collection, Kentucky State University Archives and Special Collections

Newspapers

Lexington Daily Press
Lexington Herald Leader
Lexington Leader
Lexington Herald
Lexington Morning Transcript
Lexington Observer and Recorder
Louisville Defender

Books

Bosley, Ella S. *Only Believe: Biography of Florence Jackson Brown Tolley*. Lexington: Bosley, 1999.
Byars, Lauretta Flynn. *Lexington's Colored Orphan Industrial Home: Building For the Future*. Lexington: I.B Bold Publications, 1995.
Battaile, Barton. *Lexington: Pictorial Nostalgia*. Lexington: Barton K. Battaile, 1974.
Coleman, J.W. *The Squires Sketches of Lexington*. Lexington: Henry Clay Press, 1972.
Dunnigan, Alice A. *The Fascinating Story of Black Kentuckians: Their Heritage and Traditions*. Washington, D.C.: Associated Publishers, 1982.
Ely, Melvin Patrick. *The Adventures of Amos 'N' Andy: A Social History of an American Phenomenon*. New York: The Free Press, 1991.
Goings, Kenneth W. Mammy and Uncle Mose: Black Collectibles and American Stereotyping. (Bloomington: Indiana University Press, 1994.)
House, M. Tom and Carter, R. Lisa. *Lafayette's Lexington, Kentucky*. Charleston, South Carolina: Arcadia Publishing, 1998.
Higginbotham, Evelyn Brooks, *Righteous Discontent: The Women's Movement in the Black Baptist Church, 1880–1920* Cambridge, Massachusetts, 1993

Johnson, W.D. *Biographical Sketches of Prominent Negro Men and Women of Kentucky*. Lexington, 1897.
Kerr, Betty L. and Wright Jr., John D. *Lexington: A Century in Photographs*. Lexington, Kentucky: Lexington-Fayette County Historic Commission, 1984.
Lucas, Marion B. *A History of Blacks in Kentucky: From Slavery to Segregation- 1760–1891*, Vol. 1. Frankfort, Kentucky: Kentucky Historical Society, 1992.
McIntyre, L.H. *One Grain of the Salt: The First African Baptist Church West of the Allegheny Mountains*. Lexington: Dr. L.H. McIntyre, 1986.
Peoples, T.H. *Essence of a Saga: A Complete History of the Oldest Black Baptist Congregation West of the Allegheny Mountains*. Lexington: n.p, 1990.
Reed, Billy. Transition Game: The Story of S.T. Roach. Lesington: Host Communications, Inc.
Smith, Gerald. *A Black Educator in the Segregated South: Kentucky's Rufus B. Atwood*. Lexington: University Press of Kentucky, 1994.
Waller, Greg. *Main Street Amusements: Movies and Commercial Entertainment in a Southern City, 1896–1930*. Washington: Smithsonian Institution Press, 1995.
Wright, George C. *A History of Blacks in Kentucky: In Pursuit of Equality, 1890–1980*. Vol.2 Frankfort, Kentucky: Kentucky Historical Society, 1992.
———. *Racial Violence in Kentucky, 1865–1940: Lynchings, Mob Rule, and "Legal Lynchings."* Baton Rouge: Louisiana State University Press, 1990.
———. *Life Behind the Veil: Blacks in Louisville, Kentucky*. Baton Rouge: Louisiana University Press, 1985.

Other Sources

Coleman, Jr. J. Winston. "Lexington's Slave Dealers and Their Southern Trade," *Filson Historical Club Quarterly* 12 (1938) 1–23.
Conner, Eloise, "The Slave Market in Lexington, Kentucky, 1850–1860." M.A. thesis, University of Kentucky, 1931.
Harris, Lawrence, *The Negro Population of Lexington in the Professions, Business, Education and Religion*, 1907.
Kellog, John. "The Evolution of Black Residential Areas in Lexington Kentucky, 1865–1887." *Journal of Southern History* 47 (1982): 21–52.
Lexington City Directory.
Marshall, Ann E. "Kentucky's Separate Coach Law and African American Response," *Register* 98 (2000): 241–259.
Moreland, Stephen G. "Straddling the Fence of Freedom: The Free African American Community of Antebellum Lexington." M.A. thesis, University of Kentucky, 1996.
Negro Business Directory and Fair Souvenir. Lexington, Kentucky: Standard Printing Company, 1899.
Polk's Lexington City Directory.
Thomas, Herbert A., Jr. "Victims of Circumstance: Negroes in a Southern Town, 186 5–1880" *Register* 71 (1973): 252–71.
Smith, Gerald L. "Blacks in Lexington, Kentucky: The Struggle For Civil Rights, 1945–1980 M.A. thesis, University of Kentucky, 1983.
Wilkinson, Doris. "A Guide to the African American Heritage in Downtown Lexington, Kentucky."
A Project on the African American Heritage, July 2000.
———. "Directory of Afro-American Physicians in Lexington and Fayette County From Post Reconstruction to the Pre-Civil Rights Era, 1890–1950." January 1989.